Ethics
in Tissue Establishments

Ethics
in Tissue Establishments

By

Jorge Morales Pedraza

Independent Consultant on International Affairs

World Scientific

NEW JERSEY • LONDON • SINGAPORE • BEIJING • SHANGHAI • HONG KONG • TAIPEI • CHENNAI

Published by

World Scientific Publishing Co. Pte. Ltd.
5 Toh Tuck Link, Singapore 596224
USA office: 27 Warren Street, Suite 401-402, Hackensack, NJ 07601
UK office: 57 Shelton Street, Covent Garden, London WC2H 9HE

Library of Congress Cataloging-in-Publication Data
Morales Pedraza, Jorge, author.
Ethics in tissue establishments / by Jorge Morales Pedraza ; edited by Glyn O. Phillips.
p. ; cm.
Includes bibliographical references and index.
ISBN 978-9814616751 (hardcover : alk. paper)
I. Phillips, Glyn O, editor. II. Title.
[DNLM: 1. Tissue Banks--ethics. 2. Codes of Ethics. 3. International Agencies. 4. Tissue Transplantation--ethics. QS 523]
RD120.7
174.2'97954--dc23
2014024095

British Library Cataloguing-in-Publication Data
A catalogue record for this book is available from the British Library.

Typeset by Stallion Press
Email: enquiries@stallionpress.com

Printed in Singapore

Preface

The preparation of the present book was a very complex and difficult task for me. Ethics in tissue banking is not a field that falls within my professional curriculum. My experience in tissue banking is a practical one and is associated with my former work as senior manager in the IAEA's Secretariat in charge of the programme on radiation and tissue banking, implemented by this organisation from 1972–2005.

The book has seven chapters. Chapter I gives an overall view on the current use of human tissue in certain medical treatments and in scientific medical research and on how this use has been increased in a variety of ways during the past years. These include human tissue transplantation, the utilisation of human tissue for research on new medicines, and the role of human cell lines and genetic material for studying fundamental biological processes. Nevertheless, it is important to emphasise that the use of human tissue raises ethical issues of great concern to health care professionals, biomedical researchers, ethics committees, tissue establishments and policy makers within national competent health care authorities. At the same time, society demands general respect for the human body and its parts and, for this reason, human tissue should not be used at will or abused. Practices that have been questioned include the commercial exploitation of products derived from the tissue of patients or research subjects.

Chapter II highlights the importance of ethics in the field of human tissue banking. The use of human tissues in certain medical practices has been consecrated as an effective modality to save lives and to improve the quality of life of thousands of individuals after passing specific medical treatments. Doctors and dentists use human tissue for a variety of medical purposes. Donated skin can meet critical needs in healing burn victims and in reconstructive surgery. Donated bones can be implanted to replace cancerous bones; used in knee and hip replacements and in spinal surgery; and processed into a powder for use in dental surgery. Donated heart valves can replace defective valves in young children, saving their lives.

The success rates for transplantation of human tissues have ensured that processed tissues can be used more frequently in specific medical treatments without increasing the risk of the recipient. To avoid the improper uses of the human tissues procured by a tissue establishment, it is necessary to promote and adopt certain ethical principles to be observed by tissue establishment operators and medical staff during the procurement, processing, storage, distribution and use of human tissues. The purpose of observing ethical principles is to avoid not only the abuse and unethical practices in tissue banking, but also to prevent the violation of specific regulations in force in the country. The chapter includes several ethical principles that should be observed by the tissue establishments.

Chapter III includes a model code of ethics. This model can be used as reference by interested tissue establishments during the modification of their current standards or in case that the tissue establishments have decided to prepare a new code that takes into account new developments in the ethical field.

Chapter IV highlights the importance of a code of practice for a tissue establishment. While there are inescapable acts of individual judgement involved in ethical decisions, nevertheless, it is desirable that conclusions should be reached in ways that result in as consistent a practice as possible. A way of achieving this in a given area of activity is to formulate a code of practice, providing general guidelines within which individual decisions are to be made. A code of practice is defined as *"written guidelines issued by an official body or a professional association to its members to help them comply with its ethical standards and should specify the requirements for the activities of tissue establishments for the procurement and processing of human tissues for therapeutic use and research activities"*. The scope of a code of practice should include all human tissues used for therapeutic purposes, including those used in clinical trials and research activities. The objective of a code of practice is to provide a set of principles and procedures that, when followed by tissue establishments, helps to ensure that the tissue processed will have the required quality.

Chapter V includes a model code of practice. This model can be used as reference by interested tissue establishments during the modification of their current standards or if they have decided to prepare a new code that takes into account new developments in this important field.

Chapter VI highlights the possible role of governments, the World Health Organization (WHO), the International Atomic Energy Agency (IAEA) and regional professional associations in the promotion of ethics and best practice in tissue banking. A set of proposals and recommendations to be followed by interested governments, the World Health Organization, the International Atomic Energy Agency and regional professional associations has been included.

Chapter VII includes a summary of the major topics addressed in previous chapters.

Acknowledgements

I would like to express my thanks for the invaluable support of my lovely wife, Aurora Tamara Meoqui Puig, who assumed many other family responsibilities in order to give me time to work on the preparation of this book.

I would like also to highlight the support, suggestions and proposals given by Dr. Astrid Lobo Gajiwala, Head of the Tata Memorial Hospital Tissue Bank of India, in the preparation of Chapter V of the book and by Dr. Marisa Herson, former Head of the Donor Tissue Bank of Victoria, Melbourne, Australia for her relevant role in the preparation of Chapter II. Special thanks must be given to my dear friend Professor Glyn O. Phillips, Chairman of Phillips Hydrocolloids Research Ltd, for his role as editor of the book and for his important recommendations and suggestions on all chapters.

Contents

Chapter I

General Overview

The use of human[1] tissue in certain medical treatments and in scientific medical research has increased in a variety of ways in the past years. This includes human tissue transplantation,[2] the utilisation of human tissue for research on new medicines and the role of human cell lines and genetic material for studying fundamental biological processes. Nevertheless, it is important to emphasise that the use of human tissue has raised ethical issues of great concern to health care professionals, biomedical researchers, ethics committees, tissue establishments and policy makers of the health care world and has recognised the importance of patient autonomy (Gillet, 2007).

Transplantation of human tissues is now an effective therapy across a wide range of both fatal and non-fatal diseases and in many countries from all regions. Tissue establishments[3] provide diverse types of tissues such as

[1] According to the Australia National Health and Medical Research Council (2009), human tissues are all constituent parts of the human body formed by cells. Human tissue products include samples, cellular devices, cell cultures, significantly modified cell cultures, a cellular products and even intellectual property.

[2] Human tissue transplantation is a complex process involving technical, legal and ethical aspects. Issues such as the voluntariness of tissue donations, the disequilibrium created by demand exceeding supply, cultural and religious issues, population, allogeneic vs. xenogeneic transplants and living vs. deceased donors, among others, contribute to the complexity of tissue transplantation worldwide.

[3] In this book the expression "tissue establishments" is used instead of "tissue banks".

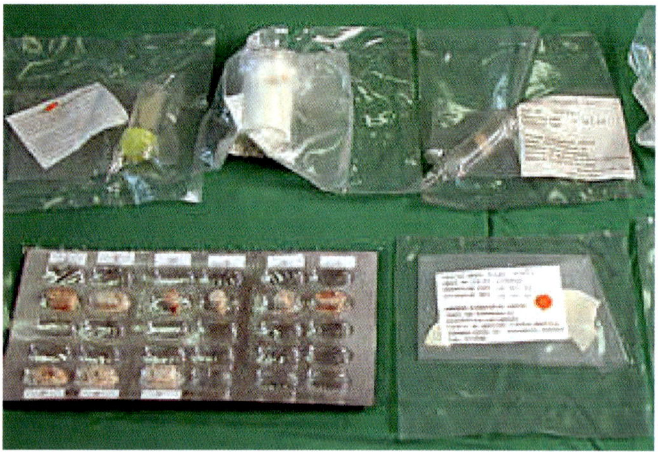

Figure 1: Life-saving medical supplies. Sterilised tissue samples ready for being used.
Source: IAEA (Courtesy of P. Pavlicek)

bone, eyes, heart valves, tendons, fascia, dura mater, sperm and skin, among others. It is estimated that between three and five million tissue transplants take place every year globally with the highest demand in the USA, though there are only poor data on the actual levels of activity.[4] The majority of transplants involve certain types of organs, but the demand for skin for treatment of burns has also increased.[5] Similarly, in solid organ

[4] In Canada it has been estimated that in ten years from now around 50% of all orthopaedic procedures will involve tissue grafts. It is expected that the foreseeable demand ranges between 34,442 and 62,098 annual demand for allograft tissue. The predicted annual usage of allograft tissue ranges between 42,589 and 72,210 grafts (Hackett, 2001). United States sales of bone grafts and bone substitutes were over US$ 500 million in 2001 as compared to approximately US$ 150 million in 1997 (Greenwald *et al.*, 2002). Today this figure is much higher.

[5] The common uses of musculoskeletal tissues in orthopaedic procedures are the following: **Bone:** Demineralised bone products (osteoinductive); cortical/cancellous — powder, chips, wedges, dowels, crest, pegs, and screws; structural — cortical segments, shafts, long bones, pelvis, and acetabulum; osteochondral long bone (cryoprotected cartilage); ribs, mandible, calvarium, and ear ossicles; **Soft Tissue:** Patellar ligament and Achilles tendon (bone block), and other assorted tendons; fascia lata, and rotator cuff; **Cartilage:** Meniscus, osteoarticular segments (fresh and cryoprotected), and costal cartilage. In 2007, in the USA, an estimated of 1.5 million musculoskeletal allografts were distributed.

Figure 2: Doctors checking packaged medical tissues for their use in medical treatment. *Source*: IAEA

transplants, although regional differences exist, there is a growing global problem of demand for different types of tissues and far-exceeding available supply.

Several problems are evident in the banking and transplanting of tissues. One of these problems is the potential for viral or bacterial disease transmission. This problem is of great concern to clinicians and patients and is one of the limiting factors that are impeding the widespread use of allograft bone and soft tissue in certain medical treatments. Another problem is the lack of global uniformity and agreement on the definition of tissue and tissue establishments. A third problem that exists, despite the potential for the transfer of infections through the transplant of allografts, is the absence of national laws for quality and safety control in most countries, including several European countries and the USA.

Undoubtedly, the use of allograft tissues will increase in the coming years and, for this reason, the safety of allografts will continue to be a critical issue for the international community and should hopefully be improved with the use of new advanced technology. Due to the need for an increase in the safety of allografts, also needed is the standardisation of the current diversity in tissue definitions, quality and safety practices, the harmonisation of national laws for tissue banking and transplantation, and the establishment of global networking and cooperation among tissue establishments.

In addition to an increase in the safety of allografts, other problems that the international community is facing, according to WHO information, are the following:

- Many countries have poorly developed access to essential human tissue transplantation;
- At the national level, in most countries, human tissue transplantation activity data is not available, hampering the development of regulatory oversight; and
- There is a significant degree of international circulation of human tissues, a large fraction of which occurs outside of any regulatory oversight.

The success rates for transplantation of human tissues which do not require immunosuppression have also ensured that such procedures are frequently the treatment of choice in the respective therapeutic areas in a group of developed and developing countries. It is, however, clear that ethically unacceptable practices occur in a number of countries and this situation should be avoided.

Despite the appropriate focus on the prevention of diseases, the global needs of patients for transplantation are not being met. The demand has outstripped the supply of tissues from deceased donors in almost all countries. An aging population, the prevalence of obesity and conditions such as osteoarthritis and osteoporosis are factors that will affect demand for allograft tissue in many countries. Clinical evidence for the use of allograft is emerging in a number of domains, but there are areas where outcomes are dictating a change in practice. A good example of this is in cardiac surgery where the longevity of allograft valves is being compared to xenografts and synthetic products. A significant use of bone tissue is required for revisions of total hip and knee procedures (Hackett, 2001).

There is also a lack of clinical expertise in some regions and countries and an inability to fund transplantation to some extent in all countries. Potential donors are reluctant to commit to donate after death and their families or legal representatives may refuse permission when approached after death.[6]

At the same time, the society demands general respect for the human body and its parts and, for this reason, human tissue should not be used at will or abused. Increasing public concern has been shown over a number of ethical issues raised by the usages of human tissue as they have evolved in the 1980s and 1990s. Practices that have been questioned include the commercial exploitation of products derived from the tissue of patients or research subjects.

It is important to understand the concept of human tissue: It means constituent parts of the human body such as: bones, skin, heart valves, cornea, tendons, arteries, veins, dura mater as well as foetal tissues obtained following abortions, such as the placenta and umbilical cord (the cord itself and the cells it contains). Human tissues can be used for a wide variety of purposes:

- **For diagnostic purposes**: To determine whether a tumour is cancerous or not by removing tissue (biopsy); in order to prove the cause of death; for toxicological studies with the aim of examining the effects of certain products like insecticides, cosmetics, and medicines on tissues;
- **For therapeutic purposes**: In this case, human tissues are mostly used for transplantation. For example, orthopaedic surgery uses fragments of bone, while skin grafts are used to treat burn victims or as dressings in the treatment of diabetics. Human tissues are also used as sources of proteins or other therapeutic substances; and
- **For research purposes**: Basic, epidemiological and clinical research. Such research has, for example, made it possible to establish a link between asbestos and lung cancer.

[6]There was broad agreement that donors should be identified and selected according to fair and explicit criteria, above all medical eligibility, equally and without explicit or implicit discrimination based on social status and wealth, race, ethnicity, national origin, colour, sex, sexual orientation, gender identity or expression, age, marital status, political belief, religion, immigration status, and mental or physical disability or gender. There was also broad agreement that consent procedures and the methods for approaching potential donors should be standardised, transparent and subject to regular external auditing, given that vulnerable groups are at risk for subtle or overt manipulation regarding the decision to donate human tissues (Schulz-Baldes *et al.*, 2007).

The most common source of human tissue is the one which is removed from the body as part of diagnosis or treatment. Tissues are also frequently removed from dead donors. Other sources include foetal tissues obtained following abortions (spontaneous or induced), as well as placenta and umbilical cords obtained at childbirth. Exceptionally, human tissues may also be obtained from healthy volunteers (skin, for example).

Human tissues are generally removed or obtained in health care institutions or medical analysis laboratories.

Human tissues can easily be stored for long periods. Once removed or collected, human tissues are subject to a series of operations which, particularly when they are intended for transplantation, comprise the following:

- Processing;
- Preserving;
- Sterilisation;
- Storage;
- Distribution; and
- Use.

Wherever tissues are removed from human beings, and possibly transplanted into other human beings, the activities involved in the collection and use of such tissues are subject to ethical requirements intended to safeguard respect for human beings, their dignity and autonomy, and for the common good. In all cases, the donation, procurement, testing, processing, preservation, sterilisation, storage and distribution of human tissues intended for human applications should comply with the highest standards of quality and safety in order to ensure a high level of health protection to donors and recipients of human tissues in all states. Nevertheless, it is important to emphasise that the clinical use of tissues of human origin for human transplantation may be constrained by limited availability of tissue sterilisation. Therefore, it is desirable that the criteria for access to such tissues are defined in a transparent manner, and based on an objective evaluation of medical needs.

Activities of procurement of human tissues as well as activities carried out by the tissue establishments require an authorisation. This authorisation must be subject to compliance with basic ethical principles and with health safety standards, which themselves are ethically imperative. For this reason, human tissue donation should not be practised unless no feasible alternatives and means are in place to effectively protect the donor's health and safety. Tissue establishments have an eminent responsibility to supervise the implementation of these regulations and ethical principles. Human tissues, the procurement of which does not satisfy ethical principles and safety regulations, should not be accepted.

There is an important and urgent need to consider, clarify and, where necessary, strengthen the ethical and legal framework within which the clinical and research uses of human tissues take place. The ethical issues relate directly to the core of respect for human beings, namely that they and their bodies should not be injured and that nothing should be done to them and their bodies without their explicit consent. The limitations of the existing framework of legal and professional regulation point to the conclusion that a coherent approach is needed to any further regulation. The regulatory framework that should be developed by governments in the field of tissue banking should have three main goals:

- To prevent the unwitting use of contaminated human tissues with the potential for transmitting infectious disease;
- To prevent improper handling or processing that might contaminate or damage human tissues; and
- To require demonstration of clinical safety and effectiveness for most human tissues that are highly processed, that are used for non-native purposes, that are combined with non-tissue components or that have systemic effects on the body.

There are four ethical principles that should be observed: a) Respect for autonomy; b) beneficence; c) non-maleficence and d) justice. These principles provide an important framework for phrasing ethical issues in transplantation. It is also important to stress that transplantation programs that could be adopted by WHO in the coming years should focus on ethics, access and safety.

There are ethical concerns that can arise in the areas of deceased and living donors as well as tissue and xenotransplants that should be overcome in order to promote tissue transplantation. Common to all four areas are questions of eligibility and safety of donor and recipient, the use of financial and other incentives to increase the number of donors, equitable access and allocation and issues of cross-border exchanges and commercialisation.

Research involving the use of human tissue, or the use of information derived from research activities involving human tissue, is considered by many experts as a fundamental cornerstone of modern medical research and knowledge. Many of the advances in the life sciences, which have contributed so much to the health, physical well-being and long life expectancy of millions of people all over the world, are based on knowledge gleaned in one way or another from human tissue research. It is expected that in the future, human tissue research will likely take a more important role as new uses for the information gained from such research are identified. Most notably, almost all forms of genetic and genomic research use human tissue, directly or indirectly, as the starting point of their investigations (The Bioethics Advisory Committee, 2002).

Lastly, it is important to emphasise the following: Some of the main problems that in the field of tissue banking need international attention arise from:

- Poor international data exchange on therapeutic use of human tissues as well as the lack of harmonisation and high costs of tissue establishment to achieve regulatory standards;
- Poor international data about the role of different techniques for the sterilisation of human tissues;
- Poor levels of education, training and research in tissue banking, inconsistent approaches to donor consent, limited or non-existent evidence of efficacy in some tissue transplantation and tissue commercialisation;
- Concerns about the self-sustainability of "not-for-profit establishment" on the one hand and excessive income of "for-profit establishment" on the other, in the context of altruistically donated human material;
- Harmonisation of international regulations in the field of tissue banking.[7] This should be achieved through global communication between

[7]According to EU Directive 2004, there is an urgent need for a unified framework in order to ensure high standards of quality and safety with respect to the procurement, testing, processing, storage and distribution of human tissues across different countries of all regions and to facilitate exchanges thereof for patients receiving this type of therapy each year. It is essential, therefore, that national provisions ensure that human tissues, whatever is their intended use, are of comparable quality and safety. The establishment of such

regulators and providers, development of global professional standards, registration of serious donor-adverse events, adoption of a coding system used for the coding, tracing, and identification of processed human tissues by different tissue establishments, and the continuous measurement and publication of transplant outcomes;

- Lack of ethical guidance and the existence of unmonitored or unregulated human tissue procurement and distribution, which represent a serious international risk to both donors and recipients of cells and tissues. For this reason, the adoption of a common model for a code of ethics and for a code of practice, which can be used as reference for the adoption of these types of codes by all tissue establishments, should be promoted. This is an important task that should be carried out by governments interested in the promotion of tissue banking and by relevant international organisations;
- The absence of an international network of tissue establishments, which can promote and strengthen the cooperation and assistance between them;
- Lack of government support to tissue banking in several countries;
- Poor public awareness strategies;
- Lack of adequate regulation of good tissue practices[8] as evidenced by many recent transmissions of infectious diseases. Problems include an absence of adverse event reporting, large numbers of small establishments and inadequate "tracking" processes making it difficult to trace tissues from donor to recipient (due to privacy issues).

---

standards, therefore, will help to reassure the public that human tissues that are procured in any country, nonetheless, carry the same guarantees as those procured in their own country or in any other country with the highest standards of quality and safety. On the other hand, the harmonisation of laws and rules in the field of research in tissue banking is likely to emerge as an important consideration in shaping the laws and rules in each jurisdiction. In a world where large-scale collaborative research projects tend to transcend national borders, there is an increasing likelihood that many countries may demand proof of each other that there is approximate equivalence in the degree of ethical and legal protection or regulation before they will allow the cross-frontier transfer of research data, or allow cross-border research collaboration, which involves access to their national tissue collections or data (The Bioethics Advisory Committee, 2002).

[8]Good tissue practice includes the methods, facilities and controls for manufacturing, which prevent contamination by infectious disease-causing organisms. Good tissue practice requires also a quality programme to prevent, detect and correct deficiencies, which could increase communicable disease risk.

Governments should take all necessary measures to ensure that any promotion and publicity activities in support of the donation of human tissues comply with the guidelines or legislative provisions laid down by the state and/or local laws and/or regulations. Such guidelines or legislative provisions should include appropriate restrictions or prohibitions on advertising the need for, or availability of, human tissues with a view to offering or seeking financial gain or anything else of comparable advantage.

The present book has the intention to provide answers to all these elements in order to move forward the field of ethics in tissue banking. This could be done by providing a model code of ethics and a model code of practice, which can be used as a reference by those tissue establishments that wish to adopt such types of codes and good tissue practice.

Chapter II

Importance of Ethics in the Field of Human Tissue Banking

General Overview

The use of human tissues in certain medical practices has been consecrated as an effective modality to save lives and to improve the quality of life of thousands of individuals undergoing specific medical treatments.

Doctors and dentists use human tissue for a variety of medical purposes. Donated skin can meet critical needs in healing burns victims and in reconstructive surgery. Donated bones can be implanted to replace cancerous bones; it can be used in knee and hip replacements and in spinal surgery; and it can be processed into a powder for use in dental surgery. Donated heart valves can replace defective valves in young children, saving their lives (Department of Health and Human Services, 2001).

The success rates for transplantation of human tissues have ensured that processed tissues can be used more frequently in specific medical treatments without increasing the risk of harming the health of the recipient. To avoid improper use of the tissues procured by a tissue establishment, it is necessary to promote and adopt certain ethical principles, which should be observed by the operators and medical staff during the procurement, processing, storage, distribution and use of human tissues. The purpose of observing ethical principles is to avoid not only the abuse and unethical practices in tissue banking, but also the violation of specific regulations in force in the country.[1]

Tissue procurement and transplantation is no longer considered an extraordinary or uncommon health care event. As the techniques become more refined, the possibility of a transplant becomes a hope for more and more people suffering from different diseases. Because the demand for human tissues is great and the supply limited, dilemmas related to allocation of resources are imminent.

There are also questions regarding the eligibility of recipients for human tissue transplant. Many concerns arise as to the identification of potential recipients. Transplantation may involve tissues from dead or living human donors, and there are dilemmas associated with each.

Because transplantation requires well-nourished tissues, procurement must occur over a specified period. The determination of when death occurs is important. Irreversible cessation of cardiopulmonary functioning is one such measures.

With living donors, issues related to voluntary informed consent or authorisation and the transplant of human tissues free of contamination are of great concern. There are some individuals who are desperate and have prompted the sale of human tissues to raise money for personal or family needs. In cases of sudden accidental death, family members may be asked to consider donation of tissues. Consider whether there can be true voluntary consent when the family is in the midst of crisis and shock. With the urgency for a decision due to time factors for tissue procurement, coercion could be a factor. In some settings, nurses are required to approach patients or families about considering tissue donation. In such situations, nurses need to be clear about their own feelings regarding

---

[1]The terms "ethics" and "morality" are often used interchangeably. However, sometimes ethics is distinguished from morality. One way of making the distinction is as follows. Morality is about minimum standards of behaviour and attitude. On the other hand, ethics is a wider notion. Ethics involves ideals and aspirations; it goes beyond minimum standards. A doctor who was competent, and was not negligent might not be engaged in immoral behaviour. Nevertheless, such a doctor might not be a good doctor. To be a good doctor implies doing more than merely complying with minimum standards. For example, a good doctor would have a caring attitude to his or her patients. So morality refers to minimum standards, whiles ethics refers to a wider field of value that embraces notions of what is good and worth aspiring to — ideals as well as minimum standards (Miller, 2002).

human tissue procurement and transplantation, and they must remember that attention to family needs takes precedence over the time constraints of tissue procurement (Bauer *et al.*, 2004).

It is important to note that current practices in human tissue transplantation raise several questions that need to be addressed jointly by clinicians, scientists, health regulators and ethicists, as well as representatives of civil society, particularly human tissue donors and recipients. Although a number of regulations on human tissue transplantation has been adopted in the past several years or is currently under discussion in several countries, national regulations and oversight of human tissue transplantation as well as ethical guidance are still non-existent or ineffective in many countries around the world. This is the reason for the existence of unmonitored or unregulated human tissue procurement and distribution, which represent a serious international risk to both donors and recipients of human tissues (Schulz-Baldes *et al.*, 2007).

Tissue banking is an interdisciplinary field of medicine more reliant than others on specialised fields and on the application of knowledge from other branches of science, in particular medical sciences, and is even more influenced by them. It is further different from other medical disciplines in that there is the urgent necessity for the inclusion of laws, norms, standards and statutory regulations, which differ in their juridical binding force (von Versen *et al.*, 2000).[2]

Tissue banking implicates a variety of ethical concerns pertaining to such values as dignity, bodily integrity, autonomy and privacy, among others. These ethical concerns have been translated into a complex and incoherent apparatus of private and public, national and international standards and provisions. This apparatus embraces, e.g., UNESCO's International Declaration on Human Genetic Data (2003), the Recommendation of the Committee of Ministers of the Council of Europe

[2]Tissue banking is a specialised medical discipline, which, in accordance with generally recognised ethical principles and conscious that human tissue donation is carried out for unselfish or charitable reasons, is concerned with the organisation and coordination of the tissue removal, processing, and preservation of tissues, their quality assurance, as well as the storage and distribution of these final products for therapeutic, diagnostic, teaching and research purposes and is controlled and licensed by official and competent national health care authorities or other authorities. In this regard, the term "tissue" includes all cells and tissues as well as the cell and tissue replacement materials of biological origin (von Versen *et al.*, 2000).

(COE) to Member States on Research on Biological Materials of Human Origin (Rec. 2006), the FDA final rule 'Human Cells, Tissues, and Cellular and Tissue-Based Products, Establishment Registration and Listing' (2001), the European Human Tissue Directive 2004/23/ EC (2004), the Standards of the American Association of Tissue Banking (AATB), the Guidelines of the Swiss Academy of Medical Sciences (2006), as well as several national laws such as the Swedish Act on Biobanks (2002) (Gassner, 2007).

Main Ethical Issues

Wherever tissues are removed from human beings, and possibly transplanted into other human beings or to the same donors, the activities involved in the procurement and use of such tissues should be subject to ethical requirements intended to safeguard respect for human beings, its dignity and autonomy.

The fact that one donor may yield several tissue transplant products, which could be used later on in a number of medical treatments or research activities, highlights the need for safety measures in the procurement, processing, storage, distribution, and use of human tissues. The impact of any misconduct during these processes may be understandably high. For this reason, each state should set itself the target to guarantee to its citizens high and ethical standards in all health care activities, particularly in the area of tissue banking. This protection must extend to all tissue donors and recipients, as well as to all health care professionals and technicians that are involved in the procurement, processing, distribution and use of human tissues in certain medical treatments or in specific research activities.

At present, the international community cannot be assured that the quality and, in particular the safety of human tissues for transplants, is properly guaranteed in all countries and regions. There are at least four main reasons that can be cited. One is the shortcomings of international and regional ethical rules and standards in the field of human tissue banking. The second is the lack of national ethical rules and standards in force in various countries. The third is the lack of proper regulatory oversight in the field of tissue banking in several countries.[3] The fourth is the lack of harmonisation of existing ethical regulations and standards. For all of the

[3]In some of the countries, particularly in the USA, there is a strong resistance to greater government oversight of tissue establishment activities.

above reasons, the adoption of ethical principles, the use of a model code of ethics and a model code of practice and the harmonisation of existing regulations and standards at international and regional levels, should be one of the highest priorities for the tissue banking community during the coming years.

Adoption of an Ethical Policy, a Code of Ethics[4] and a Code of Practice

While there are inescapable acts of individual judgment involved in ethical decisions, nevertheless, it is desirable that conclusions should be reached in ways that result in as consistent a practice as possible. A way of achieving this in a given area of activity is to formulate a code of ethics and a code of practice providing general guidelines within which individual decisions must be made. A code of ethics is a basic presentation of principles and ideals, and has a regulatory, educational and cultural integration function; a code of practice is a detailed description of the actions that are to be performed and not to be performed, and of the sanctions that attach to non-performance.

A code of ethics has two aspects: a) the content comprising the requirements, regulations, principles, ideals, and so forth; and b) the commitment of the members of an organisation to conform to, and otherwise uphold, those regulations and ideals. The commitment to such principles could require members of the organisation to undertake an oath or promise or other kind of undertaking that each member has committed to adhere to the code. A code of ethics is a good place for members of an organisation to signal their commitment to the basic laws, and thus basic moral standards of their community, including the principle of individual autonomy (Miller, 2002).

With the intention of ensuring respect to the human being and the deserved dignity and autonomy, each state should have in force an ethical policy, a code of ethics and a code of practice with the purpose of applying it to all tissue banking activities carried out in the country. This ethical

[4]The code of ethics is neither a new nor an exhaustive system of health ethics. Rather, it highlights acceptable ethical principles.

policy and the related codes should be prepared on the basis of a group of ethical principles adopted at international and regional levels, and should take into account the specific conditions prevailing in the country. These ethical principles are described in detail in the following sections.

The role of an ethical policy and related codes is to promote a culture of openness, trust and integrity in all tissue banking activities implemented in the country, and to allow human tissues processed in one country to be used in another country, with a minimum contamination risk.

It is important to note that a successful implementation of an ethical policy and related codes requires the active participation and support of all tissue establishment personnel and medical staff associated with the activities of the tissue establishment. An ethical effective conduct is a team effort in which individual members of the team should be familiar with the ethical policy, the code of ethics, the code of practice in force and the set of ethical principles adopted by the national competent health care authorities.

Tissue establishment staff should not tolerate any wrongdoings or improper ethical conduct at any time and by anyone and should take appropriate measures to act quickly to correct any deviation from the ethical policy, the code of ethics, the code of practice and the set of ethical principles adopted and in force by the national competent health care authorities in the field of tissue banking. Any violations of the code of ethics and the code of practice by some tissue establishment staff may be subject to disciplinary actions, up to and including termination of employment. In the event that the violator is the tissue establishment itself, the sanction to be applied could be equal to the suspension of the institution's operational license.

An ethical policy should ensure that the activities of a tissue establishment are conducted by all operators and medical personnel associated with the activities of the tissue establishment with professionalism and integrity. During tissue procurement, tissue establishment staff should treat the donor, the donor family, legal representative and hospital staff in a fair and respectful manner, encouraging a team environment and avoiding any conduct that may be related to unethical or compromising practices.

Every tissue establishment staff should make all necessary efforts to adopt ethical values, including efforts to increase human tissue donors within the local community, as well as to provide high-quality human tissues in a timely and responsive manner to hospitals, other medical facilities and research institutions.

There are several elements that should be considered during the discussions of any ethical policy, code of ethics and code of practice associated with the procurement, processing, sterilisation, storage, distribution and use of human tissues. Among these elements are the following:

- All tissue establishment staff should expect and have the obligation to conduct themselves at all times within high ethical standards and legal principles;
- Tissue establishments should operate by respecting all laws and regulations adopted by the national competent health care authorities in the field of tissue banking;
- No payment should be given or received regarding human tissue donations and other activities carried out by the tissue establishments, outside of those authorised by the national competent health care authorities;
- Conflicts of interest must be avoided between the tissue establishment personnel and the donors, the donor family or the legal representative;
- All tissue establishment personnel are encouraged to report any suspected wrongdoings by the staff during the fulfilment of their activities. Nevertheless, it would be expected that tissue establishment staff do their work with integrity, honesty and diligence;
- Tissue establishments should facilitate and support valuable research activities using human tissues for the welfare of the community, but within the legal and ethical framework established by the competent national health care authorities; and
- Tissue establishment staff should provide the best possible services to tissue donors, end-users and recipients, and should place the highest priority on quality, timeliness and competitiveness in providing these services.

Based on what was noted previously, the following ethical principles should be considered during the formulation of any code of ethics to be observed by operators of a tissue establishment in the future:

- Be honest and adopt an ethical conduct, including ethical handling of current or apparent conflicts of interest between personal and professional relationships;

- Comply with applicable government laws, rules and regulations in force in the country in the field of tissue banking;
- Maintain the confidentiality of data entrusted by the human tissue donors, the donor family or legal representative to the tissue establishment with regard to tissue donation and donor screening, except when authorised or legal action obligate the tissue establishment to disclose this information to duly designated national health care authorities;
- Deal fairly with tissue donors, donor families, legal representatives, medical personnel, transplant coordinators, volunteers and other hospital staff, during the procurement, processing and use of human tissues;
- Provide information that is accurate, completely objective, relevant, timely and understandable to all competent national health care authorities duly authorised to request this information;
- Proactively promote ethical behaviour among tissue establishment staff, with the purpose of creating a positive work environment within the tissue establishment and the tissue banking network; and
- Protect and ensure the proper use of tissue establishment assets and tissue donations, carefully weighing against practices that may be linked to commercialisation or other hidden agendas not authorised by the national competent health care authorities.

Other elements that can be considered during the preparation of a code of ethics are the following:

- Maintain the highest standards of professional conduct;
- Assume responsibility and accountability for individual judgments and actions;
- Gain and maintain proficiency of practice;
- Participate in efforts to establish, implement and improve standards of practice;
- Contribute to the growth of professional knowledge;
- Respect individual privacy and hold confidential all information obtained in the course of practice;
- Maintain a cooperative and respectful relationship with other transplant practitioners and health care professionals;

- Serve the public regardless of race, ethnicity, culture, social or economic status, personal political position and ideology or religious belief;
- Educate the public about donation and transplantation issues; and
- Act for protecting the public when health care and safety are endangered (Bauer, *et al.*, 2004).

Codes of ethics typically prescribe and proscribe actions. Indeed, codes of ethics are largely about actions. Nevertheless, the view that codes of ethics are simply rules that dictate what actions are to be performed, and what actions are not to be performed, is too narrow. For one thing, codes of ethics typically mention virtues and vices, as well as actions. Virtues and vices are habits or dispositions to act. As such they are not simply actions; they are elements of a person's character. For another thing, codes of ethics are, or ought to be, concerned with affective attitudes as well as actions. Attitudes are important; attitudes motivate actions (Miller, 2002).

Finally, it is important to remember the basic distinction that exists between legal norms and ethical norms. While the former are founded on the latter, there is no necessary one-to-one correspondence between each legal and ethical norm. A law may be regarded as unethical by some people (e.g., a law prescribing the death penalty for certain crimes) and likewise, an ethical norm may be regarded as unlawful in a country (e.g., one involving female genital mutilation). Hence it cannot be expected that ethical guidelines, which translate ethical principles in the form of recommendations (rather than of strict norms), will always coincide with legal prescriptions. This applies all the more to international guidelines, which are issued in the context of legal dispositions varying from one country to another (Council for International Organisations of Medical Sciences, 2008).

The following summarises. Because codes of ethics are devices that can be used to reinforce desirable behaviour and change undesirable behaviour — albeit devices that need to be used in conjunction with complaints and discipline systems, appropriate structures of reward, effective processes of conflict resolution, ethics education programmes, and so on — they need to attend not simply to the behaviour (action) itself, but also to the character (habits) and affective attitudes that condition and motivate that behaviour (Miller, 2002). Codes of ethics should not attempt to detail specific skills or knowledge that might be necessary to successfully undertake an occupation within a tissue establishment. Codes of ethics typically prescribe and proscribe actions, habits and attitudes.

However, at least two questions arise. The first question concerns the reason or reasons for prescribing some actions or other. Sometimes codes do provide reasons for their prescriptions. But in general the code is too brief to elaborate the various reasons. Nevertheless, reasons ought to be given. Hence, there is a need for a code of ethics to be supplemented by a code of practice with explanatory material.

The second question concerns the education programme. Since practical knowledge of ethical principles and ideals, and practical knowledge of their application, is not a static thing — ethical problems and the solutions to them undergo change — there is a need for ongoing revision of the code of ethics, ongoing education in relation to changes to the code of ethics, and especially on-going education in relation to the application of the principles and ideals expressed in the code. A code of ethics, and associated ethical education, ought to be an important element in initial formal and informal education programmes, an also in continuing education programmes.

Establishment of the Ethics Committees

It is important to establish an ethics committee[5] to ensure that tissue establishments and research institutions, in which human tissues are manipulated, carry out their activities respecting a group of ethical principles that

[5]Whilst the need for proper ethical review is accepted and a hierarchy of ethics committees is well established in several countries, there is still a lack of understanding, even amongst some committee members, about the remit of an ethics committee. Ethics training is not harmonised and is in some cases in the hands of the wrong individuals, who with scant knowledge of proper science take an overly harsh and unrealistic attitude to which scientific studies should or should not be permitted. This, coupled with local misinterpretations or over interpretations of relevant legislation (as in a decision to treat waste products as relevant material defined in the Human Tissue Act s53 (2004)) creates unnecessary obstructions. This only serves to demotivate scientists, and can and will lead to fewer experiments on human material. These obstacles can be removed by applying stricter criteria to who can serve on an ethics committee dealing with human tissue research and who should be permitted to run training courses (Pierscionek, 2011).

should be adopted by the competent national health care authorities, bearing in mind a group of international and regional ethical principles.

The primary role of an ethics committee in reviewing biomedical research is to contribute to safeguarding the dignity, rights, safety, and well-being of all actual or potential research participants. A cardinal principle of research involving human participants is "respect for the dignity of persons". The goals of research, while important, should never be permitted to override the health, well-being, and care of research participants (WHO, 2000).

The ethics committee should be an independent reporting body that should provide public assurance of the protection of all actual or potential research participants by reviewing and approving standards and underwriting a code of practice suitable to the activities carried out by a tissue establishment or research institution (WHO, 2000).[6]

Special mechanisms should be in place to make ethics committee operations transparent, accountable, consistent, and of high quality. The authority establishing the ethics committees should have reliable means to evaluate whether the staff and members of the ethics committees routinely follow the committee's policies, rules, and written procedures, with special attention to whether the ethical considerations articulated in international guidelines and national standards are being considered and applied consistently and coherently. In other words:

- Such evaluations are conducted by knowledgeable and unbiased people at regular, pre-defined intervals using a pre-defined format; internal assessments are supplemented periodically by independent external evaluations;
- The authority establishing the ethics committees is committed to consider and, when appropriate, follow up on the findings and recommendations of the internal and external evaluations;

[6]The ethics committee, according to Directive 2001/20/EC, is an independent body in a member state of the European Union, consisting of health care professionals and non-medical members, whose responsibility is to protect the rights, safety and well-being of human subjects involved in a clinical trial and to provide public assurance of that protection, by, among other things, expressing an opinion on the clinical trial protocol, the suitability of the investigators involved in the trial and the adequacy of facilities, and on the methods and documents to be used to inform trial subjects and obtain their informed consent.

- The results of the evaluation are of a type that can aid the ethics committees in reviewing its practice and appraising performance (rather than apportioning blame), while also assuring the public that research is being reviewed according to established standards;
- Researchers, research participants, and other interested parties have a means of lodging complaints about the ethics committee decisions; such complaints should be reviewed by an entity other than the ethics committees itself, and appropriate follow-up actions should be taken;
- Researchers have a means of discussing concerns with ethics committee members, both on general matters and in response to ethics committee decisions on particular research studies;
- Ethics committee decisions, excluding confidential information, are made publicly available, through mechanisms such as clinical trial registries, web sites, newsletters, and bulletin boards (WHO, 2011).

Countries, institutions, and communities should strive to establish ethics committees and ethical review systems that ensure the broadest possible coverage of protection for potential research participants and contribute to the highest attainable quality in the science and ethics of biomedical research. States should promote, as appropriate, the establishment of ethics committees at the national, institutional, and local levels, which are independent, multi-disciplinary, multi-sectorial, and pluralistic in nature. However, ethics committees should be established in accordance with the applicable laws and regulations of the country and in accordance with the values and principles of the communities they serve. To ensure the functioning of the ethics committees, administrative and financial support should be provided by competent national health care authorities.

It is important to ensure the impartiality of the ethics committees through carefully nominated members. These members should be chosen in a manner that an adequate representation of the community served by the tissue establishment is ensured. It is important that the ethics committees be composed of different types of professionals, such as physicians, nurses, lawyers, hospital coordinators, nuclear experts, and ethicists, as

Figure 3: Meeting room.

well as lay persons qualified to represent the cultural and moral values of the community to which the tissue establishments or the research institutions are serving.

The ethics committees should adopt a rotation policy of its members; this means a number of committee members should be replaced periodically, with the aim of blending the advantages of experience with those of fresh perspectives. To ensure that the ethics committees cannot be pressured to approve or disapproved particular research projects protocols, the charter, by-laws, policies and/or procedural rules of the ethics committees should provide that:

- The ethics committees' membership includes at least one person with no connection to the organisation that sponsors or conducts the research under review;
- Researchers, sponsors and funders may attend an ethics committee meeting to answer questions about their research project and associated documents, but they are not present when the committee reaches decisions about their proposed research;
- Senior decision-makers of the entity creating the ethics committee or of any organisation that sponsors or conducts the research reviewed by

the committee (such as the Director of a tissue establishment or other medical research institution or his or her representative), do not serve as members of the ethics committee or its Chair; and

- The authority that establishes the ethics committee ensures that its members are protected from retaliation based on positions taken with respect to committee-related matters or review of research projects (WHO, 2011).

The ethics committees should also act as an independent advisory body and carry out its activities independent of political, institutional, professional and other influences. Its work should be guided by an ethical policy, a code of ethics, a code of practice and a set of ethical principles approved by the national competent health care authorities of the country. The ethics committees should establish publicly available standard operating procedures (SOPs) that state the authority under which the committees are established, the functions and duties of the ethics committees, membership requirements,[7] the terms of appointment,[8] the conditions of appointment,[9] the offices, the structure of the secretariat, internal procedures, and the quorum requirements,[10] Ethics committees should act in accordance with their

[7]According to WHO, these are the following: The name or description of the party responsible for making appointments; the procedure for selecting members, including the method for appointing a member (e.g., by consensus, by majority vote, by direct appointment); conflicts of interest should be avoided when making appointments, but where unavoidable, there should be transparency with regard to such interests.

[8]According to the WHO, these are the following: the duration of an appointment; the policy for the renewal of an appointment; the disqualification procedure; the resignation procedure; and the replacement procedure.

[9]According to the WHO, these are the following: A member should be willing to publicise his/her full name, profession, and affiliation; all reimbursement for work and expenses, if any, within or related to an ethics committee should be recorded and made available to the public upon request; a member should sign a confidentiality agreement regarding meeting deliberations, applications, information on research participants, and related matters; in addition, all ethics committee administrative staff should sign a similar confidentiality agreement.

[10]According to WHO, these are the following: The minimum number of members required to compose a quorum (e.g., more than half the members); the professional qualification requirements (e.g., physician, lawyer, statistician, paramedical, layperson) and the distribution of those requirements over the quorum; no quorum should consist entirely of

written SOPs and will be charged with the preparation of a code of ethics. During the preparation of the code, the ethics committees should:

- Identify the purposes to be served by the code of ethics;
- Identify the format of the code of ethics, e.g., explanatory material, accompanying code of practice, among others;
- Examine the main goals, activities and the context (including organisational context) of the organisation;
- Outline the role of members of the organisation;
- Detail the main ethical requirements of members of the organisation;
- Identify the main ethical problems likely to be faced; and
- Prepare a document setting out the results of the above treatments. This is not a draft code of ethics, but rather a discussion of issues, ethical problems, and ideally a set of case studies and questions (Miller, 2002).

An application for review of the ethics of proposed biomedical research should be submitted to the ethics committee by a qualified researcher responsible for the ethical and scientific conduct of the research. The requirements for the submission of a research project for ethical review should be clearly described in an application procedure. According to WHO (2000), these requirements should include, among others, the following elements:

- The name and address of the person within the ethics committee's secretariat to whom the application is to be submitted;
- The application form;
- The format for submission;
- The documentation to be attached to the application form[11];

---

members of one profession or one gender; a quorum should include at least one member whose primary area of expertise is in a non-scientific area, and at least one member who is independent of the institution/research site.

[11]According to the WHO, this may include, among others, the following: The protocol of the proposed research, together with supporting documents and annexes, including a description of the ethical considerations involved in the research; when the research involves a study product (such as a pharmaceutical or device under investigation), an adequate summary of all safety, pharmacological, pharmaceutical, and toxicological data

- The number of copies to be submitted;
- The deadlines for submission of the application in relation to review dates;
- The expected time for notification of the decision following review, including the communication of the incompleteness of an application;
- The time frame to be followed in cases where the ethics committee requests supplementary information or changes to documents from the applicant;
- The fee structure, if any, for reviewing an application; and
- The application procedure for amendments to the protocol, the recruitment material, the potential research participant information, or the informed consent form.

The establishment of the ethics committee to supervise the routine work of a tissue establishment or the progress in a research medical institution in which human tissues are manipulated, is the appropriate mechanism to ensure the respect of all ethical aspects related to the procurement, processing, distribution and use of processed human tissues in research activities.

It is important to emphasise the following: Once a research project has been found scientifically sound, the ethics committees should consider whether any known or possible risks to human beings are justified by the expected benefits, direct or indirect, that are foreseeable to obtain from the projects under consideration, and whether the proposed research methods will minimise harm and maximise benefit.

If a proposed research project is scientifically sound and the balance of risks to anticipated benefits is reasonable, the ethics committee in charge of the revision of the proposal should then determine whether the procedures proposed for obtaining informed consent or authorisation, when

available on the study product, together with a summary of clinical experience with the study product to date; research(s)'s curriculum vitae; a description of the process used to obtain and document consent; written and other forms of information for potential research participants; informed consent form; a statement describing any compensation for study participation (including expenses and access to medical care) to be given to research participants; a description of the arrangements for indemnity, if applicable; a description of the arrangements for insurance coverage for research participants, if applicable; and a statement of agreement to comply with ethical principles set out in relevant guidelines.

applicable, are satisfactory and the process for selecting human tissues equitable. The ethics committees are also responsible for ensuring that all other ethical concerns are satisfactorily resolved both in theory and in practice, for keeping records of its decisions, and for taking measures to follow up on the conduct of ongoing research projects (Council for International Organisations of Medical Sciences, 2008).

The ethics committees have a duty to examine the progress of the research or innovative therapies.[12] It should have access to records and be

---

[12]During the examination of the progress of a specific research or innovative therapy, the following elements should be considered by the ethics committee: The appropriateness of the study design in relation to the objectives of the study, the statistical methodology (including sample size calculation), and the potential for reaching sound conclusions with the smallest number of research participants; the justification of predictable risks and inconveniences weighed against the anticipated benefits for the research participants and the concerned communities; criteria for prematurely withdrawing research participants; criteria for suspending or terminating the research as a whole; the adequacy of provisions made for monitoring and auditing the conduct of the research; the adequacy of the site, including the supporting staff, available facilities, and emergency procedures; the manner in which the results of the research will be reported and published; the characteristics of the population from which the research participants will be drawn; the means by which initial contact and recruitment is to be conducted; the means by which full information is to be conveyed to potential research participants or their representatives; inclusion and exclusion criteria for research participants; the suitability of the research(s)'s qualifications and experience for the proposed study; any plans to withdraw or withhold standard therapies for the purpose of the research, and the justification for such action; the medical care to be provided to research participants during and after the course of the research; the adequacy of medical supervision and psycho-social support for the research participants; steps to be taken if research participants voluntarily withdraw during the course of the research; the criteria for extended access to, the emergency use of, and/or the compassionate use of study products; the arrangements, if appropriate, for informing the research participant's general practitioner (family doctor), including procedures for seeking the participant's consent to do so; a description of any plans to make the study product available to the research participants following the research; a description of any financial costs to research participants; the rewards and compensations for research participants; the provisions for compensation/treatment in the case of the injury/disability/death of a research participant attributable to participation in the research; the insurance and indemnity arrangements; a description of the persons who will have access to personal data of the research participants, including medical records and biological samples; the measures taken to ensure the confidentiality and security of personal information concerning research participants; a full description of

able to substantiate that the human tissues procured are in fact being utilised for the purpose for which it was procured. Before permitting research activities involving human tissues, the ethics committee must satisfy itself:

- About the validity of a specific research or use of the human tissues proposed;
- That the objectives of the proposed use of the human tissues cannot be achieved in any other way; and
- That the researchers have the necessary facilities and skill in carrying out research activities with the human tissues that have been proposed.

Once the decision to establish an ethics committee is adopted, the committee should establish its own working rules, defining the frequency of meetings, what will be considered a quorum of members, the elaboration of the decision-making procedures, and the process for the review of decisions adopted, among others. The rules to be adopted by an ethics committee should protect the confidentiality of all documents considered by the committee, as well as the content of all discussions carried out within the committee, which were recorded.

The ethics committees generally have no authority to impose sanctions on researchers who violate ethical standards in the conduct of a research involving human tissues. They may, however, withdraw the approval of a

---

the process for obtaining informed consent, including the identification of those responsible for obtaining consent; the adequacy, completeness, and understandability of written and oral information to be given to the research participants, and, when appropriate, their legal representative(s); assurances that research participants will receive information that becomes available during the course of the research relevant to their participation (including their rights, safety, and well-being); the provisions made for receiving and responding to queries and complaints from research participants or their representatives during the course of a research project; the impact and relevance of the research on the local community and on the concerned communities from which the research participants are drawn; the steps taken to consult with the concerned communities during the course of designing the research; the influence of the community on the consent of individuals; proposed community consultation during the course of the research; the extent to which the research contributes to capacity building, such as the enhancement of local health care, research, and the ability to respond to public health needs; a description of the availability and affordability of any successful study product to the concerned communities following the research; the manner in which the results of the research will be made available to the research participants and the concerned communities (WHO, 2000).

research project, if judged necessary. They should be required to monitor the implementation of an approved research project and its progression, and to report to institutional or governmental authorities any serious or continuing non-compliance with ethical standards in the conduct of the research work. Failure to submit a report to the committee should be considered a clear and serious violation of ethical standards. If sanctions become necessary, they should be aimed at the non-compliant researchers or sponsors. They may include fines or suspension of eligibility to receive research funding, to use investigational interventions, or to exercise their profession in the future.

Summing up, it can be stated that the main requirements for establishing an ethics committee are the following:

- Members should be selected based on their experience and irreproachable conduct and should reflect the composition of the community that is serviced by the tissue establishment, or within which the research institution is working. There should be complete freedom of speech and no constraints caused by unduly lines of reporting within the ethics committee;
- The ethics committee should protect the rights and welfare of tissue donors, donor families and recipients. The primary responsibility of each member of this advisory body is to decide, independently, whether in its opinion the conduct of the proposed activity is in line with the mandate of the tissue establishment or the research institution concerned;
- Tissue establishments and institutions that undertake research activities involving human tissues should ensure that there are adequate resources to establish and/or maintain the work of the ethics committees, in accordance with relevant national regulations. This means that:
    - The ethics committees have support staff, adequate in number and training to carry out its technical and administrative responsibilities in the most efficient manner;
    - The ethics committees have adequate resources in order to allow the staff to fulfil its assigned functions, including office space and equipment and supplies (e.g., computers, stationery, telephones, photocopying machines, shredding machine) in the most efficient manner;
    - The ethics committees are in a position to conduct administrative business, to store committee files, and to keep documents secure and confidential.

- The ethics committees have access to appropriate space for the committee to meet and adequate means for members to communicate as needed between meetings;
- The ethics committees have adequate financial resources to permit the committees to produce high-quality work; and
- The ethics committees have, if considered necessary by the competent national health care authorities establishing the committees, the resources necessary to compensate its members, unless they are already being compensated for their time and effort on the committees through other means (WHO, 2011).

The underlying goals of the ethics committees should be the following:

- To promote the rights of tissue donors and recipients;
- To encourage shared decision-making between recipients (patients or their families or legal representatives, if patients are incapacitated) and their clinicians;
- To promote fair policies and procedures to increase human tissue donations;
- To promote safe and ethical practices throughout the process — from donation for transplantation; and
- To enhance the ethical scope of health care professionals and institutions.

Finally, members of the ethics committees should be trained in several topics in order to allow them to carry out their responsibilities in the best possible manner. The topics in which members of the ethics committees should be trained are: on the ethical aspects of health-related research with human participants; on how ethical considerations apply to different types of research; and on how an ethics committee conducts its review of research. This training should be provided to the ethics committee members when they join the committee and periodically during their committee service.

The training provided to ethics committee members, either directly by the appointing authorities or through cooperative arrangements with other ethics committees and/or organisations that provide education on research ethics should focus on:

- The role and responsibilities of the ethics committees, and its role vis-à-vis other relevant entities, according to relevant international guidelines

(e.g., the Council for International Organisations of Medical Societies, International Ethical Guidelines for Biomedical Research, International Ethical Guidelines for Epidemiological Research, International Council on Harmonisation, Good Clinical Practice guidelines in the case of clinical trials), national laws, and institutional policies;
- The full range of ethical considerations relevant to research with human participants;
- The application of such ethical considerations to different types of research;
- Basic aspects of research methodology and design (for members who lack such background);
- The impact of different scientific designs and objectives on the ethics of a research study; and
- The various approaches for recognising and resolving the tensions that can arise among different ethical considerations and modes of ethical reasoning (WHO, 2011).

When training is supported by research sponsors, mechanisms should be in place to ensure that the sponsor has no control over the content of the training.

Main Ethical Principles

With regard to the removal of human tissues, the main ethical principles from the donor's point of view are the following:

- Respect for the human body, even after the person's death;
- Respect for the autonomy of the donor; thus, tissue may not be removed whenever the person refuses.[13] For deceased persons, this implies that

[13] In order to exercise the right of autonomy, a patient must first possess the capacity to make decisions. When speaking of a patient's ability to decide, physicians are actually speaking of a patient's "capacity." A patient who is able to make medical decisions is considered to possess capacity. A patient who is not mentally or psychologically able to make medical decisions is considered to lack capacity. When assessing a patient's capacity, the physician must evaluate three distinct aspects of the decision-making ability: a) Patients must show that they understand the given information about diagnosis and treatment and that they appreciate the significance of the disease and its consequences. In testing for understanding, the physician might ask patients to rephrase the information he has given

tissues may not be removed if the person had refused consent or had not given authorisation for the removal of tissues during her/his lifetime;
- Protection of vulnerable people, namely people unable to give consent or authorisation or have a difficult economic situation;
- Respect for private life and medical confidentiality;
- The right to prior information on the conditions of human tissue removal and the expected use of the human tissues procured; and
- The right not to be subjected to unjust discrimination, which could result from the revelation of data collected from the donor or the family to third parties (e.g., employers and insurance companies).

The main principles affecting recipients of allografts are:

- Respect for the autonomy of the person concerned, which requires clear information on the risks and advantages of the proposed transplant;
- Respect for private life and medical confidentiality, which applies to all medical treatment;
- The right to safety, which requires prior verification of the quality and safety of the human tissue to be transplanted with regard to the risk of transmission of infectious diseases, neoplasms, and immunological diseases; and
- The right of patients to receive reasonable access to the therapeutic possibilities offered by the transplantation of human tissues.

Lastly, it is important to stress that several countries accept, as a matter of principle, that human tissue transplantation programmes be founded on the philosophy of voluntary and unpaid donation, anonymity of both donor and recipient, altruism of the donor and solidarity between donor and recipient. To support this philosophy, several governments are taking steps to encourage a strong public and non-profit sector involvement in the

---

them; b) Patients should be able to deliberate in accordance with their own values. Here, the physician might ask patients what is most important to them in making their decision; c) Patients should demonstrate an ability to communicate consistent choices regarding their decisions. Here the physician might determine patients' choices at different times to test consistency (Davenport, 1997).

provision of tissue transplantation services and the related research and development using human tissues.

The following contain a group of specific ethical principles that can be used for the preparation of an ethical policy, a code of ethics and a code of practice by the national competent health care authorities in any state interested in increasing the impact of tissue banking activities in the community.

Ethical Principles Related with the Informed Consent or Authorisation to Donate Human Tissues

The procurement of human tissues requires the prior informed and free consent of the person concerned or, in case of a deceased donor, the consent or authorisation of their next-of-kin or legal representative.[14] Several criteria have been widely agreed upon for the definition of informed consent in medical care and research practices.[15]

It is not necessary, from ethical and practical perspectives, that the tissue establishment staff or medical doctor request or confirm the consent or authorisation for tissue donation face to face. In many cases, the attending physician is not the best requester; the next-of-kin may not be the best informant. According to the experience of various states with best practices in the field of tissue banking, a good communicator or a well-trained counsellor could play these responsibilities in a better manner.

It is important to be aware that the written consent form is meant to document such consent, but is not a substitute for the activities that should be carried out by the communicator or counsellor.

---

[14]This does not apply in the case of tissue procurement ordered by a judge in the context of judicial, in particular, criminal, proceedings.

[15]Clinical ethicists stress the view that informed consent is a process, not a piece of paper in lieu of the careful approach, sharing of pertinent information and discussion of outcomes, which conduct to a meaningful, voluntary and informed consent for medical and research practice. It is important to single out that donor consent for the use of human tissue is generally required, but the requirement may be waived due to specific circumstances, such as the donor and the next-of-kin are dead, or the human tissue was in storage in the tissue establishment for a very long time and it is almost impossible to contact the donor for his/her consent for the use of the tissue, etc. Donor consent for the use of human tissue is generally required, but in some countries, the requirement may be waived by the ethics committees in appropriate circumstances and for specific research activities.

While informed consent is a fundamental ethical principle in several countries, the process involved and format of such consent, i.e., verbal or in writing, before a witness or not, explicit or presumed, etc., should be based on the legal requirements of each country.

In living donors, written informed consent must be obtained, unless there are good reasons to the contrary, such as a situation of coma, emergency, or mental incapacity, in which the consent or authorisation should be given by the next-of-kin or legal representative. Verbal consent when the participant is illiterate, should be obtained in the presence of a literate witness who should verify in writing, duly signing it, that verbal consent was obtained from the donor, including the information regarding the use of the donated human tissues, the benefits of the research, and the risks and benefits involved.

When patients are approached, we have to give them all necessary information in order to allow them to understand the concept of informed consent. There are four levels of consent, and these are the kinds of consent that the patient should be asked to give. First, they should be asked for permission to donate their tissue for specific or for unspecified uses in the future. Second, the patient should be asked to allow future data to be collected and under which conditions these data should be collected. Third, the patient should be asked for the opportunity to contact him/her in the future should that need arise in the context of long-term studies. Fourth, the patient should be given levels of options about disclosure. Do they want to have any disclosure? Do they want to have only certain forms of disclosure, or do they want to have no disclosure at all?

It is important to emphasise that in some countries, informed consent is no longer the only current practice to donate human tissues approved by the national competent health care authorities. For instance, in the United States, the practice is now to refer to the process of obtaining permission for donation from a deceased person as "authorisation" rather than informed consent. This is due to a number of reasons. First, informed consent is a legal concept with well-established principles and guidelines associated with either a medical procedure or research protocol adopted by many states. The aim is to provide the potential patient or subject the right to decide whether to become a tissue's donor or not, being aware of all the risks and benefits of undergoing a particular medical procedure or taking part in a research protocol. However, human tissue donation is neither a medical procedure nor research project, and provides no economic benefits to the patient/donor.

The second reason to move away from informed consent is the use of "First Person Consent" or "Donor Registries". In most cases, an individual registers his/her desire or intent to become a donor at the time of his/her death. Under this practice, at the time of the individual's death, the family, next-of-kin or legal representative are not given the opportunity to countermand the donor's decision to donate, although there is still a conversation about whether the individual had changed his/her mind about donation, and the medical social interview is still conducted with a knowledgeable person.

In case of living donors, the donor's consent must be given on the basis of information provided in clear and precise terms by the surgeon or the preadmission nurse.[16] The information provided to the donor should refer to:

- The procurement arrangements, in particular, concerning the free nature of the donation and the extent of its anonymity;
- Possible tissue storage time and conditions of registration of data in databases, in conformity with requirements of private life protection and medical confidentiality; and
- Foreseeable use of the human tissues (diagnostic, allograft or autograft, pharmaceutical products, research, production of cellular lines for various uses, etc.). The donor may at any time withdraw her/his consent before the human tissues are released (Quintana-Trias *et al.*, 1998).

Consent or authorisation of a donor for retrieval of human tissues after death may take different forms, depending on the national systems adopted by the country. The two most common systems used by the countries regarding human tissue donation are the following: a) explicit consent; and b) presumed consent.

---

[16] It is important to highlight, in the case of living donors, the following: Ethical issues associated with the donation of human tissues for transplantation from a living donor principally involve concern for the donors. The autonomy and welfare of the donor takes precedence over the needs of the recipient to receive the procured human tissues.

It is important to note that no retrieval of human tissues may take place, with the exception of judicial proceedings, if the party concerned formally objected while alive. Furthermore, if there has been no expression of will and the applicable system is that of presumed consent, doctors must ensure, as far as possible, that relatives or next-of-kin or legal representative have the opportunity to express the deceased person's wishes, and must take this into account (Quintana-Trias *et al.*, 1998).

In the area of cadaveric tissue transplantation, the requester may vary between programmes: the requester could be a primary care physician, a primary care nurse, or an experienced liaison person acting as a transplant coordinator from a local organ procurement organisation or a counsellor.

Lastly, it is important to emphasise the following: Widespread reluctance to donate organs and tissues from deceased donors exist in many countries throughout Africa, Asia and Latin America and the Caribbean, even when appropriate legislation is in force. Factors include financial constraints, lack of skilled staff, inadequate infrastructure, important indigenous cultural and religious beliefs and values, among others.

There is no uniformity in legislation dealing with deceased donors across Latin American countries. Legislation varies from requirement of permission from both donor and family, to required consent in order to obtain an identity card, to presumed consent. In many states, refusal by family prevails over deceased's pre-mortem consent. The situation described above can also be found in other regions as well. For instead, despite considerable success in sourcing, processing and using human tissue donations, there are many obstacles to the effective use of tissue therapies in Asia, particularly in Japan and other Islamic countries in the region. In the past several years, there has been a progressive decrease in consent from next-of-kin to recover human tissues. The reasons for this are unclear and need to be understood. According to some expert's opinion, major difficulties in enhancing tissue banking in Asia include a poor cost–benefit ratio in running tissue establishments, a lack of formal education and training for surgeons and tissue banking technologists or operators, religious beliefs and insufficient research in the region. On the other hand, the commercialisation of human tissues in Asia is causing great concern in several countries.

For this reason, and with the purpose of overcoming the situation described, a change is required in legislation to give preference to the wishes of the donors and education campaigns to increase human tissue donation from deceased donors.

Informed Consent or Authorisation in Case of Research Projects

According to Kevin and Sandie (2011), the demand for human tissue for research purposes continues to increase in many countries, driven by the desire to:

- Increase understanding of disease processes;
- Improve diagnosis;
- Develop improved pharmaceuticals;
- Improve the quality of life of terminally ill patients;
- Meet the expectations of personalised treatments; and
- Move away from animal models that are perceived to lack scientific relevance and carry their own ethical burden.

For this reason, it is important that consent or authorisation for donation is given before human tissue is actually collected[17] in order to carry out research activities. Undoubtedly, full, free and informed consent or authorisation is the cornerstone of legal and ethical legitimacy and validity of a gift of human tissue intended for research. In all cases, research projects must be previously approved by a local ethics committee and consent or authorisation must be obtained from each living donor, or from their family or next-of-kin or legal representative in case of deceased donors, before the human tissue is procured.

---

[17]There is always a potential problem around the timing of the consent or authorisation process. Tissue coordinators approach a family at a time of great distress and for some patients in hospital, awaiting surgery is just as stressful. A post-operative patient may be just as vulnerable, which reinforces the need to employ coordinators who have a good knowledge of the tissue establishment research uses of human tissues (Womack, 2003).

It is also important that medical research is subject to ethical standards that promote respect for all human subjects and that protect their health and rights.

Standards of informed consent[18] require that the donor (or the donor's family) has an adequate understanding of the procedure to retrieve human tissue for research purposes, including its risks and benefits. How the human tissue will be removed, how much of it will be removed, and how the procedure will modify the appearance of the donor's body are among the questions that should be addressed, as well as any physical risks associated with the intervention in the case of a living donor.[19] The main question here is whether the donor (or the donor's family) can share in any profits from products, tests or discoveries that result from the research. Details of how the donor (or the donor's family) will benefit should be calculated during the consent process, if this benefit is granted. In these latter cases, it is helpful to determine conditions as part of the informed consent process (Bauer *et al.*, 2004). In other words, if there is any possibility that donated human tissue samples may in the future be made available for commercial research with consequent financial benefit or gain to third parties, then this possibility must be made clear to donors from the very beginning of the process.

Some research populations are particularly vulnerable and require extra protection. These include those who cannot give or refuse consent for themselves and those who may be vulnerable to coercion or undue influence the patients (WMA, 2008). In those specific cases, the patients should be

[18]Some experts consider that the consent form for the donation of human tissue samples for research should not form part of the consent form for the taking of the tissue for therapeutic or diagnostic purposes. They recommend that, where possible, the person responsible for explaining the nature of the donation and the taking of the consent for the donation should not be the person who receives the consent for the taking of the human tissue for therapeutic or diagnostic purposes (The Bioethics Advisory Committee, 2002).

[19]There is an inherent conflict between presenting information to potential donors in a clear and simple way and between disclosing all the possible kinds of research procedures, which may be carried out on the donated human tissue sample, as well as of the benefits, which may be derived from it. Inevitably, there must be some compromise between clarity and detail in the drafting of consent forms.

clearly informed about the potential commercial use of their product and, for this reason, should be asked to release all interest for commercial use.

Physicians should consider the ethical, legal and regulatory norms and standards for research involving human subjects in their own countries, as well as applicable international norms and standards (WMA, 2008). The following elements must be stated in simple language and must be well-understood by donors or their families or legal representatives before they give consent or authorisation to use donated human tissues for research activities:

- To which research project the human tissue(s) are being donated to and what is requested;
- What is the purpose of the research;
- How the data/tissue is shared with other researchers and future projects; and
- The destination of unused or residual human tissues.

Finally, it is important to highlight the following: As long as research on human tissue in the commercial sector is regarded as "controversial" careful attention should be paid to the consent or authorisation process. In accepting the consent, especial attention should be given to the level of education of the donor in order to ensure that he/she fully understand what is the proposal to be considered, particularly if gross human tissue samples (e.g., entire organs or blocks of organs or of limbs, as opposed to human tissue slides or small human tissue blocks) are involved. Gross human tissue samples may be viewed in a very different light from small human tissue samples by the public. The issue of respectful and appropriate methods of disposal for such gross human tissue samples may have to be considered by the custodians of such samples when they are no longer needed and should be removed from the tissue establishment or collection. Researchers and institutions having responsibility for the custody, use, and disposal of such tissues should at all times be sensitive to social, cultural and religious sentiments relating to the treatment, use, and disposal of such tissues (The Bioethics Advisory Committee, 2002).

The main principles to be followed by medical doctors involved in medical research are clearly described in the World Medical Association (2000).

Surrogate Consent

In general, a surrogate is a person who stands in the position of another. In medicine, surrogates are used to assist medical doctors to make decisions when the patients lack capacity to decide. The fact that surrogates do make decisions is simply an extension of the principle of autonomy. Patients do not lose the right to make decisions about their health care just because they lose capacity; the mechanism by which that right is expressed changes.

According to Davenport (1997), it is sometimes difficult to determine who the best surrogate is. Typically it is a person who has the best interest of the patient at heart and who is acquainted with the patient's past expressions, wishes, and values so that the surrogate can make the same decision the patient would make where he is able to do so. There are several methods to determine the surrogate. Usually but not necessarily, the surrogate is a close family member. It is the duty of the physician in consultation with the health care team and other family members to determine the proper surrogate.

Most states recognise a legal document called a "Durable Power of Attorney for Health Care" wherein the patient, while still having the capacity, designates another person, typically called "an agent or the attorney" in fact, to be his surrogate should he lose the capacity to decide. Patients may sometimes expressly tell the physician their choice of a surrogate. In other instances, the patient might communicate through an informal letter or other document. It is important to distinguish a legal document from one which is legally binding. The "Durable Power of Attorney for Health Care" is a legal and legally binding document in most states. Nevertheless, it is important to highlight that because a document is not legally binding, e.g., a living will or even a handwritten note to the physician of a patient's wishes, it does not make that document illegal. It is up to the physician and those who know the context of the writing to attach the proper probative value to it.

Ethical Principles Associated with the Use of Procured Human Tissues for Medical Treatment and for Research Activities

The ethical principles associated with the use of procured human tissues can be split in two groups. The first group includes ethical principles to be applied in case of the removal of human tissues for medical treatment. The second group includes ethical principles to be applied in case of the removal of human tissues for research purpose.[20]

The following ethical principles should be included in the first group:

- Provision to the donor, or to the donor's relatives or legal representative in case of a dead donor, all information regarding the procurement of the human tissues and the process to be applied for this purpose;
- The consent from a living donor or the consent or authorisation of the next-of-kin or legal representative in the case of a deceased donor;
- Provision and maintenance of appropriate and safe systems to assure confidentiality and privacy in the recording, storage and release of data associated with the donor and the human tissues procured; and
- Accountability in the stewardship and distribution of human tissue products.

In the case of the second group, there is a group of specific ethical principles associated with the use of procured human tissues for the development of research activities in the field of human tissue banking. These principles include the following:

- Providing the donor or donor's family or legal representative with full information about the purposes of the sampling and an outline of the research proposal;
- Obtaining donor's consent in the case of living donors, or consent or authorisation in the case of deceased donors, to the use of the sample in the experiment being planned and expected outcomes;
- Obtaining donor's consent in the case of living donors, or consent or authorisation in the case of deceased donors, to storage and future use of the sample for other research purposes (secondary use);

[20]The use of human tissues to ultimately develop a new diagnostic or prognostic test for clinical use or to make discoveries in fundamental biological mechanisms, are the most common purposes for samples used in research. Each sample is, for the most part, one of many tens or hundreds of samples used to develop new understanding of human biology, and any such discoveries will relate to aggregated data, not individual results (National Health and Medical Research Council, 2009)

- Reassuring donors that all secondary use of donated human tissue samples will require approval of an accredited ethics committee;
- Reassuring donors that no tests of known clinical value for diagnosing or predicting disease on samples may be linked to them without their prior consent or authorisation;
- Providing for appropriate and secure storage of human tissue samples for the agreed period of time;
- Provision and maintenance of appropriate and safe systems to assure confidentiality and privacy in the recording, storage, and release of information; and
- Accountability in the care and use of samples.

The challenge of international research ethics is to apply universal ethical principles to biomedical research in a multicultural world with a multiplicity of health care systems and considerable variation in standards of health care.

Lastly, it is important to emphasise the following: Research involving human tissues must not violate any universally applicable ethical standards, but acknowledge that, in superficial aspects, the application of the ethical principles, e.g., in relation to individual autonomy and informed consent or authorisation, needs to take account of cultural values, while respecting absolutely the ethical standards (Council for International Organisations of Medical Sciences, 2008).

According to Bauer and others (2004), there are four main requirements that should be considered and used as a general guide on ethical considerations. They are neither exhaustive, nor absolute. These four requirements are the following:

- Each tissue establishment should have a mission statement, against which it can evaluate the merits of the proposed research uses of donated human tissues. Developing such a document will serve to provide a definition of what constitutes high-quality research in the view of the particular tissue establishment;
- Financial conflicts of interest can be addressed, in part, by ensuring that those making tissue allocation decisions do not have personal financial stakes in potential recipient organisations, or by sharply circumscribing

such relationships. Except in the case of smaller organisations or where no shortage of human tissues exists, no single person should have control over allocation decisions. At minimum, there should be written criteria for evaluating all proposed research projects; at best, there will be a clearly defined process for reviewing and approving the use of donated human tissues;

- Tissue establishments should be explicit about their standards of confidentiality. They should develop adequate methods to limit breaches of confidentiality, which are made known. Tissue banking guidelines and policies need be specific about the conditions under which donated human tissues will be deemed confidential. By doing so, tissue banking guidelines will be more effective in minimising potential harm to donors, donor families, as well as to future human tissue research and product development; and
- Tissue banking guidelines and policies should specify what information to address as part of the informed consent process. To do this, tissue establishments will already need to be clear about their mission, financial arrangements, and level of confidentiality they intend to practice. It is only after receiving the required information that the donor (or the donor's family) can make an informed decision about whether to provide human tissue samples to the facility. Towards this goal, the information to be addressed should be presented in clear and understandable language.

Ethical Principles Related to the Use of Surgical Human Tissue Residues

Medical treatment for which consent has been given may involve the removal of human tissues for the purpose of diagnosis or medical treatment. There may be also surplus human tissues after the diagnosis and medical treatment have been provided for. This excess is usually discarded and destroyed. Such leftover human tissues, and also material archived during diagnosis and medical treatment may, however, be made available for scientific research, medical training and scholarship or for medical audit under specific conditions. It is thus relevant to recommend that when a patient consents to medical treatment involving the removal of specific human tissues, it should include also the consent to the subsequent disposal or storage of the surplus tissues and to any further acceptable use, if this is possible, provided that this use is regulated by appropriate ethical, legal, and professional standards (Nuffield Council of Bioethics, 1995).

Undoubtedly, specific surgical human tissue residues are currently one of the major sources of human tissues for allografts in many countries. However, in some countries their procurement during operations is often unregulated and this could be a way to be followed by those who wish to ignore ethical principles associated with the procurement of human tissues. Measures should be adopted by the national competent health care authorities of all countries to avoid this from happening, and to ensure that surgical human tissue residues are used following defined rules and respecting ethical principles and standards.

Ethical Principles Related with the Confidentiality Access of the Donor and Recipient Information

The protection of the confidentiality of the donor and recipient information is the most important and sensitive activity to be carried out by a tissue establishment, by a facility in which the human tissues are going to be procured, by a hospital where the human tissues will be used or by a research medical centre that has the intention to use human tissues for research purposes.

Privacy belongs to each person and, as such, it cannot be taken away from that person unless he/she wishes to share it. Confidentiality, on the other hand, means that the information shared with other persons will not be spread abroad and will be used only for the purposes intended. A patients' sharing of private information imposes a duty of confidentiality on health care providers. That duty means providers will share information only on a need-to-know basis.

How can we assure the privacy of the information provided by donors and recipients? The privacy of the information of both donor and recipient can be assured, for example, by coding all donated specimens and products with a unique donor/product identifier. The patient identifier should correspond to the one used in the clinical database and, whilst maintaining tissue traceability, should avoid the establishment of a link between the donor's and the recipient's identities. Access to donor and patient identification should be restricted to a limited group of authorised personnel.

According to Bauer and others (2004), confidentiality of the patient information should be treated by all tissue establishments as an important value to be protected. Nevertheless, it is important to recognise that there are different levels among methods to curtail breaches of confidentiality. These are the following:

- **Identified**: The human tissue source is known and the individual's identity is tied to the sample;
- **Identifiable**: The human tissue source is tied to the specimen through the use of a link (e.g., a code number), but the identity of the source is not directly known without tracing the link;
- **Anonymised**: The human tissue source's identity is irrevocably unlinked from the specimen, so that the individual's identity cannot be discerned (i.e., the tissue is not identifiable); and
- **Anonymous**: The human tissue source's identity is never known, since the specimen is collected with no identifiers at all (i.e., the sample is unidentified).

Anonymity is achieved when human tissue made available for research will not have any personally identifiable links. This is one of the most effective ways to maintain confidentiality. However, absolute confidentiality is nearly impossible to achieve in practice; nor is it always sought. Indeed, once human tissue samples are anonymised, their potential uses in research are diminished — findings associated with human tissue samples cannot be linked back to information regarding the sample's source of origin.

The issue of whether the human tissues are stored as anonymised or identified specimens requires attention. If the human tissue is identified, the question whether researchers may access the donor's medical records arises. If this will be permitted, safeguards must be put into place to protect the donor's (or donor family's) confidentiality, even prior to the informed consent or authorisation process.

All necessary measures should be taken by all tissue establishments and other hospital personnel involved in the procurement of human tissues, with the purpose of ensuring that prospective donors of tissues obtain adequate assurances regarding the confidentiality of any health-related information provided to the authorised personnel, the results of tests on their donations, as well as any future traceability of their donation.

Ethical Principles Related to the Protection of Health of Donors and Recipients

No substance of human origin is free from the risk of disease transmission, independently of the process or the sterilisation technique used as part of the tissue processing. Thus, human tissues, in particular those intended for transplantation to third parties or for the provision of pharmaceutical specialities, must undergo advance testing to provide maximum health guarantees in accordance with the state of the art (Quintana-Trias *et al.*, 1998).

Believing that human tissue transplantation is an elective procedure in most circumstances where other alternatives may be available, tissue establishments should accept the responsibility to investigate any data that may contribute to minimise risk during the transplantation of the processed human tissues. Tissues obtained from donors where a risk assessment cannot be fully performed or it is not possible to ensure the quality and accuracy of the various tests the processed human tissues have undergone, should not be used for any purpose.

There should be provisions in the law allowing the tissue establishments to have universal access to private information related to the medical status of donors, including autopsy reports, hospital records, etc., with the purpose of avoiding the procurement of contaminated human tissues. Families and donors should be made aware of this right and why this action is needed.

Ethical Principles Related with Human Body Integrity

The integrity of the human body is one of the most important ethical principles to be observed by any tissue establishment during the procurement of human tissues from a donor, living or dead. When human tissues are procured from a deceased person, due regard should be paid to the integrity of the donor's body, avoiding unnecessary damage during the procurement of the tissues. Many members of the community hold the belief that selling human tissues involves treating the human body as an object or merchandise, and is thus inherently disrespectful of the body of a living person or the retention of a departed. Respect for the human person involves respecting the human body because the latter is intimate to the person and constitutive of the human identity (National Health and Medical Research Council, 2009).

The feelings of the relatives and their religion and culture beliefs, as well as to their opinion regarding the process of tissue procurement and their potential use of the procured human tissues in the future should be fully respected. Only consented or authorised specific human tissues should be procured and its use should be according to the donor's wishes or the decision adopted by their relatives or legal representative.

It is an obligation of the tissue establishment or the retrieval agency to conduct full reconstruction of the body before its return to the family for burial rituals. Respect for the cultural and religious beliefs are crucial; retrieval areas and incisions should be limited to those disclosed and accepted by consenting relatives during the informed consent process or by the authorisation given by the donor or relatives or legal representatives. Any interventions that may preclude families to undertake the desired burial ceremony to their loved ones following their religious and cultural beliefs must be avoided.

Ethical Principles Related to the Distribution of Human Tissues for Medical Use

The medical use of human tissues is inevitably constrained by its limited availability and, for this reason, all necessary precautions should be taken to ensure the safety of the patients and the donor as well as the voluntary nature of human tissue donations.

Undoubtedly, the distribution of human tissues is one of the most sensitive issues within the tissue banking community and, for this reason, should be carried out on the basis of the principle of justice. This means that it should be done after an objective evaluation of medical needs and ensuring equitable access to all patients, independently of their social status and wealth, race, ethnicity, national origin, sex, sexual orientation, gender identity, age, marital status, religious belief, immigration status, and mental or physical disability, colour of the skin, political thinking, among others. The ethical principle "first to come first to serve", should be accepted by all tissue establishments and hospitals involved in tissue procurement and transplantation.

It is important to stress that compliance with international quality and safety standards should be mandatory to guarantee the safety of recipients, even if this implies a reduced availability of human tissues. Traceability (that is, the capacity to trace tissues from the donor to recipients and vice versa) and long-term follow-up of living donors and recipients of human tissues are central elements of safety and quality management. Many experts envisaged for the future the ability to coordinate the traceability of human tissues in a common surveillance system with universal donor identification numbers. The adoption of a unified system for the coding, tracing and identification of processed human tissues is one of the relevant tasks to be carried in the coming years by national competent health care authorities interested in the promotion and support of tissue banking in their respective countries. Many governments are urging the international community to adopt minimal standards for procurement and processing as the surest way of helping interested countries to balance quality, safety and human tissue availability (Schulz-Baldes *et al.*, 2007).

Ethical Principles Related with the Commercialisation of Human Tissues

In an ideal scenario, tissue establishments should have the necessary resources for its operation within the public health care system. For this reason, tissue banking activities should be carried out preferable by "not-for-profit" organisations. In such case, revenue would result from costs recovered at the time of tissue distribution, which should include expenses related to the procurement, processing, sterilisation, storage and distribution of the tissues. Surplus in revenue must be reinvested with the purpose of supporting tissue establishment activities in the future or to improve the tissue establishment's facility. On the contrary, private enterprises or "for-profit" organisations operate not necessarily by expected health outcomes, but only by the financial interests of shareholders who directly benefit from the profits obtained.

Undoubtedly, the commercialisation of human tissues is a challenging issue. Nevertheless, it is important to note that there is an overwhelming opinion within the international community that states should adhere to the principle that the donation of human tissues should remain as a non-profit activity. This means that in general, donation of human tissues should remain unpaid, because the payment can unduly induce vulnerability among poor living donors or constitute a conflict of interest for next-of-kin or legal representatives in deceased donation, and is likely to result in inequities in donation. Some experts are also concerned that paying tissues increases the likelihood of inaccurate responses on donor-history questionnaires, resulting in transplanted materials carrying an undetected disease.

Simultaneously, the need to remove financial disincentives for human tissue donation was recognised by various national competent health care authorities in a number of countries. Therefore, compensation for travel expenses, loss of profits or other expenses actually incurred in donation may be tolerated and must be transparent and regularly audited. General consensus also existed that "for-profit" organisations should not be involved in promoting human tissue donation or discussing it with potential donors, surrogates, next of kin or legal representatives to avoid conflicts of interest (Schulz-Baldes *et al.*, 2007).

If commercialisation of human tissues is to be ethically permissible in certain cases, consent practices also need to be extended to ensure full disclosure of the possible commercial outcomes that occur throughout the chain of custody. The altruistic nature of donation in several countries is such that many donors do not enquire about how the industry is funded, nor do they enquire about the potential for profit to be generated or the uses to which their donation may be put. Potential commercial uses may change that attitude. The need is to be able not only to inform donors of commercial uses, but also to be able to inform them that commercial uses are strictly limited by effective ethical regulations. Currently, that is not the case and there is a danger that commercialisation without ethical regulations will undermine existing transplantation and research practices because the latter depend upon donation of tissues (National Health and Medical Research Council, 2009). For this reason, regulations that minimise commercial conflicts of interest in the processing and possibly the distribution of human tissues are considered necessary and should be adopted in each country by the national competent health care authorities.

However, in emerging fields such as biotechnology-enhanced products, the public system may be unable to fully absorb the resources needed to make possible access to value-added products. In this specific example, private companies may have a role to play, but under certain regulations to be embraced by the national competent health care authorities, with the aim of avoiding unethical practices. The question is about the level of the actions that these companies may play in the tissue banking sector, without compromising the altruistic principles of tissue donation and the common good. Whichever these boundaries may be, it is important to highlight that "for-profit" tissue establishments set up by private investors should be subject to the same licensing and monitoring requirements carried out by the national competent health care authorities, as well as transparent auditing processes in relation to set costs, profit margins and distribution arrangements established for "not-for-profit" tissue establishments.

It is important to note also that some states consider ethically acceptable, under certain circumstances, to provide monetary compensation for donors or their families for the constraints associated with human tissue removal (e.g., travel expenses, loss of earnings, etc.). In the United States, for example, US federal law allows fees for the recovering, processing and transporting of human tissue (Gassner, 2007).

So far, however, the arguments in favour of the altruistic nature of human tissue donation have prevailed and many states have laws and regulations already in force prohibiting any payment for human tissue donation that may be perceived as direct incentives. The position adopted by these states are based on solidarity principles and is inspired by the desire to avoid the human person being regarded as a merchandise or object that can be on sale as a whole or by part for a certain price.[21] Another argument used by this group of states to support their position is that they want to avoid all danger of exploitation of the financially underprivileged individuals in the community which, despite precarious health conditions, are ready to donate tissue primarily for financial reasons or their families for

[21]Commercialisation of products derived from human tissue thus needs to take into account whether such activities implicitly or explicitly, directly or indirectly, involve treating the body of the person as an object. The commercialisation also needs to address the ability to maintain equity of access to the benefits derived from human tissue products) (National Health and Medical Research Council, 2009).

constraints associated with human tissue removal (e.g., travel expenses, loss of earnings, etc.) are allowed.[22]

However, if commercialisation is going to be permitted under certain conditions, national competent health care authorities should be sure that the following considerations will not be breached:

- **Community Benefit**: The need to protect the community's interest in benefits from such products being available to those who need them on an equitable basis (Justice and Beneficence);
- **Genomic Significance**: The significance to families and individuals of genomic information that may be contained in a human tissue product (Respect for the Human Person);
- **Commodification of the Human Body**: The significance of the human body and the need to prevent a person's body being treated as an object (Respect for the Human Person);
- **Product Value**: The significance of preserving community benefits of a product where the value of the product derives from properties that are unique to a particular individual or family, and which may restrict access to the product if the value is set by market forces and restricted ownership (Justice and Beneficence); and
- **Perverse Incentives**: The need to avoid the creation of incentives whereby those donating or collecting human tissue, transforming the tissue and commercialising derived products is led to behave in ways they would not otherwise behave or which may place donors or themselves at risk or which may result in unintended negative or harmful consequences (Justice) (National Health and Medical Research Council, 2009).

In circumstances in which the human tissue product has a value that is unique to its donor or their family, commercial use of the product could be seen as exploiting the uniqueness of the donor rather than being a novel

[22]The British Association of Tissue Banking (BATB), Belgium and Spain, have adopted policies and laws that simply ban all commercial dealings in human tissues. The BATB state "there shall be no commercial dealing in human tissue", and the Spanish government holds that "the human body and its parts shall not, as such, give rise to financial gain" and, as specified in The Crown Order of 13 June 1986, the government of Belgium simply forbids the sale of body/body parts and profit from donation (Bauer *et al.*, 2004).

approach or process. Commercialising and generating a profit from a human tissue product with a singular value may also raise community concerns, if people feel that the donor should share the winnings. This would constitute material incentive and may erode community benefit and the altruistic nature of the country donor system, if people start to withhold donations unless profits were made. For this reason, ethical guidelines should prohibit commercial use of human tissue products, if the value of a product is derived from a characteristic that is unique to the donor (National Health and Medical Research Council, 2009).

Examples of commercialisation of products derived from human tissue in a research environment include:

- Modification of human cells for storage where the transfer incurs a fee that covers more costs than those associated with storage and handling of the donated human tissue;
- Manipulation of human tissues that permits them to be exchanged for use in research where the transfer incurs a fee;
- Extraction of valuable products such as DNA, RNA, protein and the creation of tissue microarrays from human pathology specimens that result in a product that can be transferred for a fee;
- Derivation of data from human specimens, which is valuable; that is, where a fee can be charged for access;
- Intellectual property arising from any of the activities mentioned above and profits generated from the commercialisation or sale of that intellectual property; and
- Transformation and manufacture of a human tissue product into a form that is used as a consumer product, patient therapeutic device or human transplantation where profits are derived (National Health and Medical Research Council, 2009).

Figure 4 depicts the life cycle of human tissue products and provides an overview of when exchange, trade and commercialisation may occur.

As a consequence, in some countries, views about legislators, authorities and non-governmental organisations about the acceptability of commercial tissue establishments vary to a substantial extent (Bauer, 2004). At present, the community will continue to benefit if the already developing practices

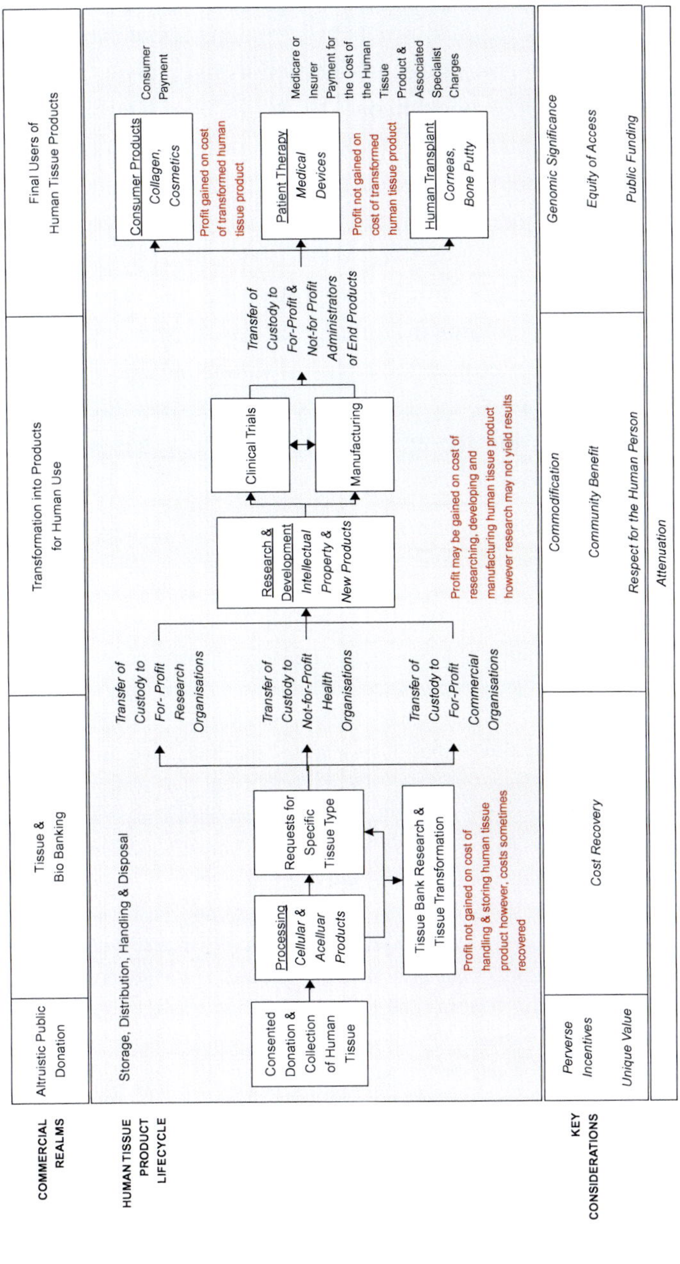

Figure 4: Human tissue life-cycle.

Source: National Health and Medical Research Council (2009)

of trade and commercialisation of products derived from human tissue are permitted to continue, within an environment regulated by ethical guidelines. These guidelines should allow decision-making about exemptions for certain categories of human tissue products. For this reason, the existing limitation, restriction or even ban on "for-profit" commercialisation of human tissue for transplantation should be in principle retained, but in some circumstances, products derived from human tissue (including cellular devices, cell cultures, significantly modified cell cultures, products and intellectual property), should be used commercially, provided that there are effective guidelines in place to protect the interests of the community and ensure the continued equitable access to the national health care system, as well as to protect the rights of donors and families.[23]

There is a gap between the existing guidelines and legislation for donated human tissue, and the current practices of exchange, trade and

[23] Some experts found it overly simplistic to frame stewardship by contrasting "for-profit" with "not-for-profit" organisations. All organisations that process or distribute human tissues can produce a surplus of income over expense, but the framework for using this surplus differs. "Not-for-profit" organisations are, at least in theory, subject to rules that tightly control the extent to which individuals may receive financial and material benefits; accordingly, surpluses must be used in ways consistent with the organisation's purpose, such as in improving human tissue services or supporting other services when the human tissue activity is a unit within a publicly funded health system. In "for-profit" organisations, in contrast, surpluses that are not reinvested are distributed among the owners (such as the shareholders of corporations) and/or lead to higher salaries for the managers. However, the apparent distinction between "for-profit" and "not-for-profit" organisations is often blurred in practice. "Not-for-profit" organisations may own or collaborate with "for-profit" subsidiaries, and in countries where human tissue organisations do not receive public funding, patients may have to rely on services of "for-profit" organisations to access necessary medical care. Furthermore, "for-profit" organisations are sometimes in a better position to invest in high-quality facilities and/or research and development, and may thereby promote efficient use of donated human tissues and improvement of services. This can help to ensure enhanced benefits from the donation for patients, which is also an ethical imperative. Finally, the organisational structure itself does not indicate the amount of income. "For-profit" organisations can generate little profit, while "not-for-profit" organisations can have large surpluses. What matters from a normative perspective is the way income is managed and the effects that efforts to generate surplus revenues have on stewardship, efficiency, transparency, accountability, fair pricing, responsiveness to local or national health needs and fair allocation. These criteria are more important in evaluating human tissue organisations normatively than their formal profit-making status (Schulz-Baldes, *et al.*, 2007).

commercialisation of human tissue products. Based on the existence of this gap, there is a need to provide guidance to those dealing with human tissue products, about when it would be ethically permissible and what restrictions are needed to protect individuals and the common good.[24]

Extended forms of cost recovery (recovering costs for more than the handling, storage and distribution of human tissue products) could challenge important values that are inherent in the country's donor system.[25] But in some instances, that type of cost is required in order to maintain and build the availability of human tissue and human tissue products.

Lastly, it is important to be aware, in the specific case of research activities, on the following: Financial incentives to academic researchers could undermine scientific standards of integrity. Beyond this concern, commercial tissue banking gives rise to a plethora of broader cultural, religious, social, and psychological issues in the treatment of the human body and its parts (Nelkin, 1998).

[24] In principle, the following preliminary ethical criteria for organisations processing or distributing human tissues with a profit-making orientation was accepted: Donors, surrogates, next-of-kin or legal representatives should be informed accordingly; the quality, safety and price of human tissues should be at least comparable to those from "not-for-profit" organisations; and the profit-making orientation should not compromise equitable access to tissue establishment and hospital services related to tissue transplantation.

[25] If cost recovery and other commercial schemes are insufficient to generate a robust commercial environment whilst protecting individuals and community interests, public funding may be a plausible alternative. Public funding and the goodwill of organisations that typically absorb costs such as human resources and power may support the infrastructure for ongoing research and development. Charitable donations may also allow purchase of capital items such as freezers and microscopes. Where human sample repositories and tissue culture repositories are closely associated with publicly funded research institutions, there may be an option to perform contract work on behalf of commercial entities. That is, external commercial entities could make application to have processes undertaken within the repository in response to their research questions. For this research, a fee would be payable to the repository and this would enable additional revenue to be drawn without the need to transfer a human tissue outside of the repository. This approach has several advantages including the separation of collection, processing and management of the human tissue and tissue cultures from commercial uses which may draw a profit. There is a possibility that "not-for-profit" organisations could serve a similar role, provided that cost recovery and the use of funds generated are transparent to the human tissue donors (National Health and Medical Research Council, 2009).

Chapter III

A Model Code of Ethics for Tissue Establishments

Introduction

Ethical practice in the field of tissue banking requires the setting of principles, the identification of possible deviations, and the establishment of mechanisms that will detect and impede abuses or violations that may occur during the procurement, processing, sterilisation, storage, distribution and use of human tissues for transplantation.

While there are inescapable acts of individual judgment involved in ethical decisions, however, it is desirable that conclusions should be accomplished in ways that result in as consistent a practice as possible. A way of achieving this is to elaborate a code of ethics and a code of practice providing general guidelines within which individual decisions are to be made.

A code of ethics is a written set of guidelines issued by an organisation to its workers and management to help them conduct their actions in accordance with its primary values and ethical standards. It has a regulatory, educational and cultural integration functions and can be considered a basic presentation of principles and ideals. A code of practice is a detailed description of the actions that are to be performed and not to be performed, and of the sanctions that attach to non-performance.

Why are codes of ethics important to the international tissue banking community? As foundation documents, they can provide the framework that tissue establishment staff need to carry out their responsibilities in the most effective and efficient manner. A code of ethics can clearly articulate unacceptable behaviour as well as provide a vision for which the staff is striving. Undoubtedly, a fundamental mechanism for ensuring professionalism is a code of ethics.

According to Gilman (2005), it is important to highlight that the use of a code of ethics can have a positive impact in several ways:

- First, increase the probability that tissue establishment staff will behave in certain ways. They do this partially by focusing on the character of their actions and partly by focusing on sanctions for violations of the code. In addition, reliance on a code of ethics can reduce the sacrifice involved in an ethical act;
- Second, a good code of ethics can focus tissue establishment staff on actions that result in doing the right things for the right reasons. Ethical behaviour should become a habit and an effective code of ethics will allow tissue establishment staff to examine their actions against expected standards;
- Third, a code of ethics does not take away one's own moral autonomy or absolve the tissue establishment staff from the obligation to reason. A code of ethics provides at most a strong prima facie reason to behave in a certain manner. However, this can be overridden by strong reasoned objection. The expectation is that the norm does not break the code of ethics adopted and, if such violations occurred, they can only be justified because of a higher ethical principle; and
- Fourth, a code of ethics can function as a professional statement. That is, it expresses the tissue establishment staff's commitments to a specific set of moral standards. This has both cognitive and emotional value. Cognitively, it gives a person joining a tissue establishment, a clear set of values to which they are expected to subscribe.

A code of ethics serves six purposes. These are the following:

- Identifies the core values on which the tissue establishment mission should be established;
- Summarises broad ethical principles that reflect the tissue establishment core values and establishes a set of specific ethical standards that should be used to guide tissue establishment practice;
- Help a tissue establishment to identify relevant considerations when tissue establishment obligations conflict or ethical uncertainties arise;

- Provides ethical standards to which the general public can hold the tissue establishment staff accountable; and
- Socialises new tissue establishment staff to the tissue establishment mission, values, ethical principles and ethical standards.

A code of ethics articulates standards that the tissue establishment can use to assess whether their staff has engaged or not in unethical conduct during the procurement, processing, sterilisation, storage and distribution of human tissues. The tissue establishment should have formal procedures to adjudicate about ethical complaints filed against their staff. In subscribing to a code of ethics, tissue establishment staff are required to cooperate in its implementation, participate in adjudication proceedings, and abide by any disciplinary rulings or sanctions based on it adopted by the Director of the tissue establishment.

According to Muller (2002), the content of a code of ethics should ideally:

- Describe not only minimum standards, but also occupational ideals; in so doing they should include not only action guiding principles, but also virtues and desirable attitudes;
- Contain a statement to the effect that minimum standards ought not to be compromised, even in the face of internal pressure from the tissue establishment to which one belongs or external pressure from outside organisations and groups;
- Contain a statement to the effect that tissue establishment staff ought to obey the just and reasonable laws of the community, since they reflect the just and reasonable standards acceptable to the community;
- Contain a statement expressing the commitment of the tissue establishment staff not discriminating on the basis of social status and wealth, race, ethnicity, national origin, colour, sex, sexual orientation, gender identity, age, marital status, political belief, religion, immigration status and mental or physical disability;
- Contain also a statement to the effect that tissue establishment staff ought to obey the just and reasonable regulations governing their activities. If tissue establishment staff believe that any of these regulations are unjust or unreasonable, they should provide a written communication, citing reasons, to the Director of the tissue establishment;

- Contain an integrity statement to the effect that tissue establishment staff ought to avoid telling lies and do what they say they will do;
- Identify the most important principles, rights and ideas to be included in the code;
- Contain a statement or statements committing tissue establishment staff to respect the relevant rights of donors and recipients to privacy and confidentiality;
- Contain a statement to the effect that complaints and disciplinary processes ought to conform to the principles of independence, reasonableness and fairness;
- Contain a statement to the effect that tissue establishment staff ought only undertake work that they are competent to perform or have been trained for;
- Contain a statement to the effect that tissue establishment staff ought to undertake their work conscientiously, and with efficiency and effectiveness;
- Contain a statement concerning the need for adequate initial and ongoing training and education for tissue establishment staff, in order to ensure that they keep up to date with recent developments in the field of tissue banking;
- Address the issue of occupational or organisational culture in relation to wrongdoing or incompetence on the part of tissue establishment staff and medical doctors and other professionals and technicians. Tissue establishment staff shall not remain silent or try to protect other staff when they perform harmful or incompetent actions in relation to the procurement, processing, and use of human tissue;
- Address problematic ethical issues that tissue establishment staff confront in relation to the provision of medical services and conflicts of interest arising from various sources;
- Contain a statement in relation to the collective responsibility of tissue establishment staff to report on any failure of other staff to meet minimum standards; and
- Contain a statement in relation to loyalty and cooperation among tissue establishment staff and other medical staff in the procurement, processing, and use of human tissues.

The above elements associated with the elaboration of a code of ethics were identified with the aim of assisting interested tissue establishments in the preparation of their own code of ethics or in the modification of the one in force. However, it is important to emphasise the following: A code of ethics cannot guarantee ethical behaviour of all tissue establishment staff. Moreover, a code of ethics cannot resolve all ethical issues or disputes or capture the richness and complexity involved in striving to make responsible choices within the activities associated with a tissue establishment. Rather, a code of ethics sets forth values, ethical principles and ethical standards to which tissue establishment staff aspire and by which their actions can be judged. The ethical behaviour of tissue establishment staff should result from their personal commitment to engage in ethical practice. A code of ethics should reflect the commitment of all staff to uphold tissue establishment values and to act ethically. Principles and standards must be applied by the staff, which identify moral questions and, in good faith, seek to make reliable ethical judgments.

Process for Developing a Code of Ethics

There are a number of different processes necessary to develop a code of ethics. These are the following:

Step 1. Establishment of an ethics committee: The ethics committee should assume the responsibility for drafting the code of ethics. The ethics committee should involve different experts in the field of tissue banking and in the field of ethics, such as medical doctors involved in the work of the tissue establishment, transplant coordinators and representatives of the civil society, among others. Membership of the ethics committee should be for a fixed term. A degree of continuity of membership is desirable. So provision should be made for only half of the terms of members to expire at the same time. The ethics committee should:

- Identify the purposes to be served by the code of ethics to be elaborated;
- Define the format of the code of ethics;

- Examine the main goals, activities and the context (including organisational context) of the tissue establishment;
- Outline the role of the tissue establishment staff;
- Detail the main ethical requirements of tissue establishment staff and other medical personnel involved in the procurement, processing, sterilisation, storage, distribution and utilisation of human tissues;
- Identify the main ethical problems likely to be confronted by the tissue establishment staff during the procurement, processing, sterilisation, storage, distribution and utilisation of human tissues; and
- Prepare a document setting out the results of the above treatments. This document is not a draft code of ethics; rather it is a preliminary set of principles, various issues for discussion, and a list of questions. The document is to be used as a guideline during the research phase.

Step 2. Drafting the code of ethics: In light of the discussion held in step 1, a draft code of ethics and accompanying materials should be prepared by the ethics committee.

Step 3. Consultation among interested parties: All members of the ethics committee involved in the preparation of the code of ethics should receive the draft that has been prepared.

Step 4. Preparation of the final version of code of ethics: Based on the comments received during the implementation of step 3, the members of the ethics committee should be in a position to prepare the final version of the code. This version should be distributed to all members of the ethics committee and other experts and authorities that the committee considered appropriate for the purposes of receiving final comments and the approval of the Director of the tissue establishment and other national competent health care authorities.

Step 5. Final approval of the code of ethics.

Step 6. Review of the code of ethics: There should be a formal review of the code of ethics at certain intervals by the ethics committee, the Director of the tissue establishment, and by the national competent health care authorities. The review of the code of ethics should be done following all of the above steps.

I. Objectives and Applicability

Objectives

A code of ethics should establish what the Director of the tissue establishment expects of the staff and what they can expect from the Director of the tissue establishment. It describes the values and principles that all staff of the tissue establishment should follow.

A code of ethics should describe procedures to help tissue establishment staff to make ethical decisions and report and deal with violations of the values, principles, rules and policies established by the tissue establishment. This code of ethics should help tissue establishment staff:

- To resolve doubts related to conduct and ethical behaviour in the workplace;
- To obtain and give confidential advice and information to donors, recipients, next-of-kin, legal representatives, hospital staff and national competent health care authorities, among others;
- To provide services to donors and recipients only in the context of a professional relationship, based, when appropriate, on valid informed consent or authorisation granted to the procurement of human tissues;
- To inform donors and recipients, in a clear and understandable language, of the purpose of the transplant of human tissues, risks related to this transplant, relevant costs, reasonable alternatives, and donors' and recipients' rights to deny or withdraw consent or authorisation given to the procurement of the human tissues;
- To give living donors, relatives of living and deceased donors, next-of-kin and legal representatives the opportunity to ask questions related to the procurement of the human tissues;
- To understand how tissue establishment's policies and procedures regarding conduct and ethics apply to the tissue establishment staff;
- To feel confident that tissue establishment staff will conduct, in dealings with donors, recipients, relatives and next-of-kin, legal representatives, medical hospital staff and other personnel such as government

representatives, national competent health care authorities and private hospitals, in an appropriate and ethical manner;

- To treat each individual in a caring and respectful manner, mindful of individual differences and cultural and ethnic diversity;
- To act honestly and responsibly and promote ethical practices in tissue establishment;
- To bring suspected violations of the code of ethics and other relevant tissue establishment policies and procedures to the attention of the Director of the tissue establishment and to other appropriate national competent health care authorities; and
- To continually strive to increase their professional knowledge and skills in the field of tissue banking and to apply them in practice.

The adherence to the code of ethics represents a personal and professional commitment to tissue establishment values of fairness, excellence, solidarity, respect and integrity.

Applicability

A code of ethics should apply to everyone who works in a tissue establishment regardless of the type of contract held, the duration of the appointment or the responsibilities assigned within or outside the tissue establishment. When tissue establishment staff sign the appointment contract accepting employment with the tissue establishment, they are considered to have acknowledged that compliance with tissue establishment rules and policies constitute conditions of the employment. Consequently, tissue establishment staff are expected to know and comply with the code of ethics as well as other tissue establishment policies, regulations and provisions that govern the staff conduct.

The code of ethics in force should not apply to tissue establishment suppliers, vendors, contractors and business partners working outside of the tissue establishment. However, it expects that they will familiarise themselves with the code of ethics adopted and will respect the ethical principles included in the code.

II. General Ethical Principles and Values

Basic Ethical Principles

The present code of ethics is founded on basic principles of ethical behaviour[1] and is consistent with the proposal for a code of practice proposed in Morales (2011), the content of the IAEA's Standards, and the IAEA Public Awareness Strategies. The main principles are the following:

1. **Respect for autonomy:** The principle of autonomy stands for the proposition that an adult with capacity to decide has a full right to decide what may be done to his body. This is a right recognised in ethics, medical practice and laws. Because of autonomy, patients may refuse any proffered procedure, treatment, or even the advice of their physicians. The fact that this refusal is seen as ill-advised or even irrational by the physician does not counter moral, social and legal norms which hold that competent patients have the right to determine their destinies. However, when assessing a patient's capacity, the physician must evaluate three distinct aspects of decision-making ability:

   a) Patients must demonstrate that they understand the given information about diagnosis and treatment and that they appreciate the significance of the disease and its consequences. In testing for understanding, the physician might ask patients to rephrase the information he/she has given to them;
   b) Patients should be able to deliberate in accordance with their own values. Here, the physician might ask patients what is most important to them in making their decision. Patients should demonstrate an ability to communicate consistent choices regarding their decisions. Here the physician might determine patients' choices at different times to prove consistency.

[1] According to the Belmont Report, the expression "basic ethical principles" refers to those general judgments that serve as a basic justification for the many particular ethical prescriptions and evaluations of human actions. Four basic principles, among those generally accepted are particularly relevant to the ethics of research involving human subjects. These principles are: a) respect for autonomy; b) beneficence; c) non-maleficence; and d) justice.

2. **Beneficence**: The principle of beneficence stands for the proposition that it is the physician's duty to do good for his patient. This is certainly a foundational principle of medical practice finding its roots in Hippocrates. For centuries, beneficence was actualised through the process of the patient presenting herself to the physician for examination and inquiry and then following the advice of the physician. In recent decades, societal demands for self-determination have sometimes brought this principle into conflict with autonomy.

3. **Non-maleficence:** Often joined with beneficence is the term, "non-maleficence", which stands for the Hippocratic duty to "do no harm". One can detect conflicts between beneficence and non-maleficence in almost any clinical situation. The dichotomy between the two principles is the foundation for "risk/benefit" analysis.

4. **Justice:** All patients should have equitable access to high-quality health care; this means giving each person or groups what he/she or they are due. It can be measured in terms of fairness, equality, need, or by any other measure.

In addition to these basic ethical principles, the following additional ethical principles presently relevant for social science research in health in India could be considered:

- **Essentiality:** For undertaking research, it is necessary to make all possible efforts to stimulate and give equal consideration to existing literature/knowledge and its relevance, and the alternatives available on the subject/issue under the study;
- **Maximisation of public interest and of social justice:** Research is a social activity, carried out for the benefit of society. It should be undertaken with the motive of maximisation of public interest and social justice;
- **Knowledge, ability and commitment to do research:** Sincere commitment to research in general and to the relevant subject in particular, and readiness to acquire adequate knowledge, ability and skill for undertaking particular research, are essential prerequisites for good and ethical research;
- **Respect and protection of autonomy, rights and dignity of donors:** Research involving participation of individual(s) must not only respect,

but also protect the autonomy, the rights and the dignity of participants. The participation of individual(s) must be voluntary and based on informed consent;

- **Privacy, anonymity and confidentiality:** All information and records supplied by donors or obtained directly or indirectly on/about the donors are confidential. For revealing or sharing any information that may identify donors, permission of the donors is essential;
- **Precaution and risk minimisation:** All research carries some risk to the donors and to society. Taking adequate precautions and minimising and mitigating risks is, therefore, essential;
- **Non-exploitation:** Research must not unnecessarily consume the time of donors and other participants or make them incur undue loss of resources and income. It should not expose them to dangers due to participation in the research. The relationship within the research team, including student and junior members, should be based on the principle of non-exploitation. The contribution of each member of the research team should be properly acknowledged and recognised;
- **Public domain:** All persons and organisations connected to research should make adequate efforts to make public in an appropriate manner and form, and at the appropriate time, information on the research undertaken and the relevant results and implications of completed research;
- **Accountability and transparency:** The conduct of research must be fair, honest and transparent. It is desirable that institutions and researchers are amenable to social and financial review of their research by an appropriate and responsible social body. They should also make appropriate arrangements for the preservation of research records for a reasonable period of time; and
- **Totality of responsibility:** The responsibility for the due observance of all principles of ethics and guidelines devolves in all those directly or indirectly associated with the research. They include institution(s) where the research is conducted, researcher(s), sponsors/funders and those who publish material generated from research.

III. Ethical Framework

If tissue establishment staff are having difficulty in deciding about their own behaviour or if they are unsure if the actions of others are in conformity with the code of ethics in force, answering these questions may help to find the proper course of action:

- Are my actions consistent with tissue establishment values?
- Do I have all the facts correctly?
- Have I gone over the facts carefully?
- Who will benefit from my actions?
- What is the best decision for the tissue establishment?
- How will my decisions and actions reflect on the activities of the tissue establishment?
- What are the results of my choices?
- How will my actions look to others?
- Would I want my actions widely publicised?
- Am I following the spirit as well as the letter of the tissue establishment's rules or policies?

Tissue establishment staff should never hesitate to ask questions, express concerns or make reports to his/her immediate supervisor or the Director of the tissue establishment about any issue about the activity of the tissue establishment or the behaviour of the staff. Tissue establishment staff should feel free to consult their immediate supervisor or the Director of the tissue establishment or any office or advisory body established within the tissue establishment for ethical issues, including the ethics committee, if necessary, particularly if the staff are unsure about a decision that should be adopted. Tissue establishment staff are not expected to have all the answers to ethical issues that may come up in the course of doing their job, but they are expected to ask for help, if they have any doubt about what to do in a specific situation.

IV. Creating a Culture of Compliance and Prevention

Rights, Responsibilities and Obligations

All personnel working in a tissue establishment should:

- Accept the code of ethics approved and in force;
- Follow applicable rules and regulations in force for the tissue establishment;

- Give honest and impartial advice and make that information available to the donors, recipients, relatives, next-of-kin, legal representatives, national competent health care authorities, medical staff as well as to any other staff associated with the work of the tissue establishment;
- Ensure proper, effective and efficient use of the tissue establishment's resources, including human tissue procured and processed, facilities, equipment and materials;
- Ensure transparency while respecting the obligation to maintain confidentiality of all medical information obtained from the donors and recipients;
- Perform all duties assigned by the Director of the tissue establishment so that confidence and trust in the integrity, objectivity and impartiality of the tissue establishment are conserved and enhanced within the community;
- Avoid even the appearance of impropriety in all actions, in the conduct, and in the decisions related to the activities of the tissue establishment;
- While fulfilling the official duties and responsibilities within the tissue establishment, make decisions that are in the best interests of the donors, recipients, relatives, next-of-kin or legal representatives, and the tissue establishment, based on objective criteria;
- Encourage, advocate and promote appropriate conduct and ethical behaviour in the workplace, and implement, monitor and enforce the code of ethics and related policies in the day-to-day work in the tissue establishment; and
- Encourage the Director of the tissue establishment to review the code of ethics adopted from time to time.

It is important to highlight that any person who wants to raise issues related to the code of ethics in force in the tissue establishment should have the right to do so and use the established channels for this purpose.

Duties of Managers and Supervisors

Managers and supervisors in a tissue establishment have the following responsibilities:

- Upholding the code of ethics in force and ensuring that the highest level of ethical conduct is exhibited at all times;

- Being familiar with the code of ethics and being able to explain to the tissue establishment staff their rights, responsibilities and obligations;
- Encouraging and allowing tissue establishment staff to participate in training activities sponsored by the tissue establishment or other national competent health care authorities on ethical issues;
- Handling confidentially and expeditiously any reported violation of the code of ethics that may be brought to their attention, and ensuring that others act accordingly;
- Providing tissue establishment staff with a copy of the code of ethics in force and advising that they are required to read, understand and adhere to the code as part of their employment contract with the tissue establishment;
- Briefing new tissue establishment staff on the code of ethics in force during orientation sessions;
- Handling with confidence all reported violations of the code of ethics in force;
- Taking timely action to investigate and respond to reported violations of the code of ethics or of any other tissue establishment's policy in force;
- Taking appropriate administrative or disciplinary measures in response to violations of the code of ethics or of any other tissue establishment's policy in force;
- Ensuring that anyone who reports a suspected violation of the code of ethics in force is not subject to retaliation;
- Ensuring that mechanisms and assistance are in place to help tissue establishment staff raise, discuss and resolve issues of concern related to the code of ethics and to any other tissue establishment's policy in force; and
- Encouraging and sustaining an on-going dialogue on values, conduct and ethics in order to address specific issues and challenges as they arise within the tissue establishment.

Tissue establishment staff that provides supervision or consultation should have the necessary knowledge and skill to supervise or consult appropriately and should do so only within their areas of knowledge and competence. Tissue establishment staff that provides supervision or consultation is responsible for setting clear, appropriate and culturally sensitive boundaries and to act within these boundaries. Tissue establishment staff should also not engage in any dual or multiple relationships with supervisors in whom there is a risk of exploitation of or potential harm to the supervised. Tissue establishment staff who provides supervision should evaluate supervisory performance in a manner that is fair and respectful.

Duty to Comply

The Director of the tissue establishment should place utmost importance on the ethical conduct of all tissue establishment staff and should not tolerate any violation of the code of ethics or other policies, regulations and provisions governing conduct within the tissue establishment. Obeying the code of ethics in force — both in its spirit and its letter — is the foundation on which tissue establishment ethical standards rest. Each of the tissue establishment staff has a responsibility to comply with tissue establishment's rules and relevant laws, standards, and regulations of the State in which the tissue establishment operates as well.

Disciplinary Measures

If the tissue establishment staff fails to follow the provisions of the code of ethics or any standards or code of practices in force within the tissue establishment, the staff may be subject to disciplinary measures. Depending on the gravity of the offence, the tissue establishment staff may be subject to one or more of the following disciplinary actions:

- A written reprimand;
- Suspension from duty without pay;
- Reassignment with or without reduction in salary;
- Dismissal for misconduct; and
- Summary dismissal for serious misconduct.

Reporting

Tissue establishment staff should be encouraged to report known or suspected violations of the code of ethics in force to his/her immediate supervisor or the Director of the tissue establishment. Tissue establishment staff may also report to the above persons, information obtained from others regarding a suspected violation of the code of ethics or of any other tissue establishment's policy, standards and regulations in force. Tissue establishment staff who consider that a colleague has acted unethically should seek resolution by discussing their concerns with the colleague, when feasible and when such discussion is likely to be fertile. When necessary, tissue establishment staff who considers that a colleague has acted unethically should take action through appropriate formal channels within the tissue establishment structure. At the same time, tissue establishment staff should defend and assist colleagues who are unjustly charged with unethical conduct.

Confidentiality

Tissue establishment staff should take all appropriate steps to ensure that reports and medical information about the donors and recipients are handled confidentially. Nevertheless, it is possible that the obligation to investigate or address any detected violations of the code of ethics or any tissue establishment's policy, standards and regulations in force, will override staff wish for confidentiality.

Investigations

All reported violations of the code of ethics in force shall be investigated as promptly, thoroughly and confidentially as possible, in accordance with tissue establishment's written procedures. Investigations will generally be conducted by the Director of the tissue establishment or a person designated for this specific task. If necessary, outside investigators or counsel to assist in the investigation could be hired. When appropriate, the Director of the tissue establishment should advise, in writing, the person preparing the report on the status of the investigation and should require from time to time how the investigation is being carried out.

The Duty to Cooperate

Tissue establishment staff should cooperate fully in any informal or formal investigations of any alleged violation of the code of ethics in force, and may not destroy or alter any documents, lie to or mislead investigators or prevent the collection of any information related to the objective of the investigation that is carried out within the tissue establishment.

Prohibition Against Retaliation[2]

It should be considered as a violation of the code of ethics in force to retaliate against anyone who reports possible unethical behaviour or misconduct to their direct supervisor, the Director of the tissue establishment or to any other national competent health care authorities.

V. Standards of Conduct

Respect for Colleagues and Other Personnel

Tissue establishment's policy in force should prohibit discrimination against or harassment of persons working within the tissue establishment. Harassment makes the workplace unpleasant, humiliating or intimidating for the person or group targeted and reduces the effectiveness of everyone. Tissue establishment staff must treat all persons working in the tissue establishment with dignity and respect.

Tissue establishment staff should provide accurately and fairly the qualifications, views and obligations of their fellows. Tissue establishment staff should also avoid unwarranted negative criticism of colleagues in communications with donors, recipients, relatives, next-of-kin, surrogates and legal representatives or with any other professionals. Unwarranted negative criticism may include demeaning comments that refer to a colleagues' level of competence or to individuals' attributes such as social status and wealth, race, ethnicity, national origin, colour, sex, sexual orientation, gender identity, age, marital status, political position, religion, beliefs, immigration status and mental or physical disability.

Tissue establishment staff should cooperate with social work colleagues and with colleagues of other professions when such cooperation serves the well-being of donors and recipients. Tissue establishment staff

---

[2]Retaliation means harm done to persons in retribution for raising good faith concerns or violations of the code of ethics or any other tissue establishment's standards and regulations in force.

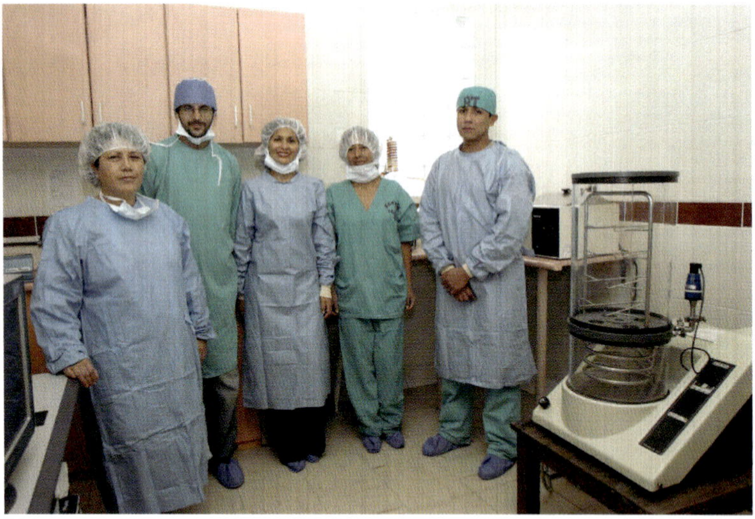

Figure 5: Rosa Guerzoni Chambergo Tissue Bank (RGCTB) in the Child's Health Institute.
Source: Courtesy of Emma Castro

should not take advantage of a dispute between a colleague and an employer to obtain a position or otherwise advance the staff's own interests. In addition, tissue establishment staff should not exploit donors, recipients, relatives, next-of-kin, surrogates and legal representatives in disputes with colleagues or engage donors and recipients, in any inappropriate discussion of conflicts between tissue establishment staff and their colleagues.

Personal Obligations

Tissue establishment staff should be solely responsible for the consequences of any failure to comply with applicable national laws and regulations in force related to the activities of the tissue establishment, particularly during the procurement of tissues from living or deceased donors or during the processing of the procured human tissue within the tissue establishment.

In addition, tissue establishment staff should be responsible for executing successfully all duties and tasks assigned to them by their immediate supervisor or the Director of the tissue establishment during the procurement and processing of tissues. Failure to do so should be considered a violation of the code of ethics in force and subject to disciplinary or administrative action.

When donors and recipients are not literate or have difficulty understanding the primary language used by medical doctors, tissue establishment staff should take steps to ensure comprehension by donors and recipients. This may include providing donors and recipients with a detailed verbal explanation of the medical doctor's information.

In instances when donors and recipients lack the capacity to provide informed consent or authorisation, tissue establishment staff should protect donors and recipients' interests by seeking permission from an appropriate third party (relatives, surrogates, next-of-kin or legal representatives), informing donors and recipients consistent with the donors and recipients level of understanding. In such instances tissue establishment staff should seek to ensure that the third party acts in a manner consistent with donors and recipients wishes and interests. Tissue establishment staff should take reasonable steps to enhance such donors and the recipients' ability to give informed consent or authorisation.

Tissue establishment staff should provide advice and represent themselves as competent only within the boundaries of their education, training, license, certification, consultation received, supervised experience or other relevant professional experience. Tissue establishment staff should also provide advice in substantive areas or use intervention techniques or approaches that are new to them only after engaging in appropriate study, training, consultation and supervision from tissue establishment staff who are competent in those interventions or techniques. When generally recognised standards do not exist with respect to an emerging area of practice, tissue establishment staff should exercise careful judgment and take responsible steps (including appropriate education, research, training, consultation and supervision) to ensure the competence of their work and to protect donors and recipients from harm.

Tissue establishment staff should understand culture and its function in human behaviour and society, recognising the strengths that exist in all cultures. Tissue establishment staff should have a knowledge base of their donor and recipient cultures and be able to demonstrate competence in the provision of advice or services that are sensitive to donor and recipient cultures.

Tissue establishment staff should respect donors and recipients' right to privacy and should not solicit private information from them, unless it is essential to provide appropriate advice or services. Once private information is shared, standards of confidentiality should be applied. Social workers may disclose confidential information, when appropriate, with valid consent or authorisation from a donor and recipient or a person legally authorised to consent on behalf of a donor and recipient.

Tissue establishment staff should also protect the confidentiality of all information obtained in the course of their professional service, except for compelling professional reasons. A general principle that should be followed by the tissue establishment staff is that he/she should not keep information confidential when disclosure is necessary to prevent serious, foreseeable and imminent harm to a donor or recipient. In all instances, tissue establishment staff should disclose the least amount of confidential information necessary to achieve the desired purpose. Only information that is directly relevant to the purpose for which the disclosure is made should be revealed.

Social workers should inform donors and recipients, to the extent possible, about the disclosure of confidential information and the potential consequences, when feasible before the disclosure is made. This applies whether tissue establishment staff discloses confidential information on the basis of a legal requirement, client consent or authorisation. In this case, tissue establishment staff should discuss with donors and recipients and other interested parties the nature of confidentiality and limitations of donors and recipients' right to confidentiality. Tissue establishment staff should review the donors' and recipients' circumstances where confidential information may be requested and where disclosure of confidential information may be legally required.

When tissue establishment staff provides counselling services to families, surrogates and legal representatives should seek agreement among the parties involved concerning each individual's right to confidentiality and obligation to preserve the confidentiality of information shared by others. Tissue establishment staff should inform participants in individual or group counselling that tissue establishment staff cannot guarantee that all participants will honour such agreements. It is important to highlight that tissue establishment staff should not disclose confidential information to third parties unless donors and recipients have authorised such disclosure. In addition, staff should not discuss confidential information in any setting unless privacy can be ensured. For this reason, tissue establishment staff should not discuss confidential information in public or semi-public areas.

Tissue establishment staff should also protect the confidentiality of donors and recipients during legal proceedings to the extent permitted by law. When a court of law or other legally authorised body orders tissue establishment staff to disclose confidential or privileged information without a client's consent and such disclosure could cause harm to the client, tissue establishment staff should request that the court withdraw the order or limit the order as narrowly as possible or maintain the records under seal, unavailable for public inspection.

Finally, tissue establishment staff should protect the confidentiality of donors' and recipients' written and electronic records and other sensitive information and should take reasonable steps to ensure that these records are stored in a secure location and that records are not available to others who are not authorised to have access. Tissue establishment staff should take precautions to ensure and maintain the confidentiality of information transmitted to other parties through the use of computers, electronic mail, facsimile machines, telephones and telephone answering machines, and other electronic or computer technology. Disclosure of confidential information should be avoided whenever possible.

Tissue establishment staff should not disclose confidential information when discussing donor and recipients with consultants unless the donors and recipients have consented to disclosure of such information or there is a compelling need for such disclosure.

Romance in the Workplace

Consensual intimate relationships between tissue establishment staff should not interfere with their work or create an environment where other persons working in the tissue establishment might feel uncomfortable or disadvantaged as a result of this relationship.

In addition, tissue establishment staff should under no circumstances engage in sexual activities or sexual contact with donors and recipients relatives, next-of-kin, surrogates or legal representatives whether such contact is consensual or forced. Tissue establishment staff should not engage in sexual activities or sexual contact with donors' and recipients' relatives or other individuals with whom donors and recipients maintain a close personal relationship when there is a risk of exploitation or potential harm to the donors and recipients.

Sexual activity or sexual contact with donors' and recipients' relatives or other individuals with whom donors and recipients maintain a personal relationship has the potential to be harmful to the client and may make it difficult for the tissue establishment staff involved in such activities to maintain appropriate professional boundaries.

Tissue establishment staff should also not engage in sexual activities or sexual contact with former donors and recipients because of the potential harm to the donors and recipients. If tissue establishment staff engage in conduct contrary to this prohibition or claim that an exception to this prohibition is warranted because of extraordinary circumstances, it is a tissue establishment staff — not their donors and recipients — who assume the full burden of demonstrating that the former donors and recipients have not been exploited, coerced or manipulated, intentionally or unintentionally. Tissue establishment staff should not provide clinical services to individuals with whom they have had a prior sexual relationship. Providing clinical services to a former sexual partner has the potential to be harmful to the individual and is likely to make it difficult for the tissue establishment staff and individual to maintain appropriate professional boundaries.

Finally, it is important to highlight that tissue establishment staff should not sexually harass donors and recipients as well as relatives, surrogate or legal representatives. Sexual harassment includes sexual advances, sexual solicitation, requests for sexual favours and other verbal or physical conduct of a sexual nature. Tissue establishment staff should not solicit a private fee or other remuneration for providing advice or any other services to donors and recipients who are entitled to such available services through the tissue establishment or hospital.

Violence in the Workplace

All tissue establishments should provide a safe work environment for all staff and will never tolerate violence or threats of any kind committed by or against someone working for the tissue establishment. The staff of the tissue establishment involved in any kind of violence in the workplace should be considered as a violation of the code of ethics in force and should be subject to disciplinary or administrative actions.

Drugs and Alcohol Abuse

All tissue establishments should be free from illegal drugs and alcohol abuse. Tissue establishment staff must always be able to perform their duties free from the effects of drugs or alcohol. Consequently, tissue establishment staff should avoid any such behaviour that prevents other staff from performing their duties and work objectives or that might bring the tissue establishment's reputation into disrepute. In case that the tissue establishment staff are involved in drugs and/or alcohol abuse, the code of ethics in force should be applied immediately and corrective measures adopted.

Conflicts of Interest

A conflict of interest occurs when the financial and personal interests, occupation, social commitments or personal or business relationships could reasonably interfere — or appear to interfere — with the ability of the tissue establishment staff to reach reasonable and impartial decisions regarding the work of the tissue establishment. Even if there is no evidence that the staff have done something improper, a conflict of interest can create an appearance of impropriety that can undermine confidence in the ability of the staff to act properly or that can damage the reputation of the tissue establishment.

Avoiding and preventing even the appearance of a conflict of interest is one of the main means by which tissue establishment staff can maintain public confidence in the impartiality and objectivity of the tissue establishment. A conflict of interest arises under the following situations:

- There is a clash between tissue establishment staff or private interests and their responsibilities within the tissue establishment;

- Tissue establishment staff engages in a business or personal relationship that may not be in the best interest of the tissue establishment;
- Tissue establishment staff or their family has a business interest in an enterprise (possibly family-owned) which could compromise the loyalty of the staff for the tissue establishment;
- Someone might reasonably question whether tissue establishment's public actions or decisions are influenced by personal or private interests or the interests of someone closely related to the tissue establishment staff by blood or marriage,[3] friends or individuals with whom they have a significant relationship or affiliation outside of the tissue establishment;
- Tissue establishment staff are in a position to use contacts or position in the tissue establishment to advance personal interests of those of someone closely related to it by blood or marriage, friends, former colleagues or individuals with whom the tissue establishment staff have a significant relationship or affiliation outside the tissue establishment;
- Tissue establishment staff provided sterilised tissues to a recipient with whom it shares personal relations, such as someone closely related to the tissue establishment's staff by blood or marriage, friends, former colleagues or individuals with whom the tissue establishment staff have a significant relationship or affiliation outside the tissue establishment, ignoring or violating the procedures established; and
- Tissue establishment staff should not accept payment, directly or indirectly, for the unduly supply of sterilised tissues or benefit from someone in the hopes of ensuring a particular decision or improperly influence future suppliers.

Disclosing Conflicts of Interest

If the tissue establishment staff think that a real or apparent conflict of interest may exist or if the tissue establishment staff have any doubts in this regard about its personal interests, the interests of someone closely

[3]A person is closely related to the tissue establishment staff by blood or marriage if they are mother, father, brother, sister, son, daughter, father-in-law, mother-in-law, son-in-law, daughter-in-law, sister-in-law, brother-in-law, grandmother, grandfather, grandson, granddaughter, uncle, aunt, nephew, niece, husband, wife, step-parent, step-child, step-brother, step-sister, and guardian or ward.

related to the tissue establishment staff by blood or marriage or the interests of friends or individuals with whom the tissue establishment staff have a significant relationship or affiliation outside the tissue establishment, then these staff must immediately disclose all of the relevant facts to their immediate supervisor or the Director of the tissue establishment, before participating in any activities or taking any decision about issues at hand. The Director of the tissue establishment has the responsibility to conduct a timely evaluation of any real or apparent conflict of interest disclosed, and should promptly inform the staff of its decision.

Abstention Where a Conflict of Interest Exists

If the tissue establishment staff have or intend to have a conflict of interest, they should not take part in any activity or decision that would directly or preferentially benefit their personal, financial or professional interests, the interests of someone closely related to the staff by blood or marriage, friends, former colleagues or people with whom they have an important relationship or affiliation outside the tissue establishment.

Waiver of Conflict of Interest

Only the Director of the tissue establishment can waive real or apparent conflicts of interest if it, at its sole discretion, determines that:

- The situation is unlikely to adversely impact the best interests of the tissue establishment;
- The conflict of interest is so remote or insignificant that it cannot reasonably be regarded as likely to influence the tissue establishment staff behaviour; or
- The interests of the tissue establishment outweigh the concern that a reasonable person may have regarding the integrity and/or objectivity of the activity in question.

The measures outlined below are intended to minimise the possibility of a real or apparent conflict. Conflict of interest issues are particularly fact-specific. As a consequence, it is not possible to describe every conceivable situation that could give rise to a conflict of interest. It becomes the responsibility of the tissue establishment staff to bring out the facts of any such situation and seek guidance from their immediate supervisor or the Director of the tissue establishment, if they entertain any doubt about a potential conflict of interest in which he/she could be involved.

Conflicts Due to Personal and Business Relationships

Tissue establishment staff should not use their position within the tissue establishment for any personal benefit, the endorsement of any products, service or businesses or for the private gain of any person closely related to the tissue establishment staff by blood or marriage, friends, former colleagues or individuals with whom they have a significant relationship or affiliation outside the tissue establishment.

In all instances, tissue establishment staff should ensure that their procurement actions comply with tissue establishment standards. If the staff have questions or doubts regarding any specific situation that may affect or be perceived as affecting their objectivity or impartiality, they should consult the Director of the tissue establishment.

Gifts From Sources Outside the Tissue Establishment

Gifts[4] given to the tissue establishment staff by anyone outside the tissue establishment for activities and/or events related to official duties should only be accepted if the gift is infrequent and of minimal value and the gift does not compromise or in any way appear to compromise the integrity of the tissue establishment staff or that of the tissue establishment itself. Otherwise, the tissue establishment staff should not, directly or indirectly, solicit or accept any gift from anyone outside the tissue establishment who

[4]The term "gift" includes any cash, gratuity, favour, discount, entertainment, admission to sporting and cultural events, hospitality, loan, or any other benefit or item having monetary value. Such gifts include also services and/or gifts of training, transportation, travel, lodgings and meals, whether provided in kind, by purchase of a ticket, payment in advance, or reimbursement after the expense has been incurred.

may be in a position to influence the tissue establishment's objectivity in carrying out their duties or that may place the tissue establishment staff under obligation to the person giving the gift.

If it is not possible to decline a gift or if there is sufficient benefit to the tissue establishment to warrant acceptance of a gift, tissue establishment staff should immediately seek written authorisation from the Director of the tissue establishment, who will notify in writing as to whether the staff or the tissue establishment can keep the gift, whether the gift must be declined, or whether the gift can be donated to charity or must otherwise be disposed of.

Gifts Between Tissue Establishment Staff

As a general rule, tissue establishment staff should not directly or indirectly give gifts to or solicit contributions from another person for gifts or make donations towards gifts for a supervisor or a person in a position of dominance within the tissue establishment.

Tissue establishment staff may, however, give gifts to or accept gifts from other persons working in the tissue establishment, only if each of the following conditions is satisfied:

- The staff involved are not in a supervisor–supervised relationship. However, the tissue establishment staff may give or accept gifts on special occasions;
- In recognition of infrequently occurring occasions of personal significance such as weddings, illnesses, births or adoptions of children; and
- Upon the occasions that terminate the supervisor–supervised relationship, such as retirements, resignations or transfers. There is a personal relationship between the staff, which would justify such gifts.

Employment and Activities Outside the Tissue Establishment

The primary obligation of the tissue establishment staff is to devote their energies to the work of the tissue establishment. The staff may engage in employment or activities outside the tissue establishment if these activities do not pose a conflict with the official duties or responsibilities within the tissue establishment, and if these activities are compatible with the work and reputation of the tissue establishment.

If tissue establishment staff wish to engage in any paid or unpaid employment or activity outside of the tissue establishment, it should submit a written request to the Director of the tissue establishment for approval prior to commencing that work.

Participation in Professional Association

Tissue establishment staff may participate as a full member of any professional association established in the country or at regional and international level in the field of tissue banking. The tissue establishment staff should seek authorisation from the Director of the tissue establishment to participate in such associations.

Use of Tissue Establishment's Property and Resources

Tissue establishment staff must be extremely careful and vigilant in the use of the tissue establishment's property, materials and resources, including its time, goods, procured and processed human tissues, services, vehicles, office equipment, official records (including electronic records), telecommunications and information technology applications.

Tissue establishment staff should only use the tissue establishment's property for official purposes. The staff have a duty to protect and conserve tissue establishment's property and use it only for authorised purposes.

Under no circumstances should tissue establishment staff conduct private business of any kind using tissue establishment's property, premises and facilities without the written authorisation of the Director of the tissue establishment.

Tissue Establishment Name and Logo

The name and logo of the tissue establishment are nationally registered and protected. Anyone outside of the tissue establishment wishing to use their name or logo must submit a written request to the Director of the tissue establishment with a full justification of the need to use it.

Intellectual Property

All rights, including title, copyright and patent rights, in any work or invention that the tissue establishment staff produces or develops as part of their official duties belongs to the tissue establishment. While authors shall be given credit for publications of a technical character, the tissue establishment has the right to decide where and how to offer for publication any professional or technical paper produced in the course of the staff duties. In carrying out their daily duties, tissue establishment staff should strive to protect the tissue establishment's intellectual property by ensuring that one understands and complies with the tissue establishment's policies in force on the use, disclosure, release, reproduction, translation, distribution or licensing of the tissue establishment's intellectual property and that the staff report any unauthorised release or use of these properties, to the Director of the tissue establishment.

In performing their official duties, the tissue establishment staff may come across or be given official access to confidential or privileged information regarding the work of the tissue establishment, its staff, its partners, its suppliers, medical history of donors and recipient of the human tissues processed by the tissue establishment, among others. Unauthorised disclosure of confidential or privileged information may seriously affect the efficiency and credibility of the tissue establishment and for this reason should be avoided.

Consequently, the tissue establishment staff should ensure that they do not intentionally or accidentally share confidential or privileged information with unauthorised parties or use such information for the staff's personal benefit or for the benefit of someone closely related to the staff by blood or marriage or for the benefit of someone with whom one of the tissue establishment staff may have a close personal relationship. In addition, staff must respect the intellectual property rights of other tissue establishments.

Internal Controls

It is essential that all tissue establishments maintain accurate record keeping and internal control systems of all its activities. As such, tissue establishment staff must register all operations and prepare accurate and complete records, in accordance with established procedures on all human tissues procured and processed by the tissue establishment. It is inappropriate, for example, to inaccurately record time for reporting purposes, provide false or intentionally misleading information to the immediate supervisor or the Director of the tissue establishment, submit false or misleading invoices or falsify any official tissue establishment's documents.

Use of Official Time

Unless authorised to use working hours for other purposes or unless the staff are on officially recognised leave, tissue establishment staff should use the official time in an honest attempt to do the assigned duties. No other activity or responsibility may conflict with this obligation, unless specifically approved in writing by the Director of the tissue establishment.

Tissue establishment staff should not request, promote, direct or attempt to coerce or influence other persons to use official time to perform activities other than those required in the performance of their official duties.

Use of Office Technology

Tissue establishment telephones, computers, e-mail, internet and other technologies should only be used for legitimate business purposes. The Director of the tissue establishment or any other person duly designated by the Director has the right to monitor and review all information contained in these systems and verify how such systems are being used. Although these systems are provided to help tissue establishment staff meet official responsibilities, staff may within reason use tissue establishment's telephones or other resources such as e-mail, internet, voice mail, faxes and computers for limited personal use.

Tissue establishment staff should not make personal long-distance telephone calls or incur any other charges related to the use of tissue establishment assets for personal reasons, if such charges ultimately accrue to the tissue establishment. If there is a personal emergency or some other well-justified reason to use the tissue establishment's long-distance service for personal calls, staff should first inform it immediately to the supervisor or, in the absence of the supervisor, to the Director of the tissue establishment and promptly reimburses the tissue establishment for the costs of such calls.

Computers are provided to persons working in the tissue establishment in order to do their work. While e-mail may encourage informality, these messages are official records and may be retrieved and used by the tissue establishment whenever necessary. Tissue establishment staff should ensure that e-mails are accurate in their language and appropriate in their tone. Furthermore, tissue establishment staff is prohibited from using tissue establishment's information technology resources to access, send or forward material that is harassing, obscene, sexually oriented or defamatory.

Motor Vehicles

Tissue establishment's vehicles, in case that these vehicles exist, are available for official use only. In exceptional cases, the Director of the tissue establishment could authorise usage of a vehicle belonging to the tissue establishment for private purposes.

Chapter IV

Importance of a Code of Practice for Tissue Establishments

General Overview

A code of practice for tissue establishments is defined as "written guidelines issued by an official body or by a professional association to its members to help them comply with its ethical standards, and which should specify the requirements for the activities of tissue establishments for the procurement and processing of human tissues for therapeutic use and research activities"(Business Dictionary).[1] The scope of a code of practice should include all human tissues used for therapeutic purposes, including those used in clinical trials and research activities.

The objective of a code of practice is to provide a set of principles and procedures that, when followed by tissue establishment staff, help to ensure that the tissue processed will have the required quality.[2] The basic

[1] Codes of practice are prescriptive in style and may be referenced by regulations or certain conditions of license. They contain practice-specific requirements that must be satisfied to ensure an acceptable level of safety in dealings with human tissues and the use of the ionising radiation technique for tissue sterilisation.

[2] The purpose of a code of practice is to set down the responsibilities of tissue establishment staff in regulating their work. The purpose of workforce regulations is to protect and promote the interests of tissue establishment users. A code of practice is intended to

tenet of a code of practice is that quality cannot be tested into a product, but must be built into each product during all stages of processing. A code of practice will also reduce the likelihood of risks associated with quality and safety of all processed human tissues, and to ensure timely access to these types of products for different medical practice. For regulatory effectiveness, it is imperative that in a code of practice, applicable legislative instruments and guidelines are reviewed regularly or whenever significant concerns are raised regarding the adequacy of the content of the approved code.

There are a number of ways that the objective of a code of practice can be achieved, including the following:

- Ensuring that there is a uniform and a minimum set of processing requirements established for all human tissues;
- Facilitating compliance with processes and technical requirements through clearly written requirements;
- Achieving international harmonisation of processing requirements, where possible and appropriate, to better facilitate regional and international cooperation and reduce regulatory burden; and
- Ensuring that the existing processing requirements will allow for advances in technology or changes in industry practices correcting any legislative discrepancies identified with, including technical requirements in the existing code of practice.

A code of practice should be based on a quality system approach. It forms the basis of good practice in all tissue establishments and will be used as reference when the tissue establishments are inspected by national competent health care authorities of the country in which they are located. For this reason, a code of practice should set out safety requirements with

---

complement rather than replace or duplicate existing tissue establishment staff's policies and it forms part of the wider package of legislations, human requirements and guidance that relate to the employment of staff. Employers are responsible for making sure that they meet the standards set out in the code, provide high-quality services and promote public trust and confidence in tissue establishment activities.

respect to processing, which includes donor screening, donor testing, collection/retrieval, preservation, packaging, labeling, and quarantine; storage; record keeping; distribution; importation; error; accident and adverse reaction investigation and reporting. The objective of a code of practice is to maximize the safety of human tissues, by clearly stipulating the safety requirements adopted by the national competent health care authorities thus making them mandatory (Canada Minister of Health, 2009).[3]

To ensure that governmental regulation remains relevant and credible, it is important that a code of practice is regularly reviewed and updated. Most countries revise and update their code of practice about every five years to keep up with changes in the industry and changes in manufacturing and testing technology. The marketplace for human tissues has undergone great change during the past decade with advances in technology in manufacturing practices, as well as changes to the type and nature of human tissues produced. The Director of the tissue establishment should ensure that these advances in technology are included in a revised version of the code of practice.

Why is good management practice in all tissue establishments an important subject? The use of human tissues is increasingly popular in several countries, with widespread use among orthopaedic surgeons — particularly in knee surgery. According to C. Thomas Vangsness Jr., (2005), in the USA, more than 60,000 allografts were used in knee surgeries by members of the American Orthopaedic Society for Sports Medicine. As the use of allograft tissue increases, the safety of allografts remains an issue of paramount importance. To avoid the use of contaminated human tissues in medical practice, all tissue establishments should:

- Have a quality system in place that includes document control, change management, monitoring systems including internal audits, corrective action and management review;

[3] A code of practice should clearly distinguish between legal requirements, situations where the competent authority is insisting on something, statements of best practice, and more vague aspirations. Those storing and using human tissue need to know exactly what is unlawful and what is regarded as incompatible with holding an authority license.

- Control manufacturing processes and evaluate any changes to the process. They should validate any changes that affect the quality of the human tissue to ensure consistency of manufacture and compliance with specifications;
- Train personnel in all aspects of processing the human tissue and associated activities that affect the quality of the processed human tissues, including general training, as well as training specific to their role;
- Have premises and equipment to undertake ancillary procedures, storage and production, including quality control and dispatch areas, and equipment looking at qualification, calibration, performance verification, maintenance and the monitoring of use;
- Have documentation setting out policies, manufacturing procedures, quality control procedures, ancillary procedures and records of outcomes in all areas;
- Where applicable, have procedures for contract production and contract testing, which involves the contract giver, contract acceptor and the contracts;
- Establish a complaint and recalls system for recalling processed human tissues prior to transplantation and implantation, where indicated;
- Have a system for managing critical material, including starting materials, packaging, intermediate, bulk and finished products, reagents, culture media and reference standards. The management of critical material must review rejected, recovered, reprocessed and reworked materials;
- Ensure that the collection and processing of human tissues are undertaken in such a way as to prevent cross-contamination, mix-ups and bacterial contamination during procurement, processing operations, packaging and release for supply. All critical processes should be either verified and/or validated;
- Have quality control practices that include the control of starting materials, intermediates, bulk and finished human tissues, the test requirements, batch records review, and stability studies; and
- Where computer systems are required in connection with a step in the processing of the human tissues, ensure that the computer system meets the same quality system requirements for those manual functions that it replaces. There should be documentation from the time of the written protocol for initial verification and the prospective validation of

the computer system, including the confirmation of accuracy and reliability of the data collected directly from the equipment, backup of the system, and contingency plans if the system fails.

A code of practice sets out all the requirements for good management practice, which collectively ensures that processed human tissues consistently meet specifications. It sets the benchmark for practices that should be followed, and alternative approaches may be permitted provided it can be demonstrated that the intent of the code is met in a timely and effective manner in order to meet quality objectives. It is the tissue establishment's responsibility to determine the most effective and efficient quality process. Furthermore, it is important to note that the requirements of a code of practice are minimum requirements. Many tissue establishments have already implemented comprehensive, modern quality systems and risk management approaches that may well exceed the minimum standards. These includes:

- Implementing and monitoring written policies on: confidentiality, equal opportunities, risk assessment, substance abuse, record keeping, and the acceptance of money or personal gifts from tissue establishment users;
- Effectively managing and supervising staff to support effective practice and good conduct and supporting staff to address deficiencies in their performance;
- Having systems in place to enable tissue establishment staff to report inadequate resources or operational difficulties which might impede the delivery of safe sterilised human tissues for medical practice or research activities; and
- Supporting tissue establishment staff to meet the code of practice in force and not requiring them to do anything that would put their compliance with that code at risk.

Consistent with the basic principles outlined above, the proposed code of practice should provide for systems that are consistent with monitoring and control of processing of human tissues and facilities. The risks associated with the procurement and processing of human tissues include:

- The human tissue (donated or laboratory-cultured cells and tissues) may contain harmful viruses, bacteria or prions;

- The intended use of the human tissue may not be supported by clinical evidence; and
- The way the human tissue is processed, if appropriate processes are not adhered to, can mean that the human tissue could be contaminated or altered, converting the product into a non-efficacious one or making it non-viable for its foreseeable use.

A code of practice should not limit the development of new concepts or technologies which have been validated and which provide a level of quality assurance at least equivalent to those set out in the code.

Finally, it is important to stress that a code of practice needs to provide clarification of scientific principles and objectives that apply to emerging cellular and tissue technologies. It also needs to provide a tissue establishment with the flexibility to apply tailored approaches to manufacturing controls suitable to their product. A code of practice should also promote the harmonisation of regulatory practice. Why is this so important for the tissue banking community? According to Barbara Indech (2000), the globalization of today's marketplace impacts every sector of business, including the health care sector. Regulatory authorities and industry have long acknowledged that as national boundaries are crossed on a regular basis, the harmonisation of health care legislation — resulting in an international consensus on essential safety, efficacy, and quality principles — offers significant benefits to all parties, including the public. These benefits include enhanced public health protection on a global level (where the best elements of national health care systems are melded together); increased government efficiency, as governments rely on each other's expertise and experience; lower health care costs to the public; and the increased development and availability of advances in medical technology (including drug and medical device products).

While the benefits of harmonisation are recognised by many, the actual term "harmonisation" has different meanings to different people and is often used interchangeably with the term "mutual recognition" in the biomedical field. In the European Union (EU), a "mutual recognition agreement" (MRA) between the EU and a third (non-EU) country refers to an accord "based on the mutual acceptance of test reports, certificates, and marks of conformity issued by the conformity assessment bodies of one of the parties of the Agreement in conformity with the legislation of the other party."

In the last decade, two international task forces have been formed for the express purpose of promoting true global harmonisation of medical device and pharmaceutical regulation — the Global Harmonisation Task Force (GHTF) and the International Conference on Harmonisation (ICH). The goal of the ICH is to ensure that "good quality, safe and effective medicines are developed in the most expeditious and cost-effective manner", with elimination of unnecessary duplication of human clinical, In the other hand, the GHTF aims to achieve its goals "by developing an international consensus to develop equivalent systems with a common basis for how regulatory practices and decisions are carried out relative to medical devices." At present, four working (or study) groups comprise the GHTF, with a separate focus on product approval-related issues (i.e., regulatory requirements/pre-market review), adverse event reporting, good manufacturing practices (quality system requirements and guidance), and audits of quality systems. These groups have developed (and continue to develop) harmonised approaches to medical device regulation in each of their areas. It is expected that future GHTF efforts will be targeted toward device classification, premarket approval, and essential requirements for devices and standards. According to authorities in the industry, global medical device regulations will continue to harmonise "along the lines of a risk class-based system and ISO 9001-based GMP requirements."

The harmonisation of human tissue regulations has experienced more limited progress, despite continued efforts by several countries' regulatory authorities, as well as by international organisations. In May 1991, the Health Assembly of the WHO endorsed the Guiding Principles of Human Organ Transplantation, which recommends to member states specific conditions under which organs and tissues may be removed from living and deceased donors for the purposes of transplantation. Member states have been encouraged to consider these guidelines when formulating their organ transplantation policies. The Guiding Principles emphasise the concepts of free informed consent, donation subject to minimum age requirements, the treatment of a potential donor and subsequent determination of his death by a physician who is independent of the organ/tissue removal or implantation medical team, the resort to donation of no regenerative organs/tissues from living, non-genetically related donors as second choice to cadaveric donation, the no commercialisation of organ/tissue donation, and the equitable distribution of organs/tissues based on a recipient's medical need (vs. financial capability).

With the advent of bio-engineered medical devices, international regulatory authorities turned their focus towards harmonisation of tissue-engineered products in the mid-1990s.

For all that has been said, above it is important to consider the use of a model code of practice to promote the harmonisation of all different types of codes in force in the different countries. In chapter V a model code of practice is included for the consideration of the tissue banking community.

Chapter V

A Model Code of Practice for Tissue Establishments

Introduction

In this chapter, relevant content from various published papers has been included with the aim of using them as reference during the harmonisation of all codes of practice in force in different countries or in the elaboration or modification of a code of practice for a specific tissue establishment. Some of the content, ideas and suggestions have been collected from several papers included in the references, particularly by Morales Pedraza and Astrid Lobo (2012).

It is important to highlight that the details of procedures and practices described here are for guidance only. Each tissue establishment should consult the national legislation operating in the jurisdiction region of the tissue establishment and ensure that the procedures adopted conform to the requirements.

Purpose of a Code of Practice

A code of practice is an important adjunct to a code of ethics for tissue establishments. While the latter addresses the ethical behaviour that directs the donation, procurement, processing and distribution of human tissues for transplantation, a code of practice ensures its implementation. It contains a general description of the actions that should or should not be performed by a tissue establishment to safeguard the safety and rights of tissue donors, recipients and tissue establishment personnel, and the obligations thereof. It covers effective ways to provide safe human tissues of reliable quality for transplantation, to identify and manage risks to all stakeholders and products, to review current practices and to take corrective action when necessary, thereby guaranteeing compliance with the code of ethics in force.

All tissue establishments supplying human tissues for therapeutic or for research purposes should comply with a code of practice that details current best practices that must be observed in the selection of donors, retrieval of human tissues, testing, processing, sterilisation, storage and delivery of human tissues. While professional bodies and specialist societies have, in many instances, prepared standards or guidelines addressing these issues in relation to specific tissues, this model code of practice is presented as a framework for any tissue establishment that would like to review their own code of practice or standards or wish to prepare a new code.

Finally, it is important to highlight the following: The content of the different paragraphs and other elements included in this book can be used as reference for the elaboration of a specific code of practice and will be very useful to tissue establishment staff, surgeons using human tissues for transplantation, regulators who oversee the safety of transplantation and radiation sterilisation procedures, members of professional associations, health care service personnel in hospitals in which human tissue transplantations are performed, and intergovernmental organisations involved in transplantation issues, for example, the WHO and the IAEA, during the development of their responsibilities and tasks assigned to them. National competent health care authorities should finally approve the code of practice prepared by the tissue establishments.

Standard Operating Procedures (SOPs)

The purpose of the SOPs is to ensure the safe and efficient operations of tissue establishments. These establishments should maintain their SOPs updated taking into account that this document contain in writing all aspects included in the code of practice in force. The SOPs should be utilised to ensure that all human tissues released for transplantation meet the minimum requirements defined by the code of practice in force.

The SOPs to be adopted by a tissue establishment should meet all of the following requirements:

- Be in a standardised format;
- Be approved by the Director of the tissue establishment and by the national competent health care authorities after consulting the Advisory Board;
- Be available for use in all positions within the tissue establishment, particularly where the relevant activities are carried out;
- Include any changes to the procedures approved by the Director of the tissue establishment after consulting the Advisory Board and before being implemented; and
- Be kept up-to-date.

The format of each SOPs depends on the regulations in force in each country but should contain, at a minimum, the following:

- The type of procedure;
- The title and purpose of the procedure;
- The unique number identifying the document and indicating revision(s);
- The date that the SOPs became effective and the date(s) that it was revised;
- The signature of the authorising person and the date of authorisation;
- The page number and the total number of pages printed on each page;
- A clear outline of steps and instructions to be followed in the described procedure, which matches the details in the processing records (e.g., worksheets, forms or computer screens), if applicable;
- Staff set out categories responsible for performing all or part of the steps in the SOPs in force;
- The provided tolerance limits applied to tests; and
- Access to publications cited in support of the policies and procedures in force.

The SOPs should include, where relevant, but should not be restricted to the following:

- Standard procedures for donor consent, screening, retrieval, processing, sterilisation, preservation, testing, storage and distribution of human tissues;
- Quality assurance and quality-control policies;
- Laboratory procedures for tests performed in-house and in contracted laboratories;
- Specifications for materials used, including reagents, storage media and packaging materials;
- Personnel and facility safety procedures;
- Standard procedures for facility maintenance, cleaning and waste disposal;
- Methods for verification of the effectiveness of sterilisation procedures;
- Equipment maintenance, calibration and validation procedures;
- Environmental and microbiological conditions and the methods used for controlling, testing, and verification;
- Physiological and physical test specifications for materials;
- Methods for determination of shelf life, storage temperature, and expiry dates of each human tissue;
- Determination of insert and/or label text;
- Policies and procedures for exceptional release of human tissues;
- Procedures for adverse event reporting and corrective actions to be implemented; and
- Donor/recipient tracking and human tissue recall policies and procedures in force.

All SOPs, their modification and associated process-validation studies should be reviewed and approved by the Director of the tissue establishment after being reviewed by the Advisory Board and the Administrative Officer (dealt with in the next section). All medically related SOPs should be reviewed and approved by the Advisory Board and/or the Medical Director/Consultant. Copies of the SOPs should be available to all tissue establishment staff, and to authorised individuals for inspection upon request. Upon implementation, all SOPs should be followed as written. SOPs should be updated at regular intervals to reflect modifications or changes that the Director of the tissue establishment, the Administrative Officer or any other staff or body within the tissue establishment consider indispensable to be introduced in the SOPs in force. The Director of the tissue establishment should approve each modification or change in the SOPs.

Appropriate training should be provided to pertinent tissue establishment staff in the use of the SOPs in force. Obsolete SOPs should be archived for a minimum of 10 years or according to the period established by the laws in force in a particular country.

Scope of the Code of Practice

A code of practice specifies the main requirements for the activities of tissue establishments that process human tissues for therapeutic use within a health care system or for research activities. The scope of a code of practice includes all human tissues used for therapeutic purposes as well as those used in clinical trials and research activities.

I. Tissue Establishment's Principles, Purpose, Organisational Structure, Staff, Equipment, and Facilities

Tissue Establishment's Principles

The government shall ensure that all tissue establishments where activities of testing, processing, preservation, sterilisation, storage or distribution of human tissues intended for transplantation are undertaken have been duly accredited, designated, authorised or licensed by a national competent health care authorities for the purpose of carrying out those activities. National competent health care authorities may suspend or revoke the accreditation, designation, authorisation or licensing of a tissue establishment or of a tissue preparation process, if audits or internal control measures demonstrate that such establishment or process does not comply with the requirements of the code of practice in force. The tissue establishments should not undertake any substantial changes to its activities after being accredited without the prior written approval of the national competent health care authorities.

Observance of the following fundamental principles is essential to ensure the ethical adequacy in utilising human tissues for transplantation:

- **Thorough practice of informed consent or authorisation**: It is necessary to obtain informed consent or authorisation through providing sufficient information about retrieval of human tissue to the donor and about transplantation of human tissue to the recipient;
- **Securing respect for the donor**: Donation of human tissue is a sublime act of societal goodwill. When handling donated human tissues, a tissue establishment and transplant organisation should maintain the respect for the dignity, intention, and good faith of the donor;
- **Guarantee of the free will decision for the donor**: The potential donor has no obligation to donate human tissue and may also refuse to receive or to accept information or interview about it. The free will and intention of the donor (or the bereaved family of a deceased donor or legal representative) should be given the first priority, and no unjust pressure should be given to the donor or their families or legal representative in their decision-making process;
- **The donation should be done on a non-profit basis**: Donation of human tissue is a sublime and public act of societal goodwill, and due to this characteristic, it is necessary to make sure that there is no financial consideration given or claimed over the donation. However, a tissue establishment can claim the reasonable amount of certain expenses (e.g., cost of retrieval, sterilisation, storage, distribution, personnel, transportation, among others), which are not deemed as financial consideration. As a non-profit organisation, a tissue establishment should not quote an unfair amount greater than the actual cost in order to make profits;
- **Protection of personal data**: In the management of a tissue establishment, personal data, such as name, age, medical conditions, etc., of the donor and recipient should be protected as confidential information;
- **Fulfilment of the donor's good intentions**: In handling donated human tissues, an organisation or institute involved in tissue procurement should make the best effort to fulfil the wish of the donor, and to

secure the ethical appropriateness and respect for the good intentions of the donor; and

- **Provision of information**: As a social and public organisation, a tissue establishment is obliged to make its activities public, while adequately protecting personal and confidential information.

Purpose of a Tissue Establishment

The purpose of a tissue establishment should be clearly formulated and documented. The tissue establishment should state whether it is a government or private, free-standing entity or part of a government or private institution or if it is a "non-profit" or "for-profit" organisation.

Organisational Structure and Staff of a Tissue Establishment

The organisational structure and the number of staff in a tissue establishment will depend primarily on the volume and type of human tissues produced, the location of the tissue establishment, the support it receives from the national competent health care authorities, and the resources available. These in turn are dependent on the requirement for human tissue transplants, the availability of surgical expertise for the use of banked tissue, the level of tissue banking activities in the country, the number of human tissue donors, and access to qualified staff.

Governing Bodies

Whether tissue establishments are free-standing entities or are associated with hospitals, universities, radiation facilities or other medical institutions, it is recommended that the following governing bodies be set up to oversee and monitor the activities of the tissue establishments:

- Advisory Board;
- Tissue Establishment Committee; and
- Management Committee.

Advisory Board

The Advisory Board must comprise key personnel of the tissue establishment or the institution to which the tissue establishment is attached. These would include the Director of the tissue establishment and the Medical Director/Consultant, if this is another individual. The Management of an institution by virtue of their office could function as the Advisory Board. The functions of the Advisory Board are as follows:

- Ensure that local legal and ethical requirements are met by the tissue establishment;
- Advise on the best use of the infrastructure available, including equipment, materials and personnel, for the effective functioning of the tissue establishment;
- Review and enable implementation of the recommendations of the tissue establishment;
- Monitor the progress of the tissue establishment through regular reports and audits;
- Provide medical, technical and scientific advice and assistance as and when required;
- Ratify the code of ethics, the code of practice and the quality manual developed by the Tissue Establishment Committee;
- Provide opportunities and the necessary support for the expansion of the tissue establishment; and
- Ensure adequate training for the tissue establishment staff.

Tissue Establishment Committee

The Tissue Establishment Committee should be chaired by the Director of the tissue establishment and should have the responsibility of promoting tissue banking activities in the country or within the community where the tissue establishment is located. Members of this committee should comprise the following:

- Director of the tissue establishment;
- Medical personnel who will promote the donation, procurement and utilisation of banked human tissues;
- Radiation physicists and biologists to facilitate the use of ionising radiation technique for the sterilisation of the human tissue to be

transplanted, in case this is the technique used for the sterilisation of the human tissues processed by the tissue establishment;
- Pathologists who will facilitate the donation and donor screening processes;
- Tissue Transplant Coordinators who will identify donors and facilitate the donation of human tissues to the tissue establishment; and
- Prominent community leaders who can influence public opinion on human tissue donation with the aim of increasing the donor pool.

The Tissue Establishment Committee should meet at least once in six months for the following purposes:

- To formulate guidelines to be adopted by the tissue establishment regarding all procedures from donation and procurement to processing, packaging, and distribution;
- To formulate quality assurance policies for tissue banking to be approved by the Director of the tissue establishment;
- To promote public awareness of tissue banking; and
- To promote professional awareness of tissue procurement and transplantation.

Stand-alone tissue establishments will have to draw from their collaborators to establish a Tissue Establishment Committee, while institution-based tissue establishments have the option of drawing on their own institutional faculty.

Management Committee

The Management Committee should be chaired by the Director of the tissue establishment to oversee the day-to-day operation of the tissue establishment. The members of this committee should comprise the following:

- Director of the tissue establishment;
- Medical Director/Consultant;
- Administrative Officer; and
- Tissue establishment staff (see the next subsection).

The Management Committee should meet at least once a month with an agenda that includes the following:

- The number of deceased and living donors reported to the tissue establishment;
- The number and types of human tissues procured;
- The number and types of human tissues utilised;
- Adverse events;
- Administrative issues;
- Personnel issues;
- Equipment maintenance and repair;
- Training programs;
- Scientific projects;
- Budget for capital equipment;
- Revisions in SOPs, quality manual, quality control policies, code of ethics and code of practice; and
- Any other technical or administrative matters.

Tissue Establishment Staff

In principle, a tissue establishment should have the following minimum staff:

- Director of the tissue establishment;
- Medical Director/Consultant, if the Director of the tissue establishment is not a physician;
- Administrative Officer;
- Quality Assurance Officer;
- Processing Officer;
- Microbiologist;
- Tissue Establishment Operators or Technologists; and
- Tissue Transplant Coordinator.

The Director of the tissue establishment must identify staff to take on responsibility for key functions based on their qualifications and experience. In smaller tissue establishments, these responsibilities may be shared among the available staff. Thus, if the Director of the tissue establishment is a physician, then he/she could take on the responsibilities and functions of the Medical Director/Consultant. Alternatively, an external physician could serve as a part-time Medical Consultant. Qualified Technologists could function as Microbiologists and Tissue Transplant Coordinators. Alternatively external contracts may be held to carry out some of these key functions. However, the Quality Assurance Officer must be an individual not engaged in the tasks she/he reviews.

The tissue establishment staff must be responsible for the implementation of all policies and procedures as established by the Director of the tissue establishment. For this reason, tissue establishment staff must possess the educational background, technical qualification, experience and training necessary to ensure that all assigned tasks are performed in accordance with tissue establishment approved procedures and in the most efficient and competent manner.

The responsibilities of all tissue establishment staff must be described in a written job description. Tissue establishment staff should demonstrate competency and skill in all tasks assigned to them.

Responsibilities of the Tissue Establishment Staff

1. *Director of the Tissue Establishment*

The Director of the tissue establishment should be qualified by training and experience for the scope of activities conducted by the tissue establishment. The Director of the tissue establishment is responsible for:

- Implementing the policies approved by the Advisory Board, the SOPs, as well as any other approved regulatory documents;
- Developing and maintaining a quality assurance (QA) programme to ensure that all activities are in compliance with the tissue establishment's policies, SOPs, code of ethics and code of practice in force;
- Conducting annual internal audits according to documented procedures and ensuring that processes needed for QA are established, implemented and maintained;
- Ensuring the promotion of awareness of good laboratory practice throughout the tissue establishment;

- Developing and evaluating SOPs and ensuring the implementation of agreed and approved procedures;
- Monitoring all activities of the tissue establishment, including tissue donation, procurement, processing, packaging, sterilisation, storage and distribution, as well as research in case that the tissue establishment is authorised by the national competent health care authorities to carry out this type of activities;
- Keeping up-to-date with recent advances, professional guidelines and current research in the field of tissue banking, with a view of improving the quality and extending the range of allografts produced;
- Ensuring that donor selection criteria are in line with current guidelines in force at the state level;
- Liaising with local and national regulatory bodies and obtaining the necessary certification, registrations and licensing to carry out the activities of the tissue establishment;
- Ensuring that agreements or contracts for services with third parties, including sterilisation of human tissues in nuclear facilities, in case that the ionising radiation technique is used for the sterilisation of human tissues, are in line with a code of practice in force and with the IAEA Code of Practice for the Radiation Sterilisation of Tissue Allografts. Requirements for Validation and Routine Control adopted in 2007;
- Approving the release of all human tissues from quarantine for transplantation purposes;
- Establishing and maintaining systems for clinical feedback;
- Reviewing clinical efficacy of the human tissue transplants, continuity of the audit trail and advising third parties involved with distribution of the procured human tissues of their responsibilities;
- Addressing any adverse events reported and ensuring that corrective and preventive actions are completed, including actions to be taken for late notification of donor infection risk and recalls;
- Conducting public and professional awareness programmes to promote human tissue donation, and the products and services offered by the tissue establishment;
- The management of the resources of the tissue establishment, including the selection and installation of process equipment and the maintenance, repair and calibration of the same;

- The management of personnel, including appointment, training and documented allocation of job responsibilities;
- Identifying the training needs of the tissue establishment staff and ensuring that such training is imparted;
- Allowing the training of staff from other tissue establishments, hospitals or medical institutions in the operation and organisation of a tissue establishment and in the use of sterilised human tissues in certain medical practice, with a view to promoting the establishment of tissue establishments in other regions of the country and tissue retrieval and distribution centres across the country;
- Coordinating the tissue establishment participation/collaboration in programmes conducted by external agencies in the field of tissue banking and transplantation of human tissues; and
- Convening the Management Committee meetings to review quality and submitting reports to the Advisory Board.

2. *Medical Director/Consultant*

The Medical Director/Consultant should have a valid medical state license. He/she may also be the Director of the tissue establishment. He/she should have training and experience in evaluating and determining donor suitability, particularly with regard to infectious diseases, or use a Medical Advisory Committee or consultants to assist in those areas. The Medical Director/Consultant is responsible for:

- Establishing donor suitability criteria;
- Evaluating and determining donor acceptability;
- Reviewing and approving the medical part of the SOPs prior to the final approval of this document and its implementation;
- Authorising, in exceptional circumstances, limited human tissue release prior to completion of the donor or human tissue suitability evaluation;
- Establishing policies and procedures to address adverse events and reviewing and approving final reports of action taken; and
- Compliance with state and/or local laws and/or regulations regarding notifying appropriate parties of confirmed positive infectious disease test results.

3. *Administrative Officer*

In case an Administrative Officer is appointed, his/her main responsibility is to assist the Director of the tissue establishment in carrying out his/her responsibilities. The Administrative Officer should not be responsible for medical activities.

In general, the Administrative Officer should be responsible for administration, management, and other general activities, and should be aware of:

- All states and/or local laws and/or regulations applicable to tissue banking;
- Tissue Banking Standards adopted by the IAEA, WHO, American Association of Tissue Banks (AATB), European Association of Tissue Banks (EATB), Asia Pacific Association of Surgical Tissue Banks (APASTB), Latin American Association of Tissue Banks (ALABAT) or any other similar professional associations;
- Administrative aspects of the informed consent for donation and transplantation of human tissues, including authorisation for the same;
- The grieving process so as to enable a sensitive approach for informed consent of the bereaved next-of-kin or legal representative, in the case of potential deceased donors;
- The rights of the donor, which include the right to refuse or withdraw consent for donation without it compromising treatment, medical or otherwise; reconstruction of the body after retrieval; respect for the religious and cultural customs of the donor and next-of-kin; information regarding the intended purposes of donation; and anonymity between donor and recipient;
- The rights of the recipient, including access to safe human tissue transplants and anonymity between donor and recipient;
- Documentation and recordkeeping requirements that comply with state and/or local laws and/or regulations;
- The coding system used for facilitating the tracking of human tissue products;
- The code of ethics and the code of practice adopted by the tissue establishment;
- The main elements of the quality control system;

- Requirements for release of human tissues;
- Adverse event reporting;
- Screening and testing criteria; and
- Confidentiality and release of information.

4. *Quality Assurance Officer*

It is essential that in all cases, the quality-related functions are separate from the processing functions. Thus the Quality Assurance Officer should be a designated individual not performing the task under review. The Quality Assurance Officer's responsibilities include:

- Regular input to the review of the quality system;
- Proposing the approval or rejection of retrieved and processed human tissues as well as discontinuing processing and/or release of human tissues when there are deviations from the SOPs;
- Evaluating batch processing records;
- Reviewing processes at regular intervals;
- Performing inspections and testing;
- Preparing and monitoring agreements of services with third parties;
- Checking maintenance of premises, equipment and calibration;
- Ensuring that processes validations are completed;
- Performing and acting on internal audit programmes; and
- Assuring compliance with training programmes.

5. *Processing Officer*

The Processing Officer's responsibilities include:

- Regular input to the review of the quality system;
- Ensuring that human tissues are retrieved, processed, sterilised and stored according to the documented procedures;
- Proposing the approval of instructions relating to process operations and ensuring implementation of the same;
- Ensuring that processes records are evaluated and authorised by the designated tissue establishment staff;
- Checking the maintenance of premises, instruments and equipment;

- Ensuring that processes validations are completed; and
- Ensuring compliance with training programmes by the tissue establishment staff.

The joint responsibilities of the Quality Assurance and Processing Officers include:

- Proposing the approval of the SOPs and other relevant documents;
- Monitoring and control of the processing environment;
- Designation and monitoring of storage and quarantine practices for materials and tissues;
- Retention of records; and
- Identification, investigation and monitoring of factors, which may affect safety and quality.

6. *Microbiologist*

The Microbiologist's responsibilities include:

- Commissioning and monitoring of effective sterilisation and/or disinfection procedures, facilities and services;
- Contributing to the development of donor testing strategies;
- Carrying out the investigation of microbial contamination of human tissues and advising appropriate actions;
- Proposing strategies for monitoring and recording environmental contamination at an appropriate frequency, and isolating and identifying contaminants and their sources;
- Proposing strategies for the microbiological control of ancillary materials for processing activities;
- Proposing strategies for the specification and routine monitoring of air conditioning and filtration equipment;
- Proposing strategies for the monitoring of hygiene and cleaning practices; and
- Developing training programmes with the aim of retraining tissue establishment staff.

7. *Operators or Technologists*

Operators or Technologists should be responsible for the implementation of policies and procedures established by the Director of the tissue establishment. Duties of each Operator or Technologist should be described in written job descriptions. Operators or Technologists must demonstrate competency in the operations to which they are assigned and must possess the educational background, experience, and training sufficient to ensure that assigned tasks are performed in accordance with the established procedures. Tissue retrieval, processing, packaging and cryopreservation should be performed by trained personnel. Staff training must be documented in individual employee training files.

8. *Tissue Transplant Coordinator*

The Tissue Transplant Coordinator's responsibilities are, among others, the following:

- Extending support to bereaved families;
- Confirming the suitability of the potential donor with the referral source;
- Obtaining contact information from the next-of-kin or legal representative;
- Obtaining consent for the donation of human tissues;
- Approaching the next-of-kin or legal representative to discuss donation options (human tissues that can be donated); possible uses of the donated human tissue; a description of the recovery, testing, processing, storage and distribution of human tissues recovered; consent process; medical social history; and services available to the donor family;
- Liaising between the donor/donor hospital and the recovery team;
- Ensuring proper preparation of the body for donation, refrigeration facilities and appropriate storage and transport of human tissues;
- Documentation for donor details;
- Following up with donor families (thank you letters, donor family services, etc.); and
- Following up with the donor referral source to obtain feedback on the process.

Buildings

Tissue establishment buildings, whether they are newly constructed or modified, should be designed to fit their intended purpose and have adequate lighting, plumbing, drainage, ventilation, and space. They should be located, designed, constructed, and used with the aim of ensuring the quality of human tissues processed by the tissue establishment. Thus, the design of the facilities should prevent errors and cross-contamination. Critical procedures should facilitate the implementation of the policies and SOPs in force, minimise errors, and prevent cross-contamination. Particular attention should be paid to the workflow to ensure a sequential decrease in the bioburden of processed human tissues and prevent cross-contamination. At a minimum there should be:

- Separation of wet and dry processing areas;
- Facilities to enable aseptic handling of human tissues and the maintenance of clean working areas;
- Adequate space for the quarantine of in-process materials;
- Adequate and separate space for the storage of approved human tissues;

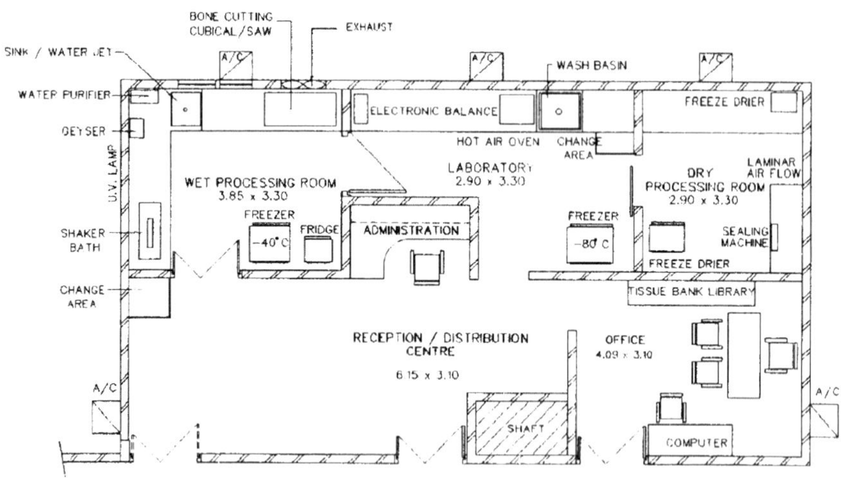

Figure 6: The TMH Tissue Bank.

Source: Courtesy of Dr. Astrid Lobo Gajiwala

- A documentation room to house records necessary for traceability and confidentiality of donors and recipients; and
- Efficient waste management system.

Where human tissues are processed in open containers, tissue establishments should have:

- Floors, walls and ceilings of non-porous smooth surfaces that are easily sanitised;
- Temperature control;
- For sterile processing, air filtered through high-efficiency particulate air (HEPA) filters with an appropriate pressure differential between zones that can be documented;
- A documented system for monitoring temperature, air supply conditions, particle numbers, and bacterial colony-forming units (environmental monitoring);
- A documented system for cleaning and disinfecting rooms and equipment;
- A documented system for gowning and laundry;
- Adequate space for staff and storage of sterile garments; and
- Access limited to authorised personnel.

Critical procedures should be performed in designated areas of adequate size and specifications. Access to certain areas of the tissue establishments should be restricted to authorised persons.

Efficient cleaning and maintenance procedures should be implemented and documented to prevent cross-contamination and exposure to blood-borne pathogens.

Equipment and Instruments

Equipment and instruments should be of appropriate quality for their intended function. Documented procedures must be established to clean and maintain all equipment and instruments to ensure efficient operation and avoid compromising the quality of the human tissue during its processing. Inspection equipment and measuring and test equipment must be calibrated to appropriate standards. All equipment and instruments must

Figure 7: Laminar airflow cabinet.

Source: Courtesy Ferdiansyah

be used in a manner which ensures that the measurement uncertainty is known and is consistent with the required measurement capability.

All tissue establishments should:

- Identify all equipment and instruments that are used during the processing of the human tissues that can affect human tissue quality;
- Specify details of the equipment type, unique identification, location, frequency and method of inspection, acceptance criteria, and the actions to be taken when results are unsatisfactory;
- Maintain calibration records for inspection equipment and measuring and test equipment;
- Identify the calibration status of test equipment; and
- Ensure that the handling and storage of inspection equipment and measuring and test equipment is such that the accuracy and fitness for use are maintained.

Equipment, instruments and non-disposable supplies that come into contact with human tissue should be built so that their surfaces do not alter the safety or quality of the tissue.

Equipment and instruments should be designed, manufactured and qualified for appropriate cleaning, and should be sterilised or decontaminated after each use. Multiple uses of disposable instruments for several donors should be excluded. A separate set of clean and sterile instruments (disposable, where appropriate) should be used for each donor. There should be SOPs for monitoring, inspection, maintenance, calibration, and clean-up procedures for each piece of equipment and instrument used. Storage equipment and instruments should be inspected on a regular scheduled basis. Refrigerators, freezers and other equipment required to maintain a specific temperature should be inspected on a regular scheduled basis. Appropriate certification and maintenance records should be maintained for all equipment and instruments.

Environmental Controls

There are four main sources of potential contamination of a human tissue after it has entered the tissue establishment:

- Processing areas;
- Personnel;
- Equipment and ancillary materials; and
- Cross-contamination from human tissues of different donors.

Environmental monitoring procedures should be established, when appropriate, as part of the QA programme. The procedures should include acceptable test parameters and corrective measures to be taken in the event of unacceptable results. The monitoring activities should be scheduled according to existing guidelines or the trend determined by previous results. They may include particulate air samplings and work surface cultures. Each monitoring activity should be documented.

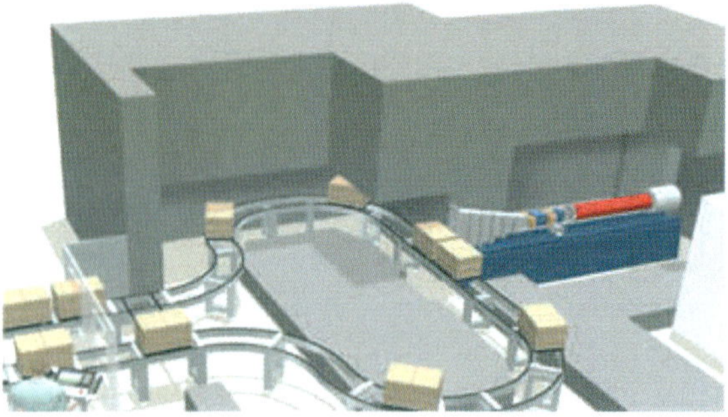

Figure 8: Electron-beam irradiator.

Source: Morales Pedraza (2009)

In order to minimise the hazard of infectious disease transmission, several steps should be undertaken by tissue establishment operators. These steps are:

1. **Careful donor selection using proper screening criteria**: Several features should be taken into consideration such as time elapsed since the death and conditions of body storage, age, social and medical history, physical examination of the body, autopsy results and serological blood testing, exclusion of potential donors who are a behaviour risk for HIV, hepatitis, and prion infections.
2. **Proper tissue processing**: Human tissue should be procured and processed under aseptic and/or as clean as possible conditions; it is recommended to keep the human tissue before sterilisation at low temperature and/or frozen to avoid micro-organism proliferation and to diminish the activity of proteolytic enzymes, which may degrade biologically important components of the human tissues, such as bone morphogenetic proteins (BMPs).
3. **Sterilisation**: Selection of a proper method, determination of bioburden, setting the sterilisation dose, and a proper validation of the procedure should be carried out in the most effective manner.

Processing Areas

All tissue establishments should establish and document requirements for the environment to which human tissue is exposed. The quality of air should be defined for each type of processing area and this will depend on the nature of the process, the type of human tissue to be processed, and the degree of handling and exposure of the human tissue. Certain features and practices are common requirements in processing areas. These include the following:

- Floors, walls and ceilings with non-porous smooth surfaces that can be cleaned easily;
- Changing area and washing facilities adjacent to the processing area to enable procedures for gowning, hygiene, and cleaning;
- Control and monitoring of the environmental conditions (particulate and microbial contamination); and
- Passage of materials and persons controlled at all times.

The rationale for the design, specification and monitoring of environmental controls is to minimise microbial and particulate contamination, and the operational and working practices should be justified to this end and documented. Controlled environments or laminar flow cabinets are effective in minimising levels of contamination. Critical work areas where human tissue is manipulated openly, either following a disinfection or sterilisation step, should be clearly identified and should be monitored according to a documented procedure.

Critical work areas, in which sterile containers, aseptically procured human tissue or disinfected human tissue are exposed to the environment, should have an air quality of grade A and should have a grade B background. This requires a HEPA-filtered air supply at a positive pressure with respect to the surrounding area. Work areas in which human tissues, materials and containers are prepared prior to disinfection or sterilisation should have an environment with air quality of at least grade C or better.

Where aseptic operations are performed, monitoring should be frequent using methods such as settle plates, air and surface sampling. Results from environmental microbiological monitoring programmes should be reviewed as part of the human tissue release stage. The routine monitoring programme for microbiological and particulate contamination should be performed according to a defined method and plan, with specified alert and action limits. Compliance with the specified requirements should be verified and the results should be documented to monitor the operational state of critical work areas or laminar flow cabinets.

Personnel

Hygiene programmes must be established and documented. They should include procedures related to health, hygiene practices and the clothing of personnel. These procedures should be understood and followed by all tissue establishment staff, particularly those with duties within processing or controlled environments. Instructions should be issued to personnel ensuring that the health conditions of relevance to the quality of the human tissues report to the Quality Assurance Officer or designated responsible person.

Every person entering the processing area should wear protective clothing appropriate to the operations being carried out.

All personnel should use hand washing facilities. The following practices should be prohibited in the processing areas: eating, drinking, smoking, chewing, and the storage of food, drink, smoking materials or personal medication.

Equipment and Ancillary Materials

Any components and materials that are in contact with human tissue during processing operations should be specified and controlled to minimise contamination and ensure that the human tissue specification is met. Any components previously in contact with other human tissue donors should be decontaminated according to the relevant guidelines in force in the tissue establishment.

Cross-Contamination from Human Tissues of Different Donors

Systems designed to prevent cross-contamination from human tissues from different donors must be in place. These include the prohibition of pooling of human tissues from multiple donors during retrieval, processing or storage, the use of designated areas for different procedures and stages of processing, and aseptic techniques.

II. Quality System

Quality can take on many forms in tissue banking. It begins with donor selection and includes the level of confidence in processing systems so that the final human tissue can be deemed both safe and effective. As we begin the twenty-first century, today's tissue establishment looks very different from its predecessors of two short decades ago. Changes have occurred in every phase of tissue banking, from donor screening to distribution practices. Today's emphasis is on prevention rather than retrospective detection. This includes process validation, employee training, establishment of control points and good records management (Kostiak, 2000). There are many reasons for considering a quality system in a tissue establishment.[1] If a tissue establishment can show that its operation has external accreditation, particularly for an internationally recognised standard such as ISO 9000 or any other equivalent recognised standards, and that tissue establishment staff have been properly trained, equipment is properly supplied and maintained, and the facility is appropriate to the work being carried out, the liability that exists when something goes wrong will be reduced and will certainly improve the tissue establishment's prestige.

Obviously, any tissue establishment hopes not to face, under any circumstance, a situation that could cause an important interruption of its activities, particularly if this situation could originate an extensive covering of the media and the public anger. The public scrutiny that comes immediately with the media involvement in a crisis situation, will affect, in one way or another the normal operations of the tissue establishment, often have a negative impact on its prestige and a substantial destruction of values. This is especially true when the crisis is not correctly managed before the public opinion and the media. For this reason, the administration of a crisis situation is an extremely important task and responsibility for the top management of a tissue establishment affected by the crisis, particularly for those in charge of providing the necessary and precise information during its development.

[1] In this book the concept of quality that is used has been included in ISO 9000. Quality is defined as "the degree to which a set of inherent characteristics fulfils requirements". An explicit definition of this concept can be found in von Versen *et al.* (2000) and is the following: "Quality is the totality of characteristics of an entity (can be an activity or a process, a product, an organisation, a system, a person or any combination thereof) that bear on its ability to satisfy stated and implied needs". Quality of a tissue is the totality of its qualities and characteristics, which make it suitable to fulfil the demands made upon it.

According to Morales Pedraza (2009), crisis situations are characterised by rich, rapidly changing information flows and by tremendous uncertainty. People in stressful situations and conditions of information-overload tend to resort to ineffective decision-making strategies. Simply providing access to information is not enough to support decision-makers. Much more effective systems are required for helping those in charge of a crisis situation to evaluate, filter, and integrate the great amount of information that the crisis generates. It is important to understand that a crisis situation is different from a routine situation, in which the traditional information systems for decision support operate, and for this reason the amount of information to be processed by persons involved in the crisis is much higher, complex, and sensitive.

In principle, the top management of a tissue establishment is used to manage certain types of crisis situations from time to time. However, their abilities are really proven when they have to manage important crises that have the potential of interrupting the normal process of the creation of values by the tissue establishment, which could affect their prestige within the community.

Not all crises situations are equal or have the same impact on the operation of a tissue establishment. They may involve a sudden financial problem, a defect in a key product or service or injuries to employees or the public. Each event is unique, requiring special tactics for handling it properly with the purpose of avoiding or reducing to the minimum any negative impact in the activities of the tissue establishment. Still, managing a crisis situation requires the respect of certain specific guidelines that help the top managers to reduce to a minimum the negative effects of a crisis situation on the activities of the tissue establishment.

Once the top management of a tissue establishment has determined that a particular event is a genuine crisis, it is important to understand the following: everything the top management of a tissue establishment does in response to the crisis will be judged from that first moment. When the crisis becomes public knowledge, the first actions adopted by the top management will be the ones most closely examined by government regulators or by other national competent health care authorities, the media, and the public.

The biggest mistake that the top management of a tissue establishment affected by a crisis can make is its denial. This is true not only for big tissue establishment affected by a crisis situation, but to medium and small tissue establishments as well. How to reduce to the minimum the effect of a crisis? There are several recommendations that need to be taken into consideration by the top management of a tissue establishment during a crisis situation, with the purpose of reducing to the minimum the negative consequences of the crisis. Some of these are mentioned here.

The first recommendation is to prepare in advance of a contingency plan in order to minimise the negative impact of a crisis situation in the normal operations of a tissue establishment. For this reason, it is extremely important to identify and announce, as soon as possible, and to all necessary persons of the tissue establishment involved in a crisis situation, which is the person authorised to talk about it to the external world, particularly the public, the media and competent government and health care authorities. The person designated to act as the spokesman should be included in any crisis management team that the tissue establishment decides to create, in order to deal in a crisis situation with the outside world.

However, "too often plans are left collecting dust on a shelf in the Director of the tissue establishment, rarely revised, let alone tested for practicality and effectiveness, thus leaving tissue establishment open to consequences of epic proportions. After something happens, some tissue establishments make the disastrous mistake of going into a state of denial, hoping the crisis will disappear on its own. But denial turns to anger and then panic — and that is the point when real mistakes are made and irreparable damage to the tissue establishment image can take place.

The second recommendation to be given to the top management of a tissue establishment involved in a crisis situation is the following: One of the first decisions that need to be made by the top management of a tissue establishment involved in a crisis situation is to move quickly during the first hours after the crisis exploded. This move is an important one, because journalists often develop the structure of their information based on what happens within these hours. Independently of the magnitude of the crisis, it is important to transmit the exact and correct information to the media, the public and to the government and other health care authorities, since it is extremely dangerous and harmful for the tissue establishment to try to manipulate the information associated with the crisis. There should be no doubt that these actions will harm the reputation and seriousness of the tissue establishment involved in a crisis, if the intention or the real fact to hide or manipulate sensitive information associated with the crisis situation is discovered.

The third recommendation is the following: The top manager of a tissue establishment involved in a crisis situation should act promptly and with determination. But the Director of the tissue establishment must think twice about entering a hostile environment just to serve the interests of photojournalists.

The fourth recommendation that needs to be considered in a crisis situation is the use of external consultants for the management of the crisis, because these persons will give the most objective advice to the top management of the tissue establishment involved in the crisis.

The fifth recommendation to be given to the top management of a tissue establishment involved in a crisis is the following: When deciding on the actions that should be taken during a crisis situation, the top management, should not only consider the losses in the short-term, but rather the long-term effects of the crisis in the future of the activities of the tissue establishment.

Any good strategy adopted by the top manager of a tissue establishment considers that the success of its works should rely upon the trust, goodwill, and the confidence of the public, the media and the government regulatory authorities. These are based upon a positive perception of their contribution to society, its procedures, transparency, good management practice, competence of its top managers and of the professional staff at all levels, as well as by its code of ethics and standards. Because of something that is done, or not, and misinformation or malicious rumor, damaging positive perception of the activities of the tissue establishment, years of work could be undone within days. In this case, all activities of the tissue establishment would face a crisis situation, and this could affect its work for years to come.

Internet, which in the past several years has become an important element of the communications infrastructure of any tissue establishment, the media, government and research medical institutions, among others, are being used to provide at least part of the means for information exchange between organisations and institutions involved in a crisis situation, and for individualised interactions with citizens, the media and the society at large. The proper use of an information system in a crisis situation is an important tool that facilitates that relevant information could reach the appropriate persons in the most effective and quick manner. The appropriate use of an information system in a crisis situation could supply decision-makers at all levels with the information they need and at the time they need it.

Supplying decision-makers with information regarding a crisis situation requires a number of capabilities that need to be in place when the crisis starts. First, the appropriate data related to the crisis situation must be collected, either during the preparation or pre-crisis phase or during the crisis-response phase. Crisis responders require retrieval information regarding the evolution of the crisis situation and access mechanisms to allow them to find and reduce to the minimum and to essential items the information they need in order to assess the situation properly. Delivery mechanisms are indispensable tools to send the appropriate information to the right people.

Importance of a Quality System

Why the adoption of a quality system is so important for a tissue establishment? A quality system defines and documents a series of systematic processes that are to be followed by all those working within a tissue establishment. These processes are designed to ensure that quality is evident in every part of the tissue establishment. The main objective of the quality system is to avoid mistakes. However, if a mistake does happen, the cause should be identified and the process amended so that it is not repeated. While the implementation of a quality system may seem overwhelmingly complex to many tissue establishments, methodical adherence to the requirements of organisational development can allow the tissue establishment to achieve goals related to quality improvement (Villalba *et al.*, 2001).

The implementation of a quality system can help the tissue establishment to establish a process control in the processing of human tissues by providing sterilised human tissues for medical treatment that comply with national and international regulatory standards and requirements.

Scope and Aim of the Tissue Establishment Quality System

A quality system should be established, documented and maintained as a means of ensuring that human tissues conform to specified requirements.

The aim of using a quality system in a tissue establishment is to ensure the safety and quality of the human tissues procured and processed by the tissue establishment in order to reduce to the minimum, medical risks to the recipients of these banked tissues.

Traceability, the capacity to trace human tissues from the donor to recipients and vice versa, and long-term follow-up of living donors and recipients of human tissues are central elements of safety and quality management.[2]

Key Elements of the Quality System

In order to reduce the risk and maximise the benefits of the transplantation of human tissues, it is necessary to operate, according to WHO (2004), an effective quality system. A quality system should include at least a number of documentation systems such as SOPs, guidelines, training and reference manuals, reporting forms, and donor records, among others. The quality system applies to each step in the process of tissue banking, including the step of donor selection and physical examination. Therefore, each tissue establishment should have guidelines on how to perform a physical examination in potential tissue donors, and registration forms to document the findings.

The key components of a sound quality system are the following:

- **Personnel and organisation**: Staff should be appropriately qualified and their tasks and responsibilities should be clearly understood and documented (usually in an organisational chart). Training requirements

[2]WHO should coordinate the traceability of organs and tissues in a common surveillance system with universal donor identification numbers, as many organ donors also donate tissues; however, such aspirations were distant for resource-poor countries. The latter urged the international community to adopt minimal standards for procurement and processing as the surest way of helping them to balance quality, safety and human tissues availability.

should be documented and training records kept. An experienced and well-trained tissue establishment staff member should be designated as a Quality Assurance Officer, with the responsibilities mentioned in section I[3];

- **Premises, equipment, instruments and materials**: Premises, equipment, and instruments must be designed, located, constructed, adapted and maintained to suit the operations to be carried out by the tissue establishment. There should be dedicated, secure and monitored areas for storage of the different categories of human tissues processed by the tissue establishment. Storage conditions should be controlled, monitored and checked with the purpose of ensuring the properties of the human tissue. Maintenance, monitoring, cleaning and calibration of equipment and instruments should be documented and records kept during the period established by the national competent health care authorities. Detailed specifications for the purchase of different reagents used by the tissue establishment during the processing of the human tissues are required;
- **Documentation and its control**: Documentation ensures that work is standardised and that there is traceability in all steps of the processing of human tissues. It should clearly state the quality requirements, organisational structures and responsibilities, the organisational policies and standards, the management and technical procedures employed and the records required. The documentation should include:
  - □ A quality manual;
  - □ Specifications for materials, labels, equipment, instruments, tissues, and reagents;
  - □ Standard operating procedures;
  - □ Records on the performance of operations; and
  - □ Protocols for audits, management of complaints, training and competency, and records of tissue establishment staff.

[3]Where a tissue establishment is operated within a large organisation with its own Quality Department and a Quality Assurance Officer, then strong working relations should be established between the tissue establishment Quality Assurance Officer and the relevant Quality Department as well as with the Director of the tissue establishment.

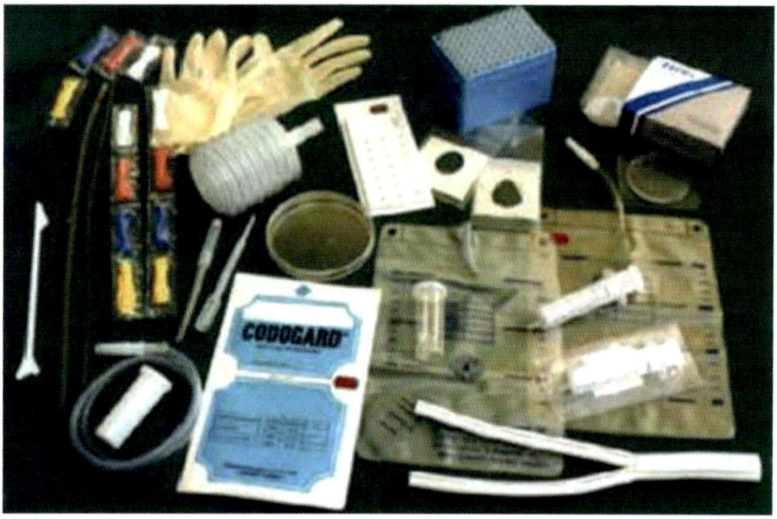

Figure 9: Medical devices.

Source: Morales Pedraza (2009)

The objectives of a thorough documentation are the following:

- To define the information and control system that should be applied;
- To minimise the risk of misinterpretation and error inherent in oral or casually written communication; and
- To provide unambiguous procedures to be followed by all tissue establishment staff.

A system for document control should identify the current revision status of any document and the holder of the document. The system should demonstrate that all controlled documents meet the following criteria:

- They are current and authorised;
- They are reviewed at regular intervals;
- Multiple copies are controlled with a distribution list;
- Obsolete documents are removed and controlled to prevent further use; and
- Changes to documents should be acted upon promptly and should include the reviewed date and the signature of the Director of the tissue establishment.

- **Selection, procurement, testing and processing/handling**: Policies and procedures for the safe selection and testing of donors need to be in place. The main steps of the human tissue procurement are the following: The first step is to know the cause of death of the donor. The next step is the treatment that was provided by the emergency room or the intensive care unit. After the treatment has been identified, the next step is the declaration of death. At this time, the procurement team is involved and the team obtains family consent. Next, human tissue recovery takes place by the surgical team in the operating room. After the donation, the donor is taken to a funeral. Human tissue procurement should be carefully controlled. Defects that may adversely affect quality must be documented and dealt with. Facilities must have adequate systems to process control, and environments must be adequately controlled. When a microbial inactivation procedure is applied to human tissues, it must be specified, documented and validated. Before new processes are implemented, they should be validated;
- **Quality control and proficiency testing**: Quality control comprises those activities that ensure that the materials and processes meet the required specifications. There should be internal quality control and, where relevant, external quality assessment (proficiency testing);
- **Traceability**: There should be in force a system that enables the path followed by each human tissue donation to be traced, from the donor to recipient(s) or to disposal;
- **Complaints, errors and accidents, adverse events and recalls**: All complaints, errors, accidents and adverse events must be investigated and documented, and appropriate corrective and preventive actions taken by the corresponding tissue establishment;
- **Self-assessment and internal and external audits**: There should be a system of internal and external audits, which allows for continuous improvement in all activities that are carried out by a tissue establishment;
- **Tissues and storage conditions**: Storage conditions, including relevant or critical parameters such as temperature, humidity and sterility should be defined, controlled, monitored, and recorded. A maximum storage time and storage conditions should be specified for each type of human tissue;

- **Distribution:** Transport parameters, such as temperature and handling, should be defined to hold the required human tissue properties. Packaging must ensure that the human tissue is preserved in the condition shown in the SOPs;
- **Final labelling for distribution**: Every unit of human tissue should be labelled with at least:
    - Identification number or code assigned to the human tissue;
    - Characteristics of the human tissue;
    - Identification of the tissue establishment that processed the human tissue; and
    - Lot number.
- **External labelling of the shipping container**: The external shipping container should be labelled with:
    - The identification of the originating tissue establishment;
    - The identification of the health care establishment of destination;
    - A statement that the package contains human tissue;
    - Recommended transport conditions of the human tissues; and
    - Safety instructions.

Quality Control

Quality controls can be classified in terms of their impact on the overall quality of the human tissue. Each of these quality controls occurs during a critical period of the development of the graft within the tissue establishment's operational system. Each quality control step can be thought of as a test that allows the graft to proceed to the next level of processing. These quality controls occur in the following areas: donor assessment, tissue procurement, tissue processing, tissue storage, and tissue distribution. Specific parameters, designed to assure a consistent level of quality, must be met during each of these stages to achieve the desired level of quality of the human tissue. Quality controls that have an indirect effect on the quality of the human tissue can also be instituted. These controls can include such functions as equipment qualification and donor records management. Together, these controls constitute the quality assurance programme (Kostiak, 2000).

Quality control is the test and/or procedures used for measuring or monitoring properties of human tissues or their sources, essential to the evaluation of their safety and efficacy (von Versen *et al.*, 2000).

According to AATB (2002), effective quality controls involve many complex components including, among others, the following:

- Obtaining complete donor medical and behavioural history information from all relevant sources, including most recent medical records;
- Obtaining valid informed consent or authorisation for donation from the donor's next-of-kin or legal representative;
- Performing tissue recovery using advanced zone and sequencing protocols to reduce the risk of graft contamination;
- Using the most reliable blood-testing methods currently available to ensure the minimum risk of infectious disease transmission;
- Using other information, such as autopsy reports, if available, to further ensure the safety of allografts;
- Employing extensive culture analysis of donor human tissue before suspending it in antimicrobial solutions;
- Using additional culture analysis as a final step in processing;
- Validating that residual antimicrobials in treatment solutions do not result in false negative culture results;
- Applying tissue-cleansing processes that further reduce the possibility of disease transmission without causing biological or mechanical harm to the allografts;
- Using human tissue preservation processes that ensure the optimal functioning of the allografts after implantation;
- Storing and transporting released allografts within temperature and packaging conditions that ensure the safety and integrity of the package in which they have been sealed; and
- Providing documented, routine, and in-depth training to tissue establishment staff to ensure knowledge in all job responsibilities.

Even if some of these steps have been performed by another organisation, such as a contracted tissue recovery agency or a tissue distributor, it is the tissue establishment's responsibility to ensure that contractors follow the tissue establishment's approved SOPs for limiting the risk of disease transmission. The tissue establishment should maintain documentation of contractors' compliance with all its SOPs. Compliance can only be ascertained by exacting audits of contractors' operations.

Quality Assurance Programme

Quality assurance in tissue banking can be defined as the overall process of building into each human tissue a level of safety and efficacy based on various controls placed on production systems.

The quality assurance component of a tissue establishment begins prior to the physical development of the tissue establishment. During the development phase, careful planning should be given to quality. Once established, quality assurance in tissue banking begins with the screening of the potential donor, perhaps the most significant quality data in the overall quality assurance programme. Quality controls in the procurement process include obtaining a sufficient serum sample from the donor, as soon as possible after death to decrease the likelihood of hemolysis.

However, the most significant changes in quality control have taken place in the area of tissue processing. Today's tissue establishment resembles a modernised manufacturing environment rather than the simple, operating room environment of processing (Kostiak, 2000).

Quality Standards

Quality standards are written norms that reflect consensus of what is needed to ensure quality; they give you a standard to measure yourself against as well as external, independent assessors and stakeholders a standard to measure you against; they also provide a basis for certification or accreditation. The contents of quality standards include:

- Management requirements, which are general requirements applicable to any organisation; and
- Technical requirements, which are specific to the technical field.

According to ISO 9000, management requirements include:

- Organisation and management;
- Quality system;
- Document control;
- Review of requests, tenders and contracts;
- Subcontracting;
- Purchasing services and supplies;
- Service to the client;
- Complaints;
- Control of non-conforming work;
- Corrective actions;
- Preventive actions;
- Control of records;
- Internal audits; and
- Management reviews.

According to ISO 9000, technical requirements include:

- Personnel;
- Accommodation and environmental conditions;
- Methods and method validation;
- Equipment;
- Measurement traceability;
- Sampling;
- Handling of test and calibration items;
- Assuring the quality of results; and
- Reporting on the results.

Quality Indicators

Quality indicators should include, but not be limited to:

- Donor screening and testing;
- Tissue processing procedures;
- Labelling procedures;
- Storage requirements;
- Criteria for release of the human tissues; and
- Adverse events (including post-transplantation infections), corrective actions, and evaluation.

Tissue establishment services involve significant risks to recipients if errors are made during the processing of the human tissues. National competent health care authorities should require that any facility performing tissue banking should have in force a quality management system intended to prevent the introduction, transmission, or spread of communicable disease for every step of tissue banking performed. Ongoing quality management involves verifying that these steps are done in a safe and efficacious manner. The above quality indicators address specific issues that may compromise the tissue. Specific quality indicators will depend on the services provided by the tissue establishment.

Quality Management

Current good tissue practices require the following aspects of quality management:

- Ensuring that required procedures are established and maintained;
- Ensuring the appropriate analysis and sharing of information, which could affect the potential contamination of the human tissue or the potential transmission of communicable disease by the tissue;
- Ensuring that appropriate corrective actions are taken and documented in case of contamination of human tissues;
- Ensuring proper training and education of personnel;
- Establishing and maintaining appropriate monitoring systems;
- Establishing and maintaining a system of records;
- Investigating and documenting any deviations of the SOPs and making certain required reports on these deviations; and
- Conducting evaluations, investigations, audits, and other actions necessary to ensure compliance with the regulations.

Responsibility for the Operation of the Quality System

The Director of the tissue establishment has overall responsibility for the policy, implementation, and operation of the quality system. This must be relevant to the tissue establishment goals and the needs of the organisations it supplies. All members of the tissue establishment staff should be familiar with the quality system in force and also be responsible for the quality of their work.

The responsibility for operating the quality system must be assigned to an appropriate qualified named individual who should be independent of operational management. There should be also a designated deputy who can accept this responsibility in the absence of the first named individual.

Other key personnel in the operation of the quality system should include those responsible for medical advice, microbiology, quality assurance, and tissue processing.

Review of the Quality System

The quality system should be reviewed at regular intervals by the Director of the tissue establishment and by other key personnel to ensure its suitability and effectiveness.

Quality System Requirements

All tissue establishments should define and document how the requirements for quality will be met. Quality requirements form the basis of all quality assurance and quality control programmes. Quality requirements should be defined not only for the final product, but also for the starting material collected, reagents, equipment and instruments used, staff competences, testing techniques, packing materials, and labels and process intermediates.

These quality requirements should be prescribed and quantified in writing specifications. These specifications determine the quality control testing or inspection performed, on which release decisions are based.

Resources to Ensure Adequate Implementation of the Quality System

Adequate resources must be provided by national competent health care authorities at all levels to ensure effective and efficient implementation of the quality system. The Director of the tissue establishment must identify and provide adequate resources, including the assignment of trained personnel for management, performance of work, verification activities, and internal audits.

Documentation Associated with the Quality System

A quality system depends on effective and adequate documentation. All tissue establishments should establish and maintain all relevant documents relating to all aspects and stages of the tissue establishment's work. This includes SOPs and associated documents for all activities, which affect the safety or quality of the processed human tissues.

Documents and data must be reviewed and approved by the Director of the tissue establishment. Current documents should be readily identifiable to ensure that invalid or obsolete documents are not used. The revision of the documents and data must ensure the following:

- The relevant issues of appropriate documents are available at all locations where operations essential to the effective functioning of the quality system are performed;
- Invalid or obsolete documents are removed from all points of issue or use, to prevent unintended use; and
- Any obsolete documents retained for knowledge preservation or legal purposes should be suitably identified and stored.

Records Associated with the Quality System

There must be documented procedures for the maintenance of records. These should include: identification, collection, indexing, batch processing records, access, filing, storage, maintenance and disposition of quality records. These should be maintained to meet the specialised requirements of the quality system.

The minimum periods of retention for all categories of documents should be specified, justified and should take into consideration all national regulations on this issue in force. Documents should be stored and retained so that they are retrievable in facilities that provide a suitable environment to prevent damage, deterioration or loss.

The Director of the tissue establishment should define the period for which at least one copy of obsolete documents must be retained.

Where specified by the agreement or contract, the relevant quality records from third parties or service providers should also be maintained during an established period.

Donor records relating to medical and behavioural history and human tissue retrieval details should be kept for the period established by the national regulations in force on this subject. These records should show that the donated human tissue has been rejected or released by the Director of the tissue establishment or by a duly authorised person. Confidential records should be held in restricted areas accessed only by authorised personnel.

Human tissue release records should be established and maintained for each batch of human tissues, to provide traceability at least to the extent required by national regulations in force. Records should identify the quantity manufactured and that released for distribution.

All tissue establishments should maintain comprehensive records of all user complaint investigations and the main outcome of the investigations carried out and the issue of advisory notices and recalls. All tissue establishments should ensure that records include the description of the human tissue, any control number used, the name of the complainant, the nature of the complaint, the corrective or preventive actions implemented and the reply to the complainant.

Quality Failures

Quality failures include in-use product deficiencies (complaints, adverse events, etc.), failures to meet quality-control specifications, and non-compliance with procedures. Methods for detecting failures include quality control tests, inspections, quality audits, staff and end-user feedback. The ability to trace, quarantine and recall materials, consumables and products at any stage, is essential to patient safety.

Serious failures should be thoroughly registered, investigated and appropriate changes to specifications, systems and procedures implemented with the aim of preventing further failures of a similar nature in the future.

III. Informed Consent or Authorisation

Authorisation Requirements

Permission to acquire human tissues and make them available for transplantation or research purposes should be obtained through the granting of informed consent from a living donor or the authorising person, i.e., the next-of-kin or legal representative, in the case of a deceased donor, in accordance with applicable state and/or local laws and/or regulations. This permit should be conveyed in a written form called "Authorisation/ Informed Consent Form", the original or a copy of which should be maintained in the donor's record at the retrieving facility as well as in the donor's record at the tissue establishment. The Medical Director/ Consultant is responsible for the donor suitability determination.

There is a broad agreement that consent procedures and the methods for approaching potential donors should be standardised, transparent, and subject to regular external auditing, given that vulnerable groups are at risk for subtle or overt manipulation regarding the decision to donate human tissues.

Authorisation

It is important to stress that informed consent is no longer the only current practice to authorise the acquisition of human tissues and make them available for transplantation or research purposes. The practice in some countries is now to refer to the process of obtaining permission for donation from a deceased person as "authorisation" rather than informed consent. This is due to a number of reasons.

First, informed consent is a legal concept with well-established rules and guidelines associated with either a medical procedure or research protocol adopted by many countries. The purpose is to provide the potential patient or subject the right to decide whether to become a tissue's donor or not, being aware of all the risks and benefits of undergoing a particular medical procedure or participating in a research protocol. However, human tissue donation is neither a medical procedure nor research project, and provides no economic benefits to the patient/donor.

The second reason to move away from informed consent is the use of "First Person Consent" or "Donor Registries". In most countries, an individual can register his/her desire or intent to become a human tissue donor through the signing of one of the above-mentioned forms. Under this practice, at the time of the individual's death, the family, next-of-kin or legal representative are not given the opportunity to countermand the donor's decision to donate, although there is still a conversation about whether the donor had changed his/her mind about donation after the signing of the forms, and the medical social interview is still conducted with a knowledgeable person.

Authorisation/Consent Conditions

Information concerning the donation and retrieval of human tissues should be presented in a language in which the donor or authorising person is conversant and in terms that are easily understood by the donor or authorising person. Authorisation should be obtained under circumstances that provide the donor or authorising person an opportunity to ask questions and receive adequate information to give authorisation in accordance with state and/or local laws and/or regulations. The person seeking authorisation should be trained to answer appropriately the questions the donor or authorising person may have. Coercion should not be exerted in any manner to obtain permission for human tissue donation.

However, it is important to be aware of the following conditions in case of a deceased donor during contact with their families: tissue establishments must obtain consent for donation within hours following the death of a loved one. Because the family may be in shock, discussing multiple aspects of tissue donation and tissue banking — recovery, processing, distribution, commercial relationships — may go well beyond the capacity of families to comprehend what they are hearing. This specific situation reduces considerably the possibility to receive a positive answer from the donor's family.

Anonymity

Anonymity between the donor and the unrelated recipients should be strictly preserved. However, anonymity between donors and recipients should allow tracking of human tissues through anonymous identification numbers.

Essential Elements of the Authorisation/Informed Consent Form

In seeking authorisation for the donation of human tissues, the following information should be provided to the person(s) being approached for authorisation:

- A confirmation/validation of the donor's identity and in the case of a deceased donor, his or her clinical terminal condition;

- An explanation that the human tissue is a donation and that neither the donor nor the person authorising the donation in the case of a deceased donor will receive any compensation, financial or otherwise;
- A general description of the purposes (benefits) of human tissue donation;
- Identification of specific human tissues that are being requested for donation;
- An explanation that the retrieved human tissues will only be used for transplantation, therapy, medical research or educational purposes;
- A general description of the recovery process (including timing, relocation of donor, if applicable, contact information, etc.);
- An explanation that laboratory tests and a medical/social history will be completed to determine the medical suitability of the donor, including an explanation that blood samples from the donor will be tested for certain transmissible diseases;
- A statement granting access to the donor's medical records, and that the medical records may be released to other appropriate parties, if absolutely necessary;
- An explanation that costs directly related to the evaluation, recovery, preservation, and placement of the human tissues will not be charged to the family;
- An explanation regarding the impact the donation process may have on the appearance of the donor's body; and
- Any additional information required to be provided to the person(s) being approached for authorisation in accordance with state and/or local laws and/or regulations.

Additional Elements

In some situations, there may be additional information that should be known by the donor or the person authorising the donation or that might be helpful for family decision-making. If the donor's family or legal representative inquires about any of these or any other additional matters, full explanations should be provided by the designated person.

The guiding principle for the utilisation of these additional elements is to advance simplicity and reasonableness in seeking authorisation, i.e., include these elements or additional comments, if they are appropriate and might clarify any exigencies. One or more of the following elements of information may also be appropriate for communication to the person(s) being approached for authorisation, depending upon the circumstances surrounding the donation and the potential human tissue(s) to be donated:

- A description of any involvement by the Medical Examiner and/or Coroner, including an explanation that an autopsy may be performed;
- An explanation that transplantation may include reconstructive and aesthetic surgery;
- A reference to the possibility that at any time of transplantation, the donated human tissue may take a different form from what was originally recovered[4];
- An explanation that multiple organisations (non-profit and/or, in specific circumstances, for-profit) may be involved in the recovery, screening, processing and distribution of the donated human tissue(s); and
- A reference to the possibility that human tissue(s) may be transferred abroad.

Signatures and Authorisation

The Authorisation/Informed Consent Form for obtaining authorisation should contain the name, address and telephone number of the donor or, in case of deceased donors, the person authorising the donation and his/her relationship to the donor, and their signatures. It should also contain the date, signatures of the person obtaining the authorisation, at least one witness or such number of witnesses as may be required by applicable state and/or local laws and/or regulations, and any information that allows the identification of the organisation represented by the person obtaining the authorisation.

[4]Musculoskeletal tissue often is processed into many forms. These forms include bone screws, dowels, and bone chips, which have many different medical uses. These final products often bear little resemblance to human tissue; in fact, they look more like tools, hardware, supplies, and devices than what most people would call human tissue.

The Authorisation/Informed Consent Form should also contain documentation that the information provided contained all the essential elements to make a decision and a statement permitting authorisation for the procurement of human tissues.

Authorisation/Informed Consent for Deceased Donors

No removal of human tissues should take place when there is an open or presumed objection on the part of the deceased donors. Permission or confirmation of the absence of objection for human tissue donation should be obtained from the next-of-kin or legal representative. The removal of human tissues can be carried out if it does not interfere with a forensic examination or autopsy as required by law in certain states.

Tissue establishment physicians or physicians involved in the removal or transplantation of the human tissues should not pronounce death nor sign the death certificate of any individual from whom tissues will be collected.

The Authorisation/Informed Consent Form should contain only the information that would be relevant to a person authorising the donation. Such information should be accurate, should not be misleading, and should contain all the essential elements that have been indicated that would be indispensable to a decision to donate. The provision of such information should be documented along with a statement permitting authorisation of the procurement of human tissues.

When a tissue procurement organisation or other institution (e.g., a hospital) has initiated the process of obtaining authorisation for a potential human tissue donation, the tissue establishment for which the tissue is being obtained should request that the procurement organisation or other institution follow the procedure and utilise the Authorisation/Informed Consent Form that satisfies the requirements.

Authorisation/Informed Consent for Living Donors

Patient-donor, next-of-kin or legal representative authorisation to donate human tissues must be obtained in writing prior to the procurement. The donor should be given appropriate information, before the removal of the tissues, about the possible consequences of this removal, in particular medical, social, and psychological as well as the importance of the donation to the recipient.

The authorisation should include a statement that the donor has been informed that his/her name and address, as well as required records, shall be kept on file by the tissue establishment. This information should be kept until the procured human tissues are used or destroyed or during the period established by the competent state authority.

In case of a legally incapacitated person, authorisation should be obtained from the next-of-kin or legal representative, if the donor does not object to it.

The authorisation/informed consent for surgical bone donors should also include a statement that a blood sample from the donor will be tested for certain transmissible diseases and will document to whom confirmed positive test results will be reported (e.g., to the patient, the patient's physician, next-of-kin, legal representative or to the appropriate health officials, if required by applicable state and/or local laws and/or regulations). The authorisation shall be given in writing.

IV. Donor Selection

In order to maximise the benefits and minimise the risks of the transplant procedure, the suitability of an individual donor of human tissues should be based upon quality and safety. Human tissues should be retrieved and kept within appropriate time intervals to preserve the necessary biological functions. The time interval should be compatible with the period it takes to perform all the relevant investigations to ensure the quality and safety of the retrieved human tissues. Therefore, all these activities should be undertaken according to the SOPs in force, within a quality assurance programme, and should include an appropriate microbiological risk assessment.

Living and deceased donors are the source of human tissue donations. Although there are some common aspects in these two types of donors, the criteria for selection may vary between the two. Therefore, the selection procedure for deceased and living tissue donation should be described separately.

The suitability of a specific donor for a human tissue donation should be based upon medical and behavioural history, medical records review, physical examination, deceased donor autopsy findings (if an autopsy is performed) and microbiological laboratory tests. Policies and specified requirements for donor selection should be documented. This should also include exclusion factors, consent and blood sample testing.

All procedures should also cover donors donating tissue for autologous and/or directed allogeneic use.

Donor Suitability

Donor suitability criteria should be established by the Medical Director/ Consultant and each donor should be evaluated accordingly. The suitability of each donor should be determined by the Medical Director/Consultant or a licensed physician caring for the patient-donor. Donors should be identified and selected according to fair and explicit criteria, above all medical eligibility, equally, and without explicit or implicit discrimination based on social status and wealth, race, ethnicity, national origin, colour, sex, sexual orientation, gender identity, age, marital status, political belief, religion, immigration status, and mental or physical disability.

Donor screening, although extremely effective in eliminating donors with active viral infections, has many limitations. With all viral infections, there may be a window period in which the donor does not have detectable antibodies to the virus (Dodd *et al.*, 2002). The risk of implanting tissue from an HIV-infected donor via current screening and testing protocols has been estimated to be as low as 1 in 1 million. Recent work has estimated an overall risk of allograft-associated infections at about 4 in 1 million (Buck *et al.*, 1994). However, the risk of implanting tissue from donors with hepatitis B virus or HCV infection is significantly higher because of the greater prevalence of these viruses in the general population and the limitations of current testing methods (Gocke, 2005).

It is not necessary to document a physical examination, a donor risk assessment interview or medical history or a medical record review for autologous tissues.

Prior to initiation of human tissue recovery procedures, a retrieval staff member should verify the potential donor's identification as stated on the Authorisation/Informed Consent Form. Donor identity verification should

Table 1: Window period — the period between infection and the time the virus is detectable by screening tests

	Virus	
	HIV	**HCV**
Window period using FDA licensed tests	HIV antibody 22 days NAT* — 7 days	HCV Antibody 70 days NAT* — 7 clays
Blood donor estimated risk (repeat donor) (a)	with NAT* 1:2 million	with NAT* 1:2 million
Tissue donor estimated risk (b)**	without NAT* 1:55,000 with NAT* 1:173,000	without NAT* 1:42,000 with NAT* 1:421,000

*Nucleic Acid-Amplification Test

Source: (a) Stramer *et al*, NEJM 351:760–768, 2004

(b) Zou *et al*, NEJM 351:751–759, 2004

** This is difficult to estimate for tissue donors because of increased prevalence and smaller donor pool. Tissue processing methods validated to kill viruses are not included in this risk estimate.

be documented in the retrieved record prior to human tissue retrieval. Records should indicate the retrieval staff member(s) and include the source of the verification information (e.g., hospital wristband, medical examiner number, driver's license, among others).

Disease Screening Policy

The tissue establishment should have a policy for obtaining information from the patient's physician as to whether the patient/donor is at high risk for hepatitis or HIV infection or any other viral or bacterial infections or trauma to the potential retrieval site.

Donor Risk Assessment

A survey should be conducted with the donor (if living) or the deceased donor's next-of-kin, the nearest available relative, a member of the donor's household, another individual with an affinity relationship (caretaker, friend, significant life partner, etc.), and/or the primary treating physician or the legal representative using a standardised questionnaire.

Questions within the survey should be prepared using the SOPs and current state regulations and guidance as reference. The survey should also contain questions that evaluate past medical history for conditions that could constitute a contraindication to the release of human tissues for transplantation (e.g., certain infectious diseases, malignancies, and degenerative neurologic disorders), as defined in the SOPs.

The survey record should document the donor's name and the relationship between the donor and the interviewee, and should indicate the name(s) of the interviewer(s) and interviewee(s). The questionnaire should be retained as part of the donor's record.

The following questionnaire could be used in case an interview with the donor is indispensable:

- Did you suffer any infection in the past months? If so, what type of infection was it?
- Did you receive any vaccination or inoculation, or have you been injected with narcotic drugs in the past months?
- Did you have a malarial attack or did you use anti-malarial medication in the past months?
- Have you ever been infected with a sexually transmitted disease?
- Have you ever been diagnosed with jaundice or liver illness?
- Have you been in contact with patients diagnosed with jaundice/hepatitis?
- Have you been in contact with patients diagnosed with AIDS or individuals at risk for AIDS? If yes, how and when?
- Have you ever been tested for HIV/AIDS?
- Have you had homosexual intercourse? (Males only)
- Are you diagnosed with haemophilia? If yes, are you using anticoagulants?
- Are you a sexual partner of an individual for whom the answer to any of the above-mentioned questions is 'yes'?
- Have you been actively involved in prostitution, or have you been a sexual partner of an individual involved in prostitution in the past 6 months?
- Have you ever been diagnosed with a hematological disease or any malignant disorder?
- Have you ever been treated for diabetes mellitus?

- Have you ever been treated for chronic brain or neurological diseases?
- Have you ever had radiation therapy?
- Have you been diagnosed with rheumatoid arthritis?
- Have you ever been diagnosed with tuberculosis?
- Have you ever been diagnosed with any disease, other than the above-mentioned?
- Have you ever received hormonal treatment?
- Do you take any prescribed medication?
- Have you ever used any illegal drugs?
- Have you recently been exposed to hazardous or toxic materials? If yes, please specify below.
- Have you recently undergone surgery? If so, when and where? Did you get blood from a blood transfusion?
- Have you been travelling through or staying in a region exposed to a SARS epidemic, or have you been in contact with patients infected with SARS in the past months?
- Have you tattooed yourself or did you get a piercing?

The donor's risk assessment should include a review of personal alcohol and drug use and sexually transmissible diseases in the donor and partner(s). The screening process also should include any history of chemical and/or radiation exposure as well as family medical history and genetic background.

For a living donor, an abbreviated donor screening must be held at each repeat donation and reviewed by a responsible person. The abbreviated screening should determine and document any changes in the donor's medical, social and sexual history (including risk factors) since the previous donation, which would make the donor ineligible.

Review of Relevant Medical Records

Prior to human tissue donation, a preliminary review of readily available medical information should be conducted by a trained individual. This information may include medical records and test results, information derived from pertinent donor medical records, and/or conversations with attending medical staff, and/or family members.

Prior to release of human tissues for transplantation, the Medical Director/Consultant should determine donor suitability based on a review and evaluation of the donor's relevant medical records. The determination of suitability should be based on the SOPs and applicable state and/or local laws and/or regulations.

Donor Autopsy Report

If an autopsy was performed for a deceased donor, the Medical Director/Consultant should review the autopsy report or a summary of findings prior to the procurement of human tissues. If a copy of the autopsy report is not available in the donor's record, the cause of death and other pertinent findings should be documented in the donor's record. In cases where an autopsy is to be performed on a deceased donor, and it is determined that the integrity of the human tissue will be compromised by the time the report is completed, the Director of the tissue establishment should not wait for the review of the final report of the autopsy results. Instead, the presumed cause of death and other pertinent preliminary autopsy findings would be taken into consideration and documented.

If it is determined that an autopsy was not performed due to infectious disease risk or if an autopsy was performed and any special precautions were taken that would suggest risk of a communicable disease in the donor, this information should be considered carefully before the procurement of the human tissues is carried out in the donor.

Infections that Impede the Release of Allogeneic Tissues

The Medical Director/Consultant should not release allogeneic tissues for transplantation from donors who exhibit any of the following findings:

- Evidence, detected by review of relevant medical records, of significant active infection at the time of donation for relevant communicable disease agents or diseases. These include, but are not limited to: septicaemia, viral disease (e.g., HIV, viral hepatitis, WNV, SARS, rabies, etc.), human transmissible spongiform encephalopathies, untreated syphilis, clinically active tuberculosis, leprosy (Hansen's disease) or systemic mycosis; and

- Risk factors for relevant communicable disease agents or diseases specified in the code of practice.

Except for human skin, autologous donation should not be undertaken when the donor patient has or is being treated for bacteraemia or other significant bacterial infection that can be associated with bacteraemia, unless such tissues will be secondarily sterilised prior to transplantation or treated in such a manner as to minimise microbial infection.

When duramater is recovered, a qualified pathologist should perform an examination of the donor's brain.

Miscellaneous Adverse Conditions

Human tissues from donors with any of the following conditions should be evaluated by the Medical Director/Consultant for suitability for transplantation in accordance with the SOPs:

- History of autoimmune diseases;
- Ingestion of, or exposure to, toxic substances;[5] and
- Clinically significant metabolic bone disease.

Risk Factors

Human tissues should not be distributed from donors, including maternal donors of foetal or neonatal tissues, who have engaged in behaviours defined as high risk for transmission of relevant communicable disease agents or diseases. This information should be obtained via a donor risk assessment interview,[6] physical assessment/physical examination, and by a review of other available relevant medical records.

---

[5] In addition to the general exclusion criteria, the following medical conditions should also preclude musculoskeletal tissue donation: rheumatoid arthritis; systemic lupus erythematosus; polyarthritis nodosa; and sarcoidosis.

[6] The main criterion for risk assessment will be the integrity of the human tissue and all points made in the risk assessments will be clearly reflected in the SOPs which will be recorded in the same manner as the risk assessments. These assessments are based on the donor's medical and social history, clinical status, physical examination, tests and autopsy

In most circumstances, the major risk of the potential recipient is failure to obtain transplantation through, for example, tissue shortage. Other risks for the recipient may include:

- Failure of the transplant because the human tissue used is inadequate, damaged or poorly preserved and fails to function (primary tissue failure);
- Risks associated with the transplantation procedure;
- Rejection of human tissues, either acutely or over the longer term (chronic rejection);
- Disease transmission such as an infection or a malignancy;
- Contamination or damage of the human tissue in some other way during transport, processing or storage;
- Complications of immunosuppression and other concomitant therapies; and
- Recurrence of primary disease.

Malignancies

Donors with current or prior diagnosis of malignancy should be evaluated by the Medical Director/Consultant for suitability in accordance with the SOPs in force. The evaluation should include the type of malignancy and treatment prior to acceptance of a donor. The evaluation and reasons for acceptance should be documented in the donor's record.

Physical Examination of a Living Donor

Except for autologous donations, prior to the donation of human tissues from a potential living donor, a physical examination should be done by

---

(if performed). The information regarding the donor's medical/social history and clinical status can be obtained through a donor interview and a review of the donor's medical records or charts. The interview should be conducted using a medical/sexual/social history questionnaire that includes the applicable contraindications/exclusion criteria and other relevant questions required by regulations in force, and should be documented in the form of a checklist where the response/outcome for each criterion is recorded. If the donor is deceased or is unable to participate in the interview, it may be carried out with one or more individuals who can provide the necessary information, such as the donor's next-of-kin or nearest available relative, an individual with a relationship with the donor (e.g., caretaker or friend, partner), a member of the donor's household or the donor's primary physician or the legal representative. In some countries the interview may take place by telephone.

the Medical Director/Consultant or physician design or the recovery team. The donor body should be examined for general exclusion signs and for signs of infection, injury or medical intervention over donor sites that can affect the quality of the donated human tissue.

If an examination of a living donor was performed for other reasons, review of the findings of such an examination should be executed and documented in the donor's record, as well as all other examination findings. The physical examination should determine whether there is evidence of high-risk behaviour. The physical examination should also be used to determine overall general health of the donor.

Physical Assessment in a Deceased Donor

Prior to the recovery of human tissues from a potential deceased donor, a physical assessment should be made by a responsible person. This should be a recent ante-mortem or post-mortem physical assessment to identify evidence of high-risk behaviour and signs of HIV infection or hepatitis infection, other viral or bacterial infections or injury to the potential retrieval site.

If any of the following signs are observed or noted in any available record, and are deemed to be an indication of these risks, the human tissues should be rejected:

- History of chronic viral hepatitis;
- Presence of active viral hepatitis or jaundice of unknown aetiology;
- Presence or suspicion of central degenerative neurological diseases of possible infectious origin, including dementia (e.g., Alzheimer's disease, Creutzfeldt-Jakob disease or familial history of Creutzfeldt-Jakob disease and multiple sclerosis);
- Physical evidence for risk of sexually transmitted diseases such as genital ulcerative disease, herpes simplex, syphilis and chancroid (genital lesions);
- Presence or history of malignant disease. Exceptions may include primary basal cell carcinoma of the skin, histologically proven and primary brain tumour without metastasis;
- For a male donor, physical evidence consistent with anal intercourse, including perianal condyloma (insertion trauma or perianal lesions);
- Physical evidence of non-medical percutaneous drug use such as needle tracks (and/or non-medical injection sites), including examination of tattoos (which may be covered needle tracks);

- Disseminated lymphadenopathy (enlarged lymph nodes);
- Oral thrush (white spots in the mouth);
- Blue or purple spots consistent with Kaposi's sarcoma (blue/purple [grey/black] spots/ lesions);
- Physical evidence of recent tattooing, ear piercing or body piercing (tattoos/piercings should be described);
- Unexplained jaundice, hepatomegaly or Icterus. It is important to stress that hepatomegaly may not be apparent in a physical assessment unless an autopsy is performed (enlarged liver, jaundice, Icterus, etc.);
- Physical evidence of sepsis, such as unexplained generalized rash or generalized petechia (rash);
- Large scab consistent with recent smallpox immunisation (scab);
- Eczema vaccinatum (lesion, scab);
- Generalised vesicular rash and generalised vaccinia (rash);
- Severely necrotic lesion consistent with vaccine necrosum (lesion);
- Significant history of connective tissue disease (e.g., systemic lupus erythematous and rheumatoid arthritis) or any immunosuppressive treatment;
- Significant exposure to a toxic substance that may be transferred in toxic doses or damage the human tissue (e.g., cyanide, lead, mercury and gold);
- Presence or evidence of infection or prior irradiation at the site of donation;
- Unknown cause of death. If at the time of death the cause of death is unknown, an autopsy should be performed to prove this cause; and
- Corneal scarring consistent with vaccinial keratitis (abnormal ocular finding and scarring).

The physical assessment should include, in the case of human skin, the documentation of the findings and conditions that may affect the quality or quantity of human skin retrieved.

Microbiological Screening

There must be a documented policy on testing blood samples for specific infections that might be transmitted with the human tissue. The examinations should be executed for certain mandatory infectious agents by accredited testing laboratories, in line with current guidelines in force in the state. The documented policy must consider:

- Quality and validity of samples;
- Retesting in the case of living donors;
- Timing of samples in relation to the donation of human tissues;
- Testing of post-mortem samples;
- Positive sample identification; and
- Archiving of samples.

All tissue establishments should have a documented policy for donors with repeat reactive samples. There should be protocols for retesting, if appropriate, confirmatory testing, counselling of donors and contacts, and acceptance or rejection of donations.

Microbiological Controls

There are six physical methods of providing microbiological control. These are:

- Heat;
- Filtration;
- Low temperatures;
- Desiccation;
- Osmotic pressure; and
- Radiation.

There should be documented procedures for the policy and practice of the microbiological test programmes for the screening of human tissues, the processing environment, and the potential sources of contamination. All aspects of processing, which contribute to the microbiological safety and quality of the human tissues, should be controlled. Contamination should be minimised by all practical means.

Bacteriological Testing Methods

Representative samples of each retrieved human tissue have to be cultured,[7] if the human tissues are to be aseptically processed without terminal sterilisation. Samples should be taken prior to exposure of the human tissue to an antibiotic-containing solution.

The culture technique should allow for the growth of both aerobic and anaerobic bacteria as well as fungi. Results should be documented in the donor record.

Blood culture, if procurement is performed on a deceased donor, may be useful in assessing the state of the deceased donor and interpreting the cultures performed on the grafts themselves. They should be reviewed by the Medical Director/Consultant.

Bacteriological Bioburden Limits

If bacteriological testing of human tissue samples obtained at the time of donation reveals growth of low-virulence microorganisms that are usually considered non-pathogenic, the human tissue may not be administered without being further processed in a way that effectively decontaminates the tissue.

Human tissues from which high-virulence microorganisms have been isolated are not acceptable for transplantation, unless the procedure has been validated to effectively inactivate the organisms without harmful potential effects to the recipient, taking into account possible endotoxins.

Non-Microbiological Tests

The application of non-microbiological tests will depend upon the human tissues to be transplanted.

---

[7] Culturing is performed on allograft tissue to detect bacteria and fungi after aseptic tissue processing. Studies have shown that cultures are between 78% and 92% accurate, and culturing is simply not an absolute method for ensuring allograft sterility (Veen, *et al.*, 1994). In fact, the United States Pharmacopeial Convention, the standards-setting body for sterility testing and other quality-control procedures used in the medical industry, specifically states that cultures for sterility can only be used to monitor a previously validated sterilisation process and should not be construed as definitive evidence of sterilisation (United States Pharmacopeial Convention, 2002).

Blood Tests for Infectious Diseases

Testing of donor blood specimens should be performed for each human tissue donor (including maternal donors of foetal or neonatal tissue), for the purpose of infectious disease screening.

All tissue establishments should ensure that infectious disease testing is performed in accordance with the following conditions:

- Testing should be done by a laboratory that meets applicable laws and regulations of the national authority having jurisdiction over that laboratory;
- The tests should be performed using test kits that are certified as required in the regulations in force; and
- The testing laboratories should follow the test kit manufacturer's instructions with respect to the following:
  - ◻ The collection, handling, and storage of blood specimens;
  - ◻ The time frame within which samples must be tested, if applicable;
  - ◻ The procedure for testing; and
  - ◻ The interpretation of the test results.

Tissue establishments should have SOPs in force for the conduct of infectious disease tests that conform to the manufacturer's instructions. In cases where testing is performed by a contract laboratory or other establishment, the tissue establishments should ensure that the SOPs of the testing laboratory or the other establishment conform to the test kit manufacturer's instructions.

A test is considered appropriate and effective if it is licensed for the detection of the infectious disease agent or marker in accordance with the licensing requirements specified in tissue regulations in force; it is used in accordance with the test kit manufacturer's instructions; and it is used for the detection of an infectious disease marker that is relevant at the time of performing the testing.

Unless otherwise specified, in tissue-specific standards, a blood specimen should be collected at the time of donation or within 7 days prior to or after donation and, in case of a deceased person, preferably within 24 hours after death. For potential deceased tissue donors who have received blood, blood components or plasma volume expanders within 48 hours prior to death, if there is an expected hemodilution of more than 50%, then a pre-transfusion blood sample should be tested.

There should be written procedures for all significant steps in the infectious disease testing process, including the collection and use of appropriate blood specimen types and instructions for specimen handling. Procedures should conform to the manufacturer's instructions for use in specimen collection and storage. Handling procedures should be described in the SOPs.

All human tissues intended for transplantation should be from donors who are tested and found to be negative for:

- Antibodies to the human immunodeficiency virus type 1 and type 2 (anti-HIV-1 and anti-HIV-2);
- Hepatitis B surface antigen (HBsAg);
- Total antibody (IgG and IgM) to hepatitis B core antigen (anti-HBc); hepatitis B core antibodies (HBc-Ab) should be negative for tissue validation. However, if the HBc-Ab (core antigen) test is positive and the HBs-Ag (surface antigen) is negative, a confirmation cascade is necessary. If the antibodies against the surface antigen are found (HBs-Ab), the donor can then be considered to have recovered from an infection and the tissue can be used for transplantation;
- Antibodies to the hepatitis C virus (anti-HCV); and
- Syphilis (a non-treponemal or treponemal-specific assay may be performed).

Retesting of living donors for HIV and HCV at 180 days is recommended. If another method of increasing safety, rather than retesting such as antigen testing, molecular biology or viral inactivation method is used (and allowed by applicable regulation), it should be documented and validated.

Optional blood tests could be necessary for compliance with applicable state and/or local laws or regulations and/or to screen for endemic diseases as follows:

- Antigen test for HIV (p24 antigen) or HCV or validated Molecular Biology Test for HIV and HCV (e.g., PCR), if performed by an experienced laboratory;

- Antibody to human T-lymphotropic virus type I and type II (anti- HTLV-I and anti-HTLV-II) depending on the prevalence in some regions;
- Cytomegalovirus (CMV), Ebstein-Barr virus (EBV) and toxoplasmosis antibodies for immune-suppressed patients; and
- Alanine aminotransferase (ALT) for living donors.

Testing used for donor suitability should be performed by laboratories that are registered with the national competent health care authorities as an establishment for testing and are certified to perform such testing on human specimens under national laws and regulations in force. All test results should be documented in the donor's record.

Interpretation of Infectious Disease Test Results

All human tissues from donors who test repeatedly reactive on a required screening test should be quarantined and should not be used for transplantation.

Discard of allogeneic tissues should be based upon the interpretation of all infectious disease test results and should be as follows:

- Human tissue is unsuitable for transplantation if it is from a donor whose specimen has tested repeatedly reactive to a donor screening test for anti-HIV-1, anti-HIV-2, HBsAg, anti-HBc, anti-HCV, anti-HTLV-I or anti-HTLV-II;
- Human tissue is unsuitable for transplantation if it is from a donor whose specimen had a final test result of positive, repeat reactive or repeatedly reactive to a screening test using a NAT assay; and
- Human tissue from a donor reactive to syphilis using a screening assay may be used for transplantation only if the sample is found to be negative using a licensed treponema-specific confirmatory assay. If the sample was reactive for syphilis when only using a licensed treponema specific confirmatory assay, the human tissue should not be used for transplantation;

If results of additional infectious disease testing are received for tests that are not required, such test results must be included in the donor's medical records and any results of those tests should be considered when determining donor suitability. Procedures should be established for the interpretation of additional infectious disease test results. Results of all tests, including those that are optional, should be included in the donor records. All tissue establishments should have SOPs in force for the interpretation and handling of all test results, including the communication of test results to transplant physicians or to the establishments to which the human tissues are distributed. Procedures should also be established for handling the results of optional tests that become available after the human tissues have been released for distribution, and should include notification of transplant physicians or institutions to which the human tissue is distributed.

Types of Exclusion Criteria

There are two types of exclusion criteria:

- **General**: Positive results for HIV, hepatitis, and HTLV-1; and
- **Specific**: In life-threatening situations for the recipient (e.g., related Hematopoietic Progenitor Cell (HPC) donation), positive results for hepatitis are no reason for exclusion, in accordance with applicable state and/or laws and/or local regulations. In these situations, human tissues with a higher risk for recipient may be offered as long as full information is given to the recipient or, if it is not possible, to his relatives or legal representative, in case that the transplant of the human tissue is the only alternative available that can be used.

Archived Blood Samples

A blood sample from each donor should be archived, if any sample remains after testing. A policy should be established to collect and archive hematopoietic tissue samples from donors to ensure that retrospective testing can be performed as new tests are adopted for donor screening. Samples should be retained for 10 years after either the expiration date of the human tissue or, if there is no expiration date, 10 years after the date of distribution.

The requirement for such retrospective testing will be based on the degree of safety enhancement afforded by the new tests, and the availability of tests that are appropriately validated or approved by the national competent health care authorities for testing frozen specimens. If such retrospective testing is required, national competent health care authorities should inform the tissue establishments involved.

If a tissue establishment chooses to archive samples, they should have SOPs for the collection and storage for this specific task. Samples should be stored frozen, and should be kept for at least 5 years. In this case, the tissue establishment should have documentation to show that the samples are kept at the appropriate temperature throughout the storage period.

A tissue establishment may not be able to use and/or distribute human tissues that are available in their existing inventory when new tests are introduced and they are unable to perform retrospective testing using archived donor samples that have been stored appropriately.

In-house Laboratory Testing

If the tissue establishment performs laboratory tests and results are used to determine acceptability of human tissues for transplantation, then staff performing the tests should have specific training in the procedures and should be certified competent to perform the tests required.

In-house Laboratory Controls

In-house laboratory control procedures should include documentation of adequate provisions for monitoring the reliability, accuracy, precision, and performance of in-house laboratory test procedures and instruments.

In-house Laboratory Records

Records of in-house laboratory testing should include:

- Sample source and quantity;
- Tissue identification number;
- Test date and identification of the person performing the test;
- Assay methods;
- Calculations, graphs, and charts, if used;
- Test results, as well as interpretation of results;

- Testing or standardisation of reference standards, reagents or standard solutions; and
- Documentation of record review by an individual other than the operator generating the records to ensure compliance with the SOPs in force.

Notification of Positive Infectious Disease Test Results

The donor, if living, should be notified of test results as required by applicable state and/or local laws and/or regulations. For deceased donors, unless otherwise directed by state and/or local laws and/or regulations, the donor's next-of-kin or legal representative or a physician who will counsel the next-of-kin or legal representative, should be notified of confirmed positive test results that may be medically relevant as determined by the Medical Director/Consultant. All organisations involved in the collection and processing of human tissues from a donor with a repeatedly reactive (positive) infectious disease test result should be notified of the donor's status within one working day of receipt of the test results. Policies regarding notification of confirmatory testing results should be established by the Medical Director/Consultant. Test result notification should be documented.

Age Criteria

The Medical Director/Consultant and/or Tissue Establishment Committee should determine age criteria for donor suitability in accordance with human tissue-specific standards. Nevertheless, it is important to emphasise that there is no age limit for autologous tissue donation. Nevertheless, in principle, acceptable donors should be not older than 60 years of age. The Medical Director/Consultant should determine the age limits for bone and soft human tissue donors.

Monetary Compensation of Donors

Monetary inducement or goods or services of value should not be offered to a donor, deceased donor's next-of-kin, or any other third party. However, the tissue establishment involved in the procurement of the human tissue should reimburse all costs directly related to the donation and may reimburse living donors for associated costs, including compensation for restoration of lost earnings when directly attributable to the donation. Donors or their families should not be responsible for any expenses related to the retrieval of allogeneic tissues.

The costs of an organisation for collecting, processing, storing and distributing of samples may include the following:

- **Infrastructure costs**: Include laboratories, equipment, power, and necessary reagents and disposables like plasticware. One of the largest infrastructure costs is information technology platforms for laboratory management and data storage. Provision for depreciation should be costed into these expenses, for example, freezers need to be replaced approximately every seven years;
- **Staff costs**: Actual cost of employment plus on costs (tax and superannuation), training costs (including, courses and conference attendance) and human resources and management costs;
- **Fees**: Fees to any third parties such as costs levied by pathology services for the handling of any samples; and
- **Research and development costs**.

V. Handling and Control of Human Tissues, Services and Materials

Handling of Human Tissues

All tissue establishments should formulate the general scope, objectives, regulations, code of practice, and SOPs, which will be used for collecting and handling the procured human tissues in the most effective and safe manner. The overall scope and regulations of the tissue establishment should be open to the public, and should also be transparent and well known to the donors and recipients of the human tissues.

Tissue Retrieval Policies and Procedures

The Director of the tissue establishment should establish policies and procedures for the retrieval of human tissues in accordance with SOPs in force.

To ensure the correct implementation of these policies and procedures, all tissue establishments should have an organised system for the procurement and processing of human tissue and the appropriate techniques. The following elements need to be taken into account:

- A physician and the organisation that procures human tissue should obtain advance approval from the national competent health care authorities on the proceedings and the method of retrieval. The organisation should also have an established system for retrieval;
- Sufficient level of medical technology as well as respect for the deceased donor should be observed when procuring human tissues;
- Proper equipment/device and technique should be utilised to procure human tissue;
- The recipient organisation is not responsible for inferior quality of equipment/device used in the retrieval;
- Documentation proving that the recovery room environment is kept as aseptic as possible should be obtained,[8] and pre-possessing cultures must be performed during the retrieval procedure;
- Proper consent for and written agreement from the recovery hospital should be obtained prior to human tissue retrieval; and
- A tissue establishment or a relevant institution should be in charge of storage and management of retrieved records;

The ideal human tissue procurement facility should be an operating room, or another suitably validated area, depending on specific requirements for the human tissue to be procured. The following points should be considered for the human tissue retrieval procedure:

- Every effort should be made to minimise contamination during the procurement of the human tissue;
- Human tissues may be removed using an aseptic technique. Clean, non-sterile techniques may be used if validated sterilisation/decontamination of human tissues is employed. Where possible, sterile single-use

[8]However, it is important to stress that aseptically processed human tissue should not be considered sterile, and health care providers should be informed of the possible risk for bacterial infection.

instruments (disposable) should be used for human tissue retrieval and also for processing. The general area of retrieval should be documented and area access should be restricted. All working surfaces used during human tissue retrieval should be disinfected;

- Before retrieval begins, the deceased donor's skin should be prepared using an appropriate anti-bacterial agent;
- Every effort should be made to minimise the number of people present during human tissue retrieval. Retrieval should not be carried out if an autopsy is under way in the same room. If permitted by national law, it is preferable to carry out human tissue retrievals before the autopsy;
- A local sterile field using sterile drapes should always be used for procurement of human tissue;
- All instruments used during the human tissue retrieval should be sterile and stored on a back table covered with a sterile drape;
- Staff conducting the human tissue retrieval should be appropriately gowned and wear gloves and protective masks;
- The following aesthetic aspects and deceased donor reconstruction should be respected: skin should not be procured from the neck, arms, face or other areas that may affect funeral viewing. Following tissue procurement, the donor's body should be reconstructed as closely as possible to its original anatomical configuration, to enable the usual funeral proceedings to take place;
- Documentation of deceased donor reconstruction should be preserved in the donor's record; and
- Every effort should be made to ensure that the human tissue retrieval is conveniently timed to fit in with funeral arrangements and other formalities.

The Director of the tissue establishment should specify the area where human tissues are to be obtained and the general retrieval environment. Retrieval and preservation should occur within a time interval appropriate for retention of biological functions of the collected human tissues, and should be compatible with the intended use of the human tissue. On this subject, it is important to emphasise that:

- The tissue establishment anonymises the collected human tissues during the handling, use, and storage;

- The procured human tissues are recorded, documented, handled, and stored according to specific SOPs in force. Each human tissue is registered by the tissue establishment as a coded bank-number, which is linked to the donor or autopsy number, if available; the tissue establishment staff are the only ones who can break the code;
- All pathology reports are stored in the donor database together with all the donor's clinical/genetic data; and
- Quality control is performed on all collected human tissues to ensure their suitability for medical treatment or research. All samples which do not meet the parameters for quality control are either thrown away or used for different purposes (e.g., teaching or internal use within the tissue establishment).

Human Tissue Retrieval

All referral arrangements with human tissue retrieval facilities and agencies, donor referral sources, and other tissue establishments or facilities should be documented.

Detection of potential donors is the starting point for tissue transplantation. The only way to ensure that potential donors are not missed is to have a donor referral system in place with the aim of identifying and monitoring individual potential donors within donor pools in relevant hospitals or geographical areas.[9] Proactive donor detection programmes should be established in every acute hospital using specifically trained professionals in compliance with agreed protocols and ethical principles.

One of the main goals of procurement coordination is to assure continuous and effective cooperation between the different teams involved in donation, retrieval, implantation, sharing of organs and tissue banking. The responsibilities for procurement coordination include:

---

[9] Detection centre: This refers to those hospitals that collaborate in identifying potential donors. These hospitals may or may not have the capacity to diagnose death with on-going cardiac function or to correctly maintain the donor or to organise human tissue procurement. Depending on the national laws or organisational network, potential donors may be transferred to the centres assigned for procurement.

Procurement centre: This refers to hospitals with the capacity to diagnose death, to maintain donors correctly and to organise organs and tissue procurement performed by local or visiting teams. Organs are sent to the assigned transplant centre where the transplants are undertaken with respect to allocation rules. Human tissues are transferred to the tissue establishment.

- Identification of potential donors, using all the available tools and scientific knowledge to expand the donor pool as much as possible;
- Providing appropriate information for potential donor family members or legal representatives, relating to the human tissues that are to be retrieved and the purposes for which they are intended;
- Informing families or legal representatives that human tissues found to be unsuitable for clinical transplantation will be discarded or, if permission is granted, may be used for research or educational purposes;
- Ensuring consent or authorisation for donation in accordance with national regulations and maintaining the relevant documentation;
- Obtaining the donor's medical and behavioural history from appropriate relatives, legal representatives or other individuals;
- Coordinating and distributing procured human tissues to the appropriate recipients through established sharing organisations. Donor–recipient pairing should be closely examined, particularly in cases of sub-optimal donors, in order to optimise the use of donors;
- Coordinating the retrieval teams and organising the retrieval procedure;
- Assuring the safety, quality, and transparency of all the procedures performed;
- Informing families and legal representatives that reconstruction of the donor ensuring that visual appearance is not affected will be performed following retrieval; and
- Informing the doctors and nurses involved about the results of donation.

All tissue establishments should establish written procedures for interacting with operating room staff, the patient's physician or other sources/facilities for autologous tissue donation prior to retrieval. In this case, staff should confirm that informed consent for donation has been obtained in the appropriate form, following the established procedures and documented.

The following are the main steps that should be followed for the procurement of human tissues from a deceased donor:

- After notification regarding an impending brain death or cardiac death[10] has been made to the national designated organ and tissue procurement

[10]Deceased donors fall into two categories: heart-beating, and non-heart-beating donors (NHBDs). Organs are mainly retrieved from heart-beating donors, whereas tissues are procured from heart-beating and non-heart-beating donors. In some countries, organ donation from NHBDs is also permitted. Certification of death with ongoing cardiac function

organisation or tissue establishment, in the case that the human tissues are not procured by the designated organ organisation, the designated procurement organisation shall evaluate donation potential;

- The national designated organ procurement organisation and/or tissue establishment should assure that families of potential organ and tissue donors or legal representatives are made aware of the option of organ and human tissue donation and their option to decline; and
- The national designated organ procurement organisation and/or tissue establishment should, working collaboratively with the hospital, request consent for organ and/or human tissue donation in the order of priority established under current regulations and should have designated trained staff available to perform the consent process 24 hours a day, 365 days a year.

The national designated organ procurement organisation and/or tissue establishment should encourage discretion and sensitivity with regard to the circumstances, perspectives, and feelings of the families of potential organ and human tissue donors.

Human tissues must be retrieved under conditions representing the least possible danger to the donor, in properly equipped and staffed institutions duly authorised to carry out this action. The general site of retrieval should be documented and area access should be restricted. All working surfaces (e.g., back table and operating room table) used during retrieval should be scrubbed using a bactericidal/antimicrobial agent.

Surgical residues remain an important source of tissues and cells and should be collected under aseptic conditions during a surgical procedure in the operating room. They are collected where the material is removed for therapeutic purposes other than to obtain human tissue. For such

---

should follow legal requirements. Most countries recognise this state as "brain death", as defined in laws and regulations in force. Strict testing according to agreed protocols is required to establish brain death beyond doubt. Countries should review and, where necessary, enact laws to cover adequate definition of death with ongoing cardiac function. Organ retrieval from NHBDs is restricted in some countries. In those countries that permit the procedure, the method of death certification and the manner of obtaining consent prior to the retrieval procedure need to be carefully defined. NHBDs are persons with complete and irreversible cessation of all cardio-respiratory function, with consequent death. Death certification for donors who are providing only tissues should follow national regulations.

procurement of human tissue, there are no risks to the donor that are specifically related to the retrieval procedure. The same conditions as for collection of surgical residues apply also for the collection of fetal membranes (amnion and chorion) following delivery.

The anonymity policy should be respected at each stage of such collection of human tissue.

The surgical residues should be used or disposed of according to the donor's decision.

The SOPs in force should specify the time limits for the post-mortem retrieval of human tissues consistent with tissue-specific standards, where applicable. Human tissues should be retrieved soon after death, if this action is possible. Specific time limits vary with each human tissue obtained, which should be determined by the Director of the tissue establishment or the Advisory Board. Usually, procurement of human tissues should be completed within 12 hours after death. If the body has been refrigerated within 4 to 6 hours of death, procurement should preferably start within 24 hours and no later than 48 hours. If retrieval is to be delayed for deceased donors, the donors should be refrigerated as specified in the tissue-specific standards.

Methods for perioperative autologous tissue collection and transplantation should be safe, aseptic, and ensure accurate identification of autologous tissues.

Retrieval Cleaning and Preparation

Cleaning, preparing, and draping the human skin as well as technician gowning and gloving should be accomplished with the same diligence as used routinely for operative procedures. Aseptic technique should be used.

The area of excision should be devoid of hair and cleansed with an antimicrobial agent(s). Agents used should be antimicrobial skin preparation products, as specified in the SOPs in force, and should be used in accordance with manufacturers' guidelines/instructions.

Retrieval Technique

Persons performing the surgical retrieval should perform a surgical scrub of their hands and forearms prior to retrieval. A head cover, eye shields and mask should be worn at the time of scrub, and a sterile gown and gloves should be donned after the scrub.

Specific tissue recovery operations that control contamination and cross-contamination (e.g., sequencing of the human tissue recovery, use of well-defined zone recovery techniques, and isolation draping in the presence of trauma), should be implemented. During the initial incision (or retrieval), areas of skin that have abrasions or puncture wounds should be avoided. All human tissues should be recovered using aseptic technique.

Post-Retrieval Reconstruction of a Deceased Donor

Unless there is a specific request from a medical examiner, pathologist or a funeral home, the surgical incision(s) should be closed in an aesthetic fashion and the body prepared for the next stage of the retrieval or for transportation to an appropriate facility. The body should be reconstructed in accordance with the SOPs in force. Donor reconstruction should employ techniques consistent with funeral home guidelines and/or medical examiner or pathologist requests and should respect the religious belief of the donor's family. Documentation of donor reconstruction (if applicable) and disposal or handover of the body should be maintained in the donor's record.

Retrieval Records

Retrieval records should include, but not be limited to:

- Name and address of the retrieval agency;
- Date, time, place of the procedure and the identity of the staff involved in the human tissue retrieval;
- Location of the human tissue donation within the retrieval site facility, if relevant;
- Donor name, age and sex;
- Type, lot number, manufacturer, and expiration date of supplies and reagents used to recover, clean, and transport the human tissue retrieved;
- Specific human tissue retrieved; and
- Other relevant donor and human tissue information.

The following information regarding the human tissue retrieval should be documented:

- Name and address of the institution in which the human tissues were retrieved;
- Date and time the human tissues were collected;
- Name of the physician recovering the human tissues;
- Donor name, age, sex, and hospital medical record number and/or social security number or identity card number; and
- Types of human tissues recovered.

Post-Retrieval Packaging

Human tissues should be maintained at defined environmental temperatures until the time of transport to the processing centre. Maintenance of such temperatures should be documented.

Immediately following recovery, the human tissues recovered should be individually and aseptically wrapped in a manner that will prevent contamination of the contents, preserve cellular structure and viability, if desired, and allow for aseptic delivery of the specimen at the time of processing, if necessary or replantation. The container used should be labelled immediately with the donor's name, age, sex, hospital medical record number and/or social security number or identity card number and institution name. After filling and closing the container, it should not be re-opened nor the human tissue removed until further processing by the tissue establishment. All human skin retrieved should be packaged in a sterile solution immediately following retrieval.[11] The volume of transport solution should be adequate to cover the entire skin. The type, lot number, manufacturer, and

[11] In case of absence of validated sterilisation procedures, representative skin samples should be obtained according to Pharmacopeia (pathogenic and facultative pathogenic) immediately prior to final packaging for microbiologic cultures. The samples should also be cultured for the presence of fast-growing fungal organisms (Brychta, 2002). Acceptance or rejection of the human tissue should be based on the model code of practice and the SOPs adopted by the tissue establishment.

expiration date should be documented. The transport container should be fluid-tight and designed to prevent contamination of the contents.

Post Retrieval Transport

Following human tissue retrieval, it should be packaged in a manner that permits required environmental conditions to be maintained for the duration of the transportation.

Transportation temperatures do not require monitoring if the packaging and transport conditions have been validated to maintain the required environmental conditions and the established temperatures.

The transportation container should indicate that human tissue is inside and should also indicate the name and address of the retrieval institutions and processing centre (if different) in accordance with state and/or local laws and/or regulations. All human tissues processed or shipped prior to determination of donor suitability should be under quarantine, accompanied by records assuring identification of the donor and indicating that the human tissues have not been found to be suitable for transplantation (e.g., "quarantine"; "not suitable for transplant in its current form", etc.).

Human tissues should be transported to the processing/storage centre on wet ice in the time limits appropriate for the particular human tissues.

The transport container should also be transported on wet ice. The time of acceptance of the human tissues into the processing centre should be documented. The retrieved human tissues should be wrapped in an aseptic fashion with at least one moisture barrier. The retrieved human tissues should be transported at wet ice temperatures or colder. The maximum time that the retrieved human tissues should remain at wet ice temperatures, prior to either processing or freezing, should be no longer than 72 hours. The human skin transportation container should be transported at wet ice temperatures.

Review of Relevant Medical Records Before Transplantation

Prior to release of human tissues for transplantation, the Medical Director/Consultant should determine donor suitability based on a review and evaluation of the donor's relevant medical records. The determination of suitability should be based on the SOPs in force, and applicable state and/ or local laws and/or regulations.

VI. Human Tissues for Research Purposes

Basic Principles for all Medical Research

The following are the main basic principles that should be applied by a research centre in all medical research involving human tissues:

- Medical research involving human tissues must conform to generally accepted scientific principles, be based on a thorough knowledge of the scientific literature, other relevant sources of information, and on adequate laboratory and, where appropriate, animal experimentation;
- The design and performance of each experimental procedure involving human tissues should be clearly formulated in an experimental protocol. This protocol should be submitted for approval to a specially appointed ethics committee of the research centre;
- Medical research involving human tissues should be conducted only by scientifically qualified persons and under the supervision of a clinically competent medical person. The responsibility for the human tissue should always rest with a medically qualified person;
- Every medical research project involving human tissues should be preceded by careful assessment of predictable risks and burdens in comparison with foreseeable benefits of the research. The design of all studies should be publicly available;
- Physicians should abstain from engaging in research projects involving human tissues unless they are convinced that the risks involved have been adequately assessed and can be satisfactorily handled. Physicians should cease any investigation if the risks are found to outweigh the potential benefits or if there is no conclusive proof of positive and beneficial results;
- Medical research involving human tissues should only be carried out if the importance of the objective outweighs the inherent risks and burdens to the subject;
- The right of research subjects to safeguard their integrity must always be respected. Every precaution should be taken to respect the privacy

of the subject and the confidentiality of the patient information and to minimise the impact of the study on the subject's physical and mental integrity and on the personality of the subject;

- In any research in which human tissues are used, each potential donor should be adequately informed of the aims, methods, sources of funding, any possible conflicts of interest, institutional affiliations of the researcher, the anticipated benefits and potential risks[12] of the study, and the discomfort it may entail, among other relevant issues. The potential donor should be informed of the right to abstain from participation in the study. Only after ensuring that the potential donor has understood the information, should the physician obtain the donor's freely given informed consent or authorisation in writing. If the consent cannot be obtained in writing, the non-written consent should be formally witnessed and documented;
- When obtaining informed consent or authorisation for the research project, the physician should be particularly cautious if the donor is in a dependent relationship with the physician or may consent under duress. In that case, the informed consent or authorisation should be obtained by a well-informed physician who is not engaged in the research and who is completely independent of this relationship;
- For a research donor who is legally incompetent, is physically or mentally incapable of giving consent or is a legally incompetent minor, the researcher should obtain informed consent or authorisation from the authorised legal representative in accordance with applicable state law and/or regulations. These groups should not be included in research unless the study is necessary to promote the health of the population represented and the research cannot instead be performed on legally competent persons. When a subject deemed legally incompetent, such

[12]According to the Belmont report, the assessment of risks and benefits requires a careful arrayal of relevant data, including, in some cases, alternative ways of obtaining the benefits sought in the research. Thus, the assessment presents both an opportunity and a responsibility to gather systematic and comprehensive information about proposed research. For the researcher, it is a means to examine whether the proposed research is properly designed. For an ethics committee, it is a method for determining whether the risks that will be presented to donors are justified. For prospective donors, the assessment will assist the determination whether or not to participate.

as a minor child, is able to give assent to decisions about participation in research, the researcher should obtain that assent in addition to the consent or authorisation of the authorised legal representative;

- In publication of the results of the research, the researchers are obliged to preserve the accuracy of the results. Negative as well as positive results should be published or otherwise publicly available. Sources of funding, institutional affiliations and any possible conflicts of interest should be declared in the publication;
- The physician may combine medical research with medical care, only to the extent that the research is justified by its potential prophylactic, diagnostic or therapeutic value. When medical research is combined with medical care, additional standards should apply to protect the patients who are research subjects. The benefits, risks, burdens and effectiveness of a new method should be tested against those of the best current prophylactic, diagnostic, and therapeutic methods. This does not exclude the use of placebo, or no treatment, in studies where no proven prophylactic, diagnostic or therapeutic method exists;
- At the conclusion of the study, every patient should be assured of access to the best proven prophylactic, diagnostic and therapeutic methods identified by the study;
- The physician should fully inform the patient, which aspects of the medical care is related to the research; and
- In the treatment of a patient, where proven prophylactic, diagnostic and therapeutic methods do not exist or have been ineffective, the physician, with informed consent from the patient, must be free to use unproven or new prophylactic, diagnostic and therapeutic measures, if in the physician's judgment it offers hope of saving life, re-establishing health or alleviating suffering. Where possible, these measures should be made the object of research, designed to evaluate their safety and efficacy. In all cases, new information should be recorded and, where appropriate, published.

Sharing of Human Tissues for Research Activities

In medical research involving human tissues, considerations related to the well-being of the human subject should take precedence over the interests of science and society. The primary purpose of medical research involving human tissues is to improve prophylactic, diagnostic and therapeutic procedures to be used in certain medical treatments by doctors in the future and the understanding of an aetiology and pathogenesis of the different diseases. Even the best proven prophylactic, diagnostic, and therapeutic methods should continuously be challenged through research for their effectiveness, efficiency, accessibility, and quality.

Facilities providing human tissues for research and other non-transplantation purposes should develop detailed relevant specific policies and procedures for the correct use of human tissues.[13] Informed consent for research should be obtained from the donor, next-of-kin or legal representative.

All medical research should be subject to ethical standards that promote respect for all human beings and protect their health and rights. Ethical principles and standards to be followed by a researcher during the implementation of a research project are included in chapters II and III.

Written Requests

All requests for human tissues intended for research use should be submitted in writing. The request should indicate the type of human tissues requested and how it will be used as well as the name, address, and affiliation of the principal researcher's accepting responsibility for receipt of the human tissues.

The manner and context in which information is conveyed is as important as the information itself. For example, presenting information in a disorganised and rapid fashion, allowing too little time for consideration or curtailing opportunities for questioning, all may adversely affect donor's ability to make an informed choice. Because the donor's ability to understand is a function of intelligence, rationality, maturity and language, it is necessary to

[13]The issue of ownership of collected biological specimens is still in debate; the major issue is not the legal status of the samples or the tissue establishment, but who has the right and control of the use of the samples, sharing with other researchers, the prioritisation of distribution and feedback of the obtained scientific results into the database of the tissue establishment. Therefore, the term "custodianship" is more appropriate than ownership. This term implies that the tissue establishment will guarantee the safe and ethical handling of the specimens, as well as the proper use and optimal sharing with researchers and eventually safe disposal of specimens (Ravid, 2008).

The formulary that may be used for obtaining the consent or authorisation from the donor in a research project is the following:

Formulary to be used during the interview of the living donor or relatives for the donation of human tissues for research purposes

Name of the donor:

Name of the hospital: Date:

Personal data, including how the donor can be contacted	☐
Donation of tissues for research purposes is a voluntary decision	☐
Tissue to be procured for donation is a surplus of the diagnostic and therapeutic requirements	☐
Donation of tissue is confidential for others outside the medical and the procurement team	☐
Donated tissues are anonymised and the research company will not contact the donor directly	☐
Relevant medical information will be passed to recipients of the tissues and will be stored in the tissue establishment database	☐
There are no payments involved in the donation of human tissues, only cost recovered	☐
Tissues procured for research purposes may involve the issues of patents and profit	☐
Patients have been given all necessary information regarding the donation of human tissues	☐

Comments made by the donor:

Name of the Tissue Establishment Coordinator or the name of the person involved in the interview:

Signature:

____

adjust the presentation of the data to the donor's capacities. Researchers are responsible for ascertaining that the subject has comprehended the information. While there is always an obligation to ascertain that the information about risk to donors is complete and adequately comprehended, when the risks are more serious, that obligation increases.

Review and Approval

Requests for human tissues for research purposes should be reviewed and approved by the Director of the tissue establishment with the authorisation to carry out research activities after review and written approval by the Director and the ethics committee of the research medical facility involved.

Human tissues are to be used solely for the requested/approved research project and are not to be passed on to a third party without written permission from the concerned ethics committee and the Director of the tissue establishment.

The tissue establishment formulates the terms and contractual obligations of sharing/transfer of specimens/data in a "Material Transfer Agreement" and a "Tissue Recipient Statement" or any other equivalent documents in force.

Assessment of the Justifiability of Research Using Human Tissues or Human Subjects

It is important in any research involving human tissues or human subjects that benefits and risks be balanced. For this reason, the idea of systematic, non-arbitrary analysis of risks and benefits should be emulated insofar as possible. This ideal requires those making decisions about the justifiability of research to be thorough in the accumulation and assessment of information about all aspects of the research, and to consider alternatives systematically. This procedure renders the assessment of research more rigorous and precise, while making communication between members of the ethics committees and researchers less subject to misinterpretation, misinformation and conflicting judgements. Thus, there should first be a determination of the validity of the presuppositions of a specific research; then the nature, probability and magnitude of risk should be distinguished with as much clarity as possible. The method of ascertaining risks should be explicit, especially where there is no alternative to the use of such vague categories as small or slight risk. It should also be determined whether a researcher's estimate of the probability of harm or benefits is reasonable, as judged by known facts or other available studies. Assessment of the justifiability of a specific research should reflect at least the following considerations:

- Brutal or inhumane treatment of human subjects is never morally justified;

- Risks should be reduced to those necessary to achieve the research objective. It should be ascertained whether it is in fact necessary to use human subjects at all. Risk can perhaps never be completely eliminated, but it can often be reduced to a minimum by careful attention to alternative procedures;
- When research involves significant risk of serious impairment, ethics committees should be extraordinarily insistent on the justification of the risk (looking usually to the likelihood of benefit to the subject or, in some rare cases, to the manifest voluntariness of the participation);
- When vulnerable populations are involved in research, the appropriateness of involving them should itself be demonstrated. A number of variables go into such judgements, including the nature and degree of risk, the condition of the particular population involved, and the nature and level of the anticipated benefits;
- Relevant risks and benefits must be thoroughly arrayed in documents and procedures used in the informed consent process.

VII. Written Agreements or Contracts with Third Parties

Written agreements or contracts are required to define and document the relationships between the tissue establishment and any third party. The requirements for written agreements or contracts with regular review apply in the following circumstances:

- Where a third party takes responsibility for any aspect of human tissue donor selection, human tissue retrieval or human tissue processing on behalf of the tissue establishment. For example, where a Tissue Transplant Coordinator interviews a donor family on behalf of the tissue establishment;
- Where a third party provides goods or services that may affect human tissue quality or safety.
  For example, where companies hold equipment maintenance or calibration contracts with tissue establishments; where companies supply human tissue packaging and labelling to tissue establishments; where a contracted microbiologist provides testing and consultant services to a tissue establishment; where a commercial sterilisation facility sterilises human tissues on behalf of a tissue establishment; or where a cleaning contractor is employed;

- Where a tissue establishment provides services to another tissue establishment. For instance, when a tissue establishment receives, processes, and returns human tissues to another establishment or when the tissue establishment stores human tissues to be supplied to specific users on behalf of the other tissue establishment; and
- Where a tissue establishment provides finished human tissues to a user. Before accepting a request from a user, the tissue establishment should ensure that the requirements are adequately defined and documented, and that the tissue establishment has the capability to satisfy those demands.

Management of Written Agreements and Contracts

All tissue establishments should establish and maintain documented procedures for the review of all signed agreements and contracts with third parties. The details of the agreement or contract, including responsibilities, should be clearly specified, documented, and agreed between the parties. The agreement or contract should include an option for audit of procedures carried out by a third party. All tissue establishments should identify and document how an amendment to an agreement or contract is made. Records of reviews of agreements and contracts should be maintained.

All tissue establishments should:

- Evaluate and select third parties on the basis of their ability to meet the required standards, including quality system and any specific quality assurance requirements;
- Define the type and extent of control exercised by the tissue establishment over third parties. This will depend upon the type of product or service provided, on the impact of the third party product or service, on the quality of the final human tissue product and, where applicable, on the quality audit reports and/or quality records maintained by the third party;
- Establish and maintain documented procedures for the control, verification, storage, and maintenance of equipment used for processing and/or storage by another tissue establishment;
- Determine the required procedures before the adoption of human tissues for processing by another tissue establishment; and
- Establish and maintain quality records by third parties, where appropriate.

VIII. Processing and Preservation of Human Tissues

Policies and procedures for preserving, storing, and maintaining human tissue should be established by the Director of the tissue establishment, reviewed annually, and readily available in the practice setting. Policies establishing authority, responsibility, and accountability for the processing and preservation of human tissues within the practice setting should be established and maintained for all steps performed by the tissue establishment. These policies may include, but are not limited to:

- Authority and accountability for processes;
- Screening and testing criteria;
- Obtaining informed consent from the donor;
- Providing information and obtaining informed consent from the human tissue recipient;
- Evaluating culture and serology tests with appropriate interventions for positive results;
- Processing and preserving of human tissues;
- Packaging and labeling of human tissues;
- Sterilisation processes, if applicable;
- Monitoring temperature during storage;
- Maximum storage duration;
- Handling frozen human tissues if there is a freezer malfunction or power outage;
- Warming or reconstituting preserved human tissues;
- Rinsing solutions from human tissues;
- Criteria for return of unused human tissues into inventory;
- Disposing of human tissues;
- Documenting implanted and discarded human tissues in a retrievable format, and notifying recipients or recalling released human tissues;
- Responses to adverse events; and
- Responses to recalls of human tissues from tissue vendors.

The Director of the tissue establishment should establish processing and preservation methods in accordance with SOPs in force and applicable state and/or local laws and/or regulations. All human tissues should be processed, preserved, quarantined, and/or stored pursuant to such methods so as to render them suitable for clinical use. If human tissues are not to be processed immediately, it should be retained in its original wrapping. Processing of human tissues should include a disinfection period followed by rinsing, packaging and preservation, and the sterilisation of the human tissue, when applicable. Processing of cardiac and vascular tissues should be conducted so that there is a minimum alteration of the tissues.

Processing Environment

All human tissues should be processed in an aseptic fashion using sterile drapes, packs, solutions, appropriate instruments, and packaging material.

Processing steps should take place in an appropriate controlled environment. Human tissue processing in an open system should have the environmental conditions and monitoring of the area clearly defined (such as for a clean room or laminar flow cabinet). Records should be maintained to demonstrate that the area is monitored for microbiological contamination and air control.

Critical work areas should be monitored according to a documented procedure. Where aseptic operations are performed, monitoring should be frequent using methods such as settle plates, air, and surface sampling. Results from environmental microbiological monitoring programmes should be reviewed as part of the human tissue release stage. The recommended limits for microbiological monitoring of critical work areas in operation are given in Table 2.

Table 2: Air classification system for the processing of human tissues

Grade	Maximum permitted number of particles per m^3 equal to or above the size specified			
	At rest		**In operation**	
	0.5 μm	5 μm	0.5 μm	5 μm
A	3,500	0	3,500	0
B	3,500	0	350,000	2,000
C	350,000	2,000	3,500,000	20,000
D	3,500,000	20,000	Not defined	Not defined

Source: UK Department of Health

Table 3: Microbiological monitoring of critical work areas

Grade	Air sample cfu/m	Settle plates cfu/4 hours	Contact plates cfu/plate	Glove print cfu/glove
A	<1	<1	<1	<1
B	10	5	5	5
C	100	50	25	—
D	200	100	50	—

Source: UK Department of Health

The routine monitoring programme for microbiological and particulate contamination shall be executed according to a defined method and plan, with specified alert and action limits. Compliance with the specified requirements shall be verified and the results shall be documented to monitor the operational state of critical work areas or laminar flow cabinets.

Musculoskeletal human tissues and the processing of exposed human skin should be processed in a bacteriological and climate-controlled environment.

If the processing of autologous tissues is required, it should occur in a bacteriological and climate-controlled environment utilising aseptic technique.

Processing Methods

All human tissues should be processed by methods known and validated to prevent contamination and cross-contamination.

The specific methods employed for processing may vary with each type of human tissue and with the manner in which it has been retrieved. Each type of human tissue should be prepared according to a written procedure, which should be included in a code of practice and the SOPs in force, resulting in processed human tissues appropriate for safe and efficient clinical use.

In-process Controls

In-process controls should be applied as necessary during processing and packaging to ensure that each process meets requirements specified in the SOPs in force. The Director of the tissue establishment, in collaboration with technical staff and the Quality Assurance Officer, should determine when, which, and how controls are to be performed (e.g., residual moisture testing, microbial cultures of human tissues, solutions, packaging, equipment, pH measurements and post-thaw sperm quality). Sampling for in-process controls should be designed to be representative of the materials to be evaluated.

Process Validation

All steps involved during the processing of human tissues should be validated, when appropriate, to demonstrate the effectiveness of the procedures used.

When computers are used as part of a processing or quality system, the software package should be validated as well.

When validation cannot be adequately evidenced through testing, validation should be evidenced through documentation demonstrating adequate design, development, and verification and maintenance procedures.

Time Limits for Processing and Preservation Phases

The Director of the tissue establishment should establish time limits and/or other valid process-control endpoints or limits for the completion of each phase of processing and preservation of human tissues.

Processing of osteo-articular human tissues should be completed within 5 days of retrieval. Processing of human skin that is to be frozen/cryopreserved should be initiated within 10 days of retrieval, provided the skin is placed in tissue storage media, which is replaced at least every 72 hours. If the media are not changed, processing should be initiated within 96 hours of retrieval.

Tolerance Limits of Processed Human Tissues

Tissue establishments that process and preserve human tissues should include in their SOPs in force a description of the final types of human tissues, any specifically required or specifically prohibited dimensions or characteristics, and the means used to assess these characteristics. At or near the conclusion of processing, each group of human tissues should be judged according to these procedures to ascertain whether it is in conformance with the SOPs in force.

Relevant human tissue dimensions or characteristics should be recorded. All human tissues deemed to be out of conformance should not be released for transplantation. This inspection, the staff involved, and the disposition (e.g., discard, research, further processing, ready for distribution, among others) of each group of human tissues should be documented.

Pooling

Tissues from multiple donors should not be pooled during retrieval, processing, preservation or storage. If human tissues are subsequently treated in batches, a unique batch number should be assigned and added to the records of the human tissues. However, under specific circumstances, a tissue establishment may pool human tissues from different donors during processing to produce a therapeutic dose for an individual recipient.

Human Tissue Cross-Contamination

Written procedures should be prepared, validated, and followed for prevention of infectious disease contamination or cross-contamination of human tissues during processing.

Inspection of Human Tissues on Receipt at the Tissue Establishment

Tissue establishments should ensure that human tissues from within or outside the country, are quarantined until the human tissues and their associated documentation have been inspected or otherwise verified as conforming to the tissue establishment's requirements, including those relating to donor selection and testing. Verification of conformity to the requirements must be done in accordance with documented procedures. All tissue establishments should establish and maintain records that provide clear evidence that the human tissue (or its packaging) and associated documentation have been inspected on reception.

Human tissues must be correctly identified at all times. Each delivery or batch of human tissues must be allocated an identifying code, which can be related to the human tissues and be traceable to the donor through processing and storage.

Inspection of Materials on Receipt at the Tissue Establishment

Purchased materials that may affect the quality of finished human tissues should similarly be quarantined until inspection has confirmed that they comply with the agreed specifications.

Reagents and Suppliers

The reagents used in processing and preservation of human tissues should be of appropriate grade for the intended use and sterile, if indicated. A record should be made of all reagents and supplies following receipt including the type, manufacturer, lot number, date of receipt, and expiration date. The inspection of reagents and supplies should be documented, including identification of the staff performing the inspection. Possible contamination of preservation fluid should be avoided and monitored by repeated testing for bacteria and fungi.

All instruments, solutions, and supplies used to process human tissues for transplantation purpose should be sterile. All non-disposable surgical instruments and mechanical/electrical equipment used in human tissue processing should be cleaned, disinfected, and sterilised between donors according to written procedures prepared, validated, and followed for prevention of infectious disease contamination or cross-contamination during processing.

Whenever possible, reagents used for collection, processing and preservation should be approved for human use. Reagents not approved for human use may be used if reagents or procedures that include the reagent have been approved by national competent health care authorities or have been established in the medical literature to be acceptable for the purpose specified. The origin, characteristic (physical, chemical and microbiological) conditions for storage and expiry dates of reagents should be monitored and recorded. All reagents should be stored in accordance with the manufacturers' instructions.

Human Tissue Preservation, Cryopreservation, Lyophilisation, Dehydration, and Demineralisation Techniques

Cryopreservation of Human Tissues

To ensure correct processing of the human tissue, it should be removed from the disinfectant solution and then rinsed with a disinfectant-free solution. If human tissue is to be cryopreserved, it must be packaged in a cryoprotectant medium, and then frozen at a steady controlled predetermined rate with compensation for heat of crystallisation. Procedures for the cryopreservation of musculoskeletal human tissues should be established and documented. Documentation of the concentrations of cryoprotectant and nutrient or isotonic solutions in the cryopreservative solution should be maintained.

Upon termination of the freezing programme, the cryopreserved human tissue should immediately be placed in storage. Temperature fluctuation and cycling should be avoided.

Freezing of Musculoskeletal and Soft Human Tissues

If human tissue is to be frozen in order for it to be preserved, it should be frozen at a specific rate to a predetermined specific endpoint (a temperature of −40°C or colder). If human tissue is to be preserved using other methods, appropriate protocols should be defined and described in writing procedures.

Freezing of human skin should be done in a manner that ensures a slow cooling rate to maintain the structural integrity of the skin. Variable-rate cooling using insulated heat sink boxes or programmed control-rate freezing techniques are acceptable methods of human skin cryopreservation. If a programmed control-rate freezing technique is employed, a record of the freezing profile should be evaluated and approved and should become a permanent part of the processing record. Frozen human skin that has been thawed should not be returned to the skin establishment inventory. The frozen human skin should not be assigned for use to another patient, if the package has been opened.

Procedures for freezing musculoskeletal and soft human tissues should be established and documented. Freezer chamber temperature should be monitored during each freezing cycle. The thermal profile for each vial or batch should be logged with the specimen records.

The expiration time of refrigerated musculoskeletal human tissues should be 5 days from the date of recovery or established in the SOPs in force using a validated method for determining expiration dating. Human skin should be stored refrigerated for no longer than 14 days.

Control-rate Freezing: Surrogate Packages

If freezing surrogates are used for monitoring the freezing programme, the packaging should be regularly inspected and solutions and tissue changed when indicated. Monitoring for deterioration of the packaging should be performed. The processing centre should have a procedure describing the assembly of such surrogates and a means for monitoring the surrogates.

Lyophilisation of Human Tissues

There are various protocols of freeze-drying human tissues. Freeze-drying is a method for preservation and is not a sterilisation method; sterility should be assumed by aseptic protocol or by the use of additional sterilisation techniques or methods.

Procedures for lyophilising human tissue should be established and described in the SOPs in force. A quality control programme for monitoring the performance of the freeze-dryer should be documented. Each lyophilisation cycle should be monitored for shelf temperature, condenser temperature, and vacuum; values should be recorded daily. Additionally, each lyophilisation cycle should document, if applicable, the method/length of disinfection of the human tissue. Representative samples of the human tissues should be tested for residual moisture content and should not exceed 6% of initial weight by gravimetric or Karl Fischer analysis or 8% by nuclear magnetic resonance spectrometry (NMR). The final container should maintain these moisture requirements for the indicated expiration period.

Dehydration of Musculoskeletal Human Tissues

Procedures for dehydration of musculoskeletal human tissues should be established. Temperature should be monitored during each dehydration cycle and should not exceed the maximum temperature for dehydration.

Chemical Preservation of Musculoskeletal Human Tissues

Procedures for the preservation of musculoskeletal human tissues by chemical means should be validated and documented. When chemical preservation has been used, the package insert should so indicate.

Demineralised Human Bone: Calcium Residuals

Representative samples of each lot of demineralised human bone should be tested for residual calcium. Residual calcium content should not exceed 8% by a standard method.

Expiration Date

An expiration date for each human tissue should be fixed. According to AATB, the expiration time of different human tissues should not exceed the following:

- Refrigerated musculoskeletal human tissue: 5 days;
- Refrigerated human skin: 14 days;
- Frozen and cryopreserved cells and human tissue (–40° C or colder): 5 years; and
- Lyophilised or dehydrated human tissue: 5 years.

Safe duration of storage of autographs may be influenced by processing and packaging methods and should be defined by the facility, not to exceed the expiration date listed above. A process should be in place to minimise the number of autographs in storage to those that will be reimplanted. This is facilitated by periodic communication with surgeons or review of medical records to determine whether patients have survived.

Processing and Preservation Records

A record should be created to document the processing and preservation of human tissues. Processing and preservation records should include the following:

- Processing dates and responsible processing personnel;
- Tissue identification number(s) and type(s) of human tissues being processed;
- Tissue measurements (e.g., weight, dimensions and volume), as appropriate;
- Expiration date, where applicable;
- Type and quantity of human tissues sampled for in-process controls;
- Processing technique used;
- Final disposition of each human tissue retrieved and/or processed; and
- Type, lot number, manufacturer (unless noted down in other records), and expiration date, where applicable, of supplies and reagents used to process and/or preserve human tissues.

Additives

The type, amount, concentration and method of incorporation/addition of all media, cryoprotectants and any other additives used in the freezing solution/media should be specified in the SOPs in force. This information about the allograft should be made available to the implanting/transplanting physician, upon request.

IX. Human Tissue Release and Distribution

Finished human tissues must be held in quarantine until released by the Director of the tissue establishment or the Quality Assurance Officer following the SOPs in force. Human tissues must not be released from quarantine until all the activities in the documented procedures, including microbiological procedures, have been satisfactorily completed and the associated data and documentation are available and authorised. Records must identify the inspection authority responsible for making the proposal for the release of human tissues and should include a statement explaining the reasons why the human tissues have been approved for release or have been rejected.

Prior to the release of human tissues into the inventory for distribution, there should be documentation of the following:

- Approval of donor eligibility by a responsible or designated person within the tissue establishment;
- Review and approval of processing, preservation and storage records by the responsible or designated person within the tissue establishment;
- Final inspection of both the label and the container to ensure accuracy and integrity by the responsible person within the tissue establishment;
- Screening results (e.g., microbiology/processing cultures) and other test results used to determine final release. These results should be kept by the tissue establishment distributing the human tissues during the time foresee in the SOPs in force; and
- Exceptional release approved by the responsible person within the tissue establishment and transplanting physician.

The composition of the batch processing record may include the quantity of raw materials, components and intermediate products, their batch/control number, the quantity of human tissues processed, the number of finished human tissues, results of in-process controls, microbiological test results, identity of the processing personnel, details of any non-conformity to processing specifications, copies of labels and final tissue identification numbers and, where relevant, processing and/or sterilisation records.

In exceptional clinical circumstances, the limited release of non-conforming human tissue may be authorised by the Director of the tissue establishment after hearing the opinion of the Medical Director/Consultant.[14]

[14] Given the urgent and life-saving/life-enhancing nature of transplantations, it is recognised that in exceptional circumstances, a human tissue may be needed for transplantation, and a compatible human tissue may be available, but has yet to be deemed safe for transplantation as required by the code of practice and the SOPs in force. For this reason, the code of practice and the SOPs should provide a mechanism, referred to as "exceptional distribution", to allow for the distribution of human tissues that may not meet all of the requirements of the code of practice when no fully compliant human tissue is available. The intent of a code of practice is to maximise the safety of human tissues used in transplantation, not to determine

A tissue establishment that distributes human tissues under special circumstances should keep a copy of the notice of exceptional distribution in its records. Simultaneously, the transplant establishment should keep a copy of the notice of exceptional distribution in its records. The notice of exceptional distribution of human tissues should include the following information:

- The name of the transplanted human tissue;
- The provisions of a code of practice used as reference for indicating that the human tissue is not in compliance at the time of its distribution;
- The justification for the distribution of the human tissues that formed the basis for the decision of the transplant physician, dentist, the Director of the tissue establishment or Medical Director/Consultant to authorise it;
- The name of the tissue establishment that distributed the human tissues;
- The name of the transplant establishment and of the transplant physician, the Director of the tissue establishment or Medical Director/Consultant or dentist who authorised the distribution; and
- The time and date of the written authorisation of the distribution and a copy of the authorisation signed by the transplant physician, the Director of the tissue establishment or Medical Director Consultant or dentist.

In the case of a tissue establishment, documentation of a notice of exceptional distribution of human tissues should be available in its records. Similarly, follow-up assessment and testing results of the donor are to be available in the tissue establishment's records.

---

the suitability of a human tissue for a specific recipient. For human tissues to be deemed "safe" under the code of practice and the SOPs, all of the requirements should have been met. However, there are special circumstances, such as using a hepatitis C positive human tissue in a hepatitis C positive recipient, where a human tissue may be suitable, even if under the code of practice this human tissue has not been deemed "safe". Other similar situations occur when, for example, not all the information from the donor screening questionnaire is available, but the use of the human tissue is acceptable given the direness of the intended recipient's situation. In these special situations, the suitability of a human tissue is a matter of clinical discretion and/or judgement. For this reason, exceptional distribution from a source tissue establishment requires that the transplant physician and the Director of the tissue establishment/Medical Director/Consultant authorise the use of the human tissue, and that the recipient give their informed consent for that use.

A tissue establishment that has not completed the donor suitability assessment, and distributes a human tissue under exceptional circumstances, should complete the assessment and carry out any other appropriate follow-up testing after distributing the human tissue. The tissue establishment should notify the relevant transplant establishment of the results of the donor suitability assessment.

Where such human tissue is released, the rationale and conditions should be agreed by the Director of the tissue establishment, the Advisory Board, and the clinician treating the intended recipient, and should be documented in accordance with a written procedure. In these circumstances, records should be maintained and be subject to regular inspection.

Human Tissue Distribution and Dispensing Restrictions

Provision of human tissues for transplantation should be restricted to hospitals, freestanding medical facilities, tissue establishments, tissue-dispensing services, research medical institutions, and end-users (e.g., physicians, dentists, podiatrists or other medical professionals). Distribution of human tissues for therapeutic use should be based on medical criteria on an equitable basis, in accordance with state and/or local laws and/or regulations and practice.[15]

---

[15] Some experts concurred that a fair human tissue distribution could only be achieved through the regulated implementation of transparent allocation criteria and prioritisation rules, which balance utility and equity considerations in the distribution process. However, it is important to stress that medical need is considered by many experts as the primary consideration in distributing human tissues, because donors generally give tissues with the intention to help others, but recognised that medical need is vague and context-dependent. Although distribution according to medical need would imply prioritising human tissues use for life-saving purposes over life-enhancing or cosmetic purposes, there are practical limitations in effectuating such prioritisation. There is a general agreement that discriminatory criteria in the distribution process, such as ethnicity and religion should be excluded (Schulz- Baldes, *et al.*, 2007).

The transfer of material from the tissue establishment to the recipient could be formalised by a Material Transfer Statement (MTS) and a Material Transfer Agreement (MTA) signed by both parties. These documents specify the terms in which samples have been procured and the conditions and obligations under which the recipient will be able to use them. The MTS and MTA free the tissue establishments from liability concerning the use of specimens and will also define the status of intellectual properties related to the obtained results and the right to file patent applications or register them (Ravid, 2008).

Quality control and fair allocation are essential elements in the distribution of human tissues. The following elements should be taken into account when a tissue establishment distributes human tissues for transplantation:

- When a tissue establishment distributes human tissues to a transplant organisation, the allocation of human tissues should be made fairly and impartially. Selection of a recipient should be done carefully based on demand;
- All tissue establishments should provide information to the transplant organisation about the criteria, methods used, and results of donor screening tests as well as the processing procedures of procured human tissues;
- All tissue establishments must maintain confidentiality and archive records of each donation and distribution. Samples of human tissues should be kept. Human tissue transplant records about the recipients and procedures in processing and preservation of the human tissues should be available;
- All transplant organisations should maintain a log of the adverse reaction of the recipients; and
- A system that provides traceability of records should be established.

There should be written SOPs and documentation for all human tissues distributed. The SOPs will describe final verification of release, distribution, procedures, documentation and the collection of tracking information for all human tissues distributed.

The clinical team using human tissues should have instructions for contacting the tissue establishment for any question they have and should be made aware of the following:

- Actions to be taken in the event of loss of integrity of the package;
- Actions for reporting of adverse event; and
- Actions for the return or the disposal of unsuitable or unused human tissues.

Transfer of Human Tissues to Other Establishments

When a tissue establishment forwards human tissues obtained from another tissue establishment, all accompanying original labelling materials or other enclosures should be forwarded with the human tissues.

Requests for Donor Status and Human Tissue Processing Information

Donor risk assessment, human tissue-related information, and human tissue processing details should be made available to the transplanting physician upon request, except such information that may infringe upon the confidentiality of donor information.

Discarding of Human Tissues

Special provisions should be made by the tissue establishment for the handling of human tissues to be discarded in order to prevent contamination of other human tissues, the processing environment or personnel. These provisions should conform to the state and/or local laws and/or regulations for discard of human tissues and the relevant guidance on the discard of clinical waste.

X. Process Control and Safety

All tissue establishments should identify and plan the processes that directly affect the quality of the human tissues and should ensure that these processes are carried out under controlled conditions. These conditions should include:

- Use of suitable processes, equipment, instruments and a suitable working environment;
- Compliance with reference standards and/or codes, quality manuals and/or documented procedures;
- Monitoring and control of suitable process parameters and human tissue characteristics;
- Approval of processes, equipment and instruments, as appropriate; and
- Proper servicing and maintenance of equipment and instruments.

A tissue establishment that has reasonable grounds to believe that the safety of human tissues for whose processing it is responsible has been compromised by the occurrence of an error or accident during processing, should immediately take the following actions:

- Quarantine any implicated human tissues in its possession;

- Send a notice to all of the following establishments:
  - If the human tissues were imported, the establishment that imported them;
  - Any source establishment from which it received the donor referral, if applicable;
  - Any source establishment to which it made a donor referral, if applicable; and
  - Any establishment to which it distributed implicated human tissues.
- Initiate an investigation into the suspected error or accident.

The notice should include the following information:

- The reasons for its belief that the safety of the human tissues has been compromised;
- An explanation of how the safety of the implicated human tissues may have been compromised, if known;
- The donor identification codes of all implicated human tissues;
- The name of any suspected transmissible disease or disease agent, if known; and
- A statement requiring all implicated human tissues to be quarantined immediately and until further notice from the tissue establishment and specifying any other corrective action that should be considered.

The requirements for any process operations, including related equipment, instruments and personnel, should be specified and records maintained. Each time a process is carried out, conformity with the documented procedures should be confirmed by using work sheets to note the performance of each critical step or data collection. Any deviation from the documented procedures should be specified and formally reviewed for possible effects on quality.

Process control procedures should be designed to ensure that human tissues have the identity, characteristics, and quality intended. The Director of the tissue establishment should review these procedures and should approve any changes that are needed to be introduced in these procedures.

Safety of Human Tissues

The safety of human tissues is of great concern for the protection of tissue establishment staff and researchers who come in contact with this type of tissues. Human fresh post-mortem tissues and fluids may contain highly infectious agents and have potential risks of diseases that are highly communicable to other humans. All human tissues should be treated as a potential risk for such transmission and handled carefully as certain extremely hazardous infectious agents (viruses and prions) are very stable. All tissue establishments should inform all human tissue recipients about the potential hazardous nature of the human tissues to be used for transplantation and ask the recipient to sign for handling all material with the necessary safety methods. The tissue establishment cannot be liable for any health risk/damage resulting from unsafe handling of the human tissues.

All human tissue recipients are responsible for returning unused human tissues to the tissue establishment and disposing residual human tissues according to local legal, ethical and safety rules for disposal of human remains.

Safety of Personnel

Personnel engaged in the retrieval, processing, preservation or packaging of human tissues should be suitably attired. Attire should include personal protection devices to minimise the spread of transmissible pathogens among and between donors, tissues, and staff.

Work Environment

Each tissue establishment should provide and promote a safe work environment by developing, implementing, and enforcing safety procedures. These procedures should be incorporated into the code of practice and SOPs in force or included in a specific safety manual which is referenced by the SOPs in force. The procedures should be written in accordance with applicable regulations in force. All safety procedures should be approved and reviewed annually by the Director of the tissue establishment.

Safety Procedures

Safety procedures should include, but are not limited to the following:

- Instructions for contacting emergency personnel and the establishment of evacuation routes and procedures in the case of fire or natural disaster;
- Procedures for management of tissue establishment staff injury, including possible exposure to hazardous materials or blood-borne pathogens. Such procedures should require a written report of the incident, including documentation of medical care received, management notification, and actions to prevent recurrence;
- Procedures specifying the proper storage, handling, and utilisation of hazardous materials, reagents and supplies; and
- Procedures outlining the steps to be followed by cleaning biohazardous spills.

Hazardous Materials Training

A training programme should be designed to inform tissue establishment staff about chemical, biological, and radioactive hazards of the workplace as well as the use of personal protective devices to reduce the risk of exposure to these hazards.

Immunisation

All tissue establishment staff potentially exposed to human tissues should be vaccinated against possible risks and regularly checked for the level of immunity.

Hepatitis B vaccination should be provided free of charge to all non-immune personnel whose job-related responsibilities involve the potential exposure to blood-borne pathogens. Personnel files should include documentation of receipt of vaccination or refusal of immunisation with hepatitis B vaccine and actions adopted in these cases.

Hazardous Waste Disposal

Biohazardous human tissues, medical waste, and other hazardous materials utilised should be disposed of in accordance with applicable state and/or local laws and/or regulations in such a way as to minimise environmental impact and exposure of personnel.

Medical waste or hazardous material tracking records should be kept in accordance with the rules of the regulatory authority charged with management oversight.

Infections

Any tissue establishment staff and members of the recovery team shown, either by medical examination or supervisory observation, to have a serious infectious condition (e.g., an apparent illness or open lesion) that may adversely affect the safety of the human tissues should be excluded from the retrieval, processing, preservation or packaging of human tissues until the condition is determined to be resolved. All tissue establishment staff and staff members of the recovery team should be instructed to report, to supervisory personnel, any health conditions that may cause an adverse effect on human tissues.

Validation of Special Processes

Protocols for the development or significant modification of human tissue processing operations or special processes must be documented and authorised by the Director of the tissue establishment.

The protocols should include provision for verification that the procedure meets the process specification and is compatible with the human tissue specification. Each critical step that may affect human tissue quality should be qualified and validated.

All tissue establishments should subject human tissues to effective validated processes (e.g., disinfection, sterilisation or controlled rate freezing). All the control parameters of the process should be recorded. These validation data should be recorded and a re-evaluation made of any changes to the process. Details of the physical control parameters should form part of the batch processing records for whatever method of disinfection/sterilisation used by the tissue establishment. Equipment for sterilisation should be provided with recording equipment or indicators.

Where the results of the processes cannot be fully verified by subsequent inspection and testing of the human tissue, the processes must be continually monitored to ensure that the specified requirements are met.

Quality records of special processes should identify the work instruction used, the date the special process was performed, and the identity of the tissue establishment operator.

Before special processes are implemented, they should be validated to demonstrate that the processes will consistently produce human tissues in accordance with the specifications. Documented procedures should identify the specific equipment used in processing (e.g., sterilisation, refrigeration, freezing and culturing). Special processes should undergo a regular critical appraisal to ensure that they remain capable of achieving the intended results.

Where validation is not performed, the rationale and authorisation must be recorded. Similar procedures should be followed where any significant change in human tissue processing occurs involving new or modified equipment, major overhauls or change of location.

XI. Import and Export of Human Tissues[16]

National competent health care authorities should take all necessary measures to ensure that all imports of human tissues from third countries are undertaken by tissue establishments duly accredited, designated, authorised or licensed for the purpose of those activities, and that imported human tissues can be traced from the donor to the recipient and vice-versa. All tissue establishments that receive such imports from third countries should ensure that they meet standards of quality and safety equivalent to the ones laid down in their code of practice in force.

National competent health care authorities should also take all necessary measures to ensure that all exports of human tissues to third countries are undertaken by tissue establishments duly accredited, designated, authorised or licensed for the purpose of those activities. Those countries that send such exports to third countries should ensure that the exports of human

[16]Unrelated hematopoietic progenitor cell donations in 2005, as reported in the WMDA tenth annual report (WMDA, 2006), showed that nearly 42% of donations provided came from international sources. In the WMDA report for 2008, a slight rise in the percentage of donations provided from international sources to 43.8% was registered. This international movement reflects the global collaboration required for finding donor matches for recipients. Recipients may receive treatment with human tissues in one continent, and subsequently receive further treatment in another.

tissues comply with the requirements of their code of practice in force. These requirements are the following:

- The import or export of human tissues should be authorised by the national competent health care authorities; and
- The national competent health care authorities should take all necessary measures to ensure that imports and exports of human tissues meet quality and safety standards equivalent to those laid down in the code of practice in force.

XII. Sterilisation and/or Disinfection of Human Tissues

Presently, there is no universal way to clean, disinfect, or sterilise all human tissues. Individual processing facilities should establish, validate, and document antibiotic regimens and microbial surveillance methods. The SOPs in force should establish a list of organisms which necessitate discard, sterilisation and/or disinfection, if detected in human tissues.[17] The following are considered to be pathogenic, highly virulent microorganisms the presence of which in human tissues results in their being discarded:

- Fungi (yeasts and moulds);
- Clostridium;
- *Streptococcus pyogenes* (group A strep.);
- *Staphylococcus aureus*; and
- Gram-negative bacilli.

Human tissue sterilisation should be documented in the processing record. This includes the method of sterilisation used, the processing parameters, and certification of sterilisation. The type of sterilisation method used should be indicated on the container label or package insert of all human tissues exposed to the method.

---

[17] Organisms of high pathogenicity are generally endogenous, arising from the donor's gastrointestinal tract or respiratory tract (Finegold, *et al.*, 1974). Clinically significant organisms are not reduced by simple antibiotic soaks (Hirn *et al.*, 2001). Therefore, the tissue industry relies on donor screening, which includes serologic testing for viruses, physical examination of the donor, and medical background review, as well as bacterial and fungal cultures, to accept or reject human tissues for transplantation.

The different techniques for disinfection and sterilisation of human tissues that can be used are described in the following paragraphs.

Sterilisation of Human Tissues by Irradiation

International standards have been established for the radiation sterilisation of health care products, which include medical devices, medicinal products (pharmaceuticals and biological agents) and *in vitro* diagnostic products. Following intensive studies of the effects of ionising radiation[18] on the chemical, physical, and biological properties of human tissues and their components carried out by experts from different countries, it can be stated that these tissues are now sterilised using a variety of ionising radiation methods and practices. Many countries all over the world are now using the ionising radiation technique for tissue sterilisation and the Radiation Sterilisation of Tissue Allografts. Requirements for Validation and Routine Control: A Code of Practice, adopted by the IAEA in 2007.

---

[18] Ionising radiation are high-energy electromagnetic waves (such as X-rays and gamma rays) and particles (such as alpha and beta particles, neutrons, protons, and heavy nuclei) that cause substances in their paths to dissociate into ions. The spatial distribution of the ionisation depends on the kind of radiation used, its penetrating power, the location of the source, and the nature of the irradiated material. High-energy X-rays penetrate deeply; most beta particles penetrate only a few millimetres; and alpha particles penetrate only a fraction of a millimetre. However, all three produce intense ionisation along their tracks. Ionising radiation directly affects living organisms by killing cells or retarding their development and by producing gene mutations and chromosome breaks. Tissues containing elements with relatively high atomic masses, such as calcium in bones and teeth, absorb much higher doses of ionising radiation than do soft human tissues.

From clinical practice, except in radiotherapy, where deterministic effects may arise, stochastic effects, and particularly cancer in the directly exposed population, are the principal adverse health effects of exposure to ionising radiation. In general, the radiation-associated excess relative risks among the Japanese atomic bomb survivors are greater than those among medically exposed individuals, although excess absolute risks can be higher in the medically exposed groups. There is no evidence of higher radiation-associated excess relative risk among those with cancer-prone disorders, although excess absolute risks can be higher in these cancer-prone groups. Risks among occupationally exposed groups such as nuclear workforces and underground miners are generally consistent with those observed in the Japanese atomic bomb survivors (Little, 2003).

The use of the ionising radiation for tissue sterilisation should be an integral part of the overall process for processing human tissues and rendering them safe for medical use. To achieve this objective, it is important to have in place good tissue banking practice that meet international standards. This good practice should be contained in a precise written form (SOPs), and should be strictly adhered to during normal day-to-day operations in the tissue establishment. The use of the ionising radiation technique for sterilisation purpose should be the final stage of a carefully detailed and documented sequence of procedures, involving: a) Donor selection; b) Tissue retrieval; and c) Tissue processing. The use of the ionising radiation technique for human tissue sterilisation purposes requires:

- The use of a nuclear institution with experience in the use of the ionising radiation technique for sterilisation purposes;
- Staff trained in the use of the ionising radiation technique for human tissue sterilisation; and
- Specific procedures to be put in place, which will be followed by the tissue establishment and by the nuclear institution in which the human tissue will be sterilised.

The nuclear institution used as sterilisation centre should help the medical device manufacturer with test irradiations for dose settings, materials compatibility studies, and bioburden studies. These tests typically require very precise dose delivery and very little dose variation over the product. In many cases, this excludes irradiation in the normal production containers. Samples like this typically require their own procedure for loading pattern definition and dose analysis. Prior to radiation sterilisation, the tissue must be maintained at a low temperature or must be frozen to prevent proliferation of microorganisms and to diminish the action of proteolytic enzymes, which degrade biologically important components of the human tissues, such as BMPs (bone morphogenetic proteins) and even collagen, a main constituent of connective tissue allografts.

The sterilisation of human tissues should be carried out in an appropriate facility normally located outside the tissue establishment. The responsibility of obtaining a sterilised human tissue is shared between the Director of the tissue establishment and the Manager of the nuclear facility acting as the sterilisation centre. The division of responsibilities should be agreed upon between these two parties. The tissue establishment's responsibilities include, among others, the following:

- Establishing a sterilisation dose;
- Establishing the maximum acceptable sterilisation dose that will not compromise the biological and biomechanical properties of the human tissue;
- Controlling the procurement and processing process of the human tissue to be sterilised, including meeting the specifications for the human tissue sent to the nuclear facility for sterilisation purpose (such as dimensions, packaging, etc.);
- Revising the specifications of the nuclear facility, which could affect the dose distribution or validity of the sterilisation process used (e.g., product packaging, materials, dose requirements, etc.);
- Changing the control of the human tissue, including a review of variables affecting radiation sterilisation; and
- Releasing the sterilised human tissue.

An acceptable sterilisation procedure for any type of human tissue depends on defining the most radiation-resistant microorganisms, which could be present in the human tissues and the density of each of them.[19]

[19]Standardised sterilisation procedures for musculoskeletal allografts are necessary to reduce the risk of allograft-associated infections. Validating the sterilisation of bone-tissue transplants with per-acetic acid–ethanol has showed that spores of *Bacillus subtilis* and *Clostridium sporogenes,* as well as enveloped and non-enveloped viruses were inactivated effectively. Only hepatitis A virus appeared to be resistant (Pruss *et al.*, 2003). It has been observed that there was no bacterial or viral infection with the use of allografts treated with peracetic acid–ethanol in approximately 100,000 transplantations (Pruss *et al.*, 2002a). Tissues that do not allow sufficient penetration of chemical sterilisation solutions (i.e., massive allografts) should be gamma-irradiated whenever possible; the minimal doses are 25 kGy for inactivation of non-viral microorganisms and 34 kGy for viral inactivation (Pruss, *et al.*, 2002b). For validation of the human tissue sterilisation process, the recommended reduction is 5 log colony-forming units per millilitre for bacterial spores and fungi, and 4 log tissue-culture infectious doses (50%) per millilitre for viruses. In addition, testing of the donors for viral markers and single polymerase-chain-reaction analysis for at least the human immunodeficiency virus, hepatitis C virus, and hepatitis B virus should be mandatory.

If the resistance and density of microorganisms are unknown and cannot be measured directly, the worst-case scenario should be assumed. In that case, it is recommended that the highest D_{10} value for the resistant microorganisms present in the human tissue be used for setting the sterilisation dose. However, this dose should not provoke physico-chemical changes in the human tissues or affect their biological properties, such as the osteoinductive capacity and the mechanical properties of bone, and other connective tissue allografts.[20]

A Sterility Assurance Level (SAL) should be selected and the sterilisation dose should be shown to be capable of achieving that SAL. Validation methods used may include, but are not limited to biological indicators, bioburden-based methods (e.g., AAMI/ISO 11137) or may be based on a group of pre-selected microorganisms. The type of irradiation used should be indicated on the container label or package insert of all human tissues exposed to irradiation.

The nuclear institution acting as sterilisation centre does not certify sterility; instead it certifies delivery of dose according to specification. It is only able to do this if:

- Monitoring and controlling of the process parameters function according to specification, and all equipment and instrumentation are calibrated;

[20]The following are possible effects of radiation on cells: a) Cells are undamaged by the dose. Ionisation may form chemically active substances, which in some cases alter the structure of the cells. These alterations may be the same as those changes that occur naturally in the cell and may have no negative effect; b) Cells are damaged, repair the damage and operate normally: Some ionising events produce substances not normally found in the cell. These can lead to a breakdown of the cell structure and its components. Cells can repair the damage, if it is limited. Even damage to the chromosomes is usually repaired. Many thousands of chromosome aberrations (changes) occur constantly in our bodies. Cells have effective mechanisms to repair these changes; c) Cells are damaged, repair the damage and operate abnormally: If a damaged cell needs to perform a function before it has had time to repair itself, it will either be unable to perform the repair function or perform the function incorrectly or incompletely. The result may be cells that cannot perform their normal functions or that now are damaging to other cells. These altered cells may be unable to reproduce themselves or may reproduce at an uncontrolled rate. Such cells can be the underlying causes of cancers; d) Cells die as a result of the damage: If a cell is extensively damaged by radiation, or damaged in such a way that reproduction is affected, the cell may die. Radiation damage to cells may depend on how sensitive the cells are to radiation.

- Changes to processing equipment are executed in compliance with the implementation procedures in force and their requalification is in compliance for the intended use after the change;
- The evaluation of dose mapping data and processing categories are performed by suitably trained and knowledgeable personnel;
- All personnel in the sterilisation centre are competent and aware of quality management procedures and do not try to bypass them for any reason; and
- All procedures, methods, measurements and results are recorded and retained.

It is important for the nuclear institutions acting as the sterilisation centre to insist that the medical device manufacturer coordinate any changes to the product specifications with the sterilisation centre. In the absence of such coordination, all effort on the part of the sterilisation centre to achieve the correct dose will be useless. Especially for electron beam sterilisation, a change in packaging will invalidate the dose map results of the product.

The management of the sterilisation centre must be committed to quality. It shall establish quality management objectives and procedures, and ensure that objectives are achieved. Resources should be provided, responsibilities and authorities shall be defined, documented, and communicated within the centre. Typically this means that a quality assurance manager is assigned who is responsible for implementation of and adherence to the procedures.

Competence and awareness can only be a result of training. All personnel shall be trained regularly (i.e., after changes and annually) on quality procedures. The work environment influences product safety. Hence, it is advisable to establish and implement procedures regarding cleanliness and clothing of workers, address worker safety, and define quarantine rules for product and sick personnel.

The use of the ionising radiation technique as a sterilising agent offers the following unique advantages:

- The ability to destroy contaminating microorganisms with an insignificant rise in the temperature of the irradiated materials, thereby preserving their main properties and characteristics, which could influence the required function of the human tissues;

- A reliable and safe sterilisation process with no residues or radioactivity in the radiated human tissues;
- Gamma radiation easily reaches all parts of the human tissue to be sterilised due to its high penetrating power. The items should be pre-packed in hermetically sealed packages, impermeable to microorganisms before sterilisation. Consequently, the sterile shelf-life of these human tissues is practically indefinite up to the point of use;
- The continuous nature of the process allows the mechanical and fully automated handling of the human tissues for treatment, thereby virtually eliminating the human factor in the process;
- At the sterilising dose usually applied, radiation causes no significant rise in temperature making it an ideal method for sterilising biological tissues and preparations of biological origin;
- The chemical reactivity of radiation is relatively low compared with the often highly reactive gases, which may even leave toxic residues hazardous to the patient (e.g., when ethylene oxide gas is used for sterilisation purposes). The possibility of inducing a disadvantageous chemical reaction is minimal with radiation;
- The sterilising effect of radiation is instantaneous and simultaneous in the whole of the human tissue, and there is no problem similar to convection of heat or diffusion of gas; and
- The process is simple, precise, easy to control and can be applied accurately to achieve sterility; only one process variable (exposure time or dose) needs to be controlled to achieve a SAL of 10^{-6}. In contrast, sterilisation by ethylene oxide gas needs seven variables (temperature, time, pressure, vacuum, gas concentration, packaging, and humidity), and steam sterilisation needs six variables (temperature, time, pressure, vacuum, packaging, and humidity) to be controlled.

The most common sources of ionising radiation are Cobalt 60, Caesium 130, electron beam, and X-ray. Identification of the irradiation source, the dosimetry, and completed certificate of irradiation should be documented in the processing record. The sterilisation dose used must be validated and supported by data.

Ethylene Oxide

Care should be taken when using ethylene oxide for sterilisation purposes since the residues may have toxic effects, particularly for musculoskeletal allografts.

Following appropriate processing procedures, the human tissues are placed in ethylene-oxide-permeable containers and exposed to the ethylene oxide gas mixture following the manufacturer's suggested guidelines. The conditions of exposure may need to be individualised depending upon the nature of the human tissue to be sterilised.

Following ethylene oxide sterilisation, an appropriate aeration procedure should be followed, to allow removal of residual ethylene oxide and/or its breakdown products (ethylene chlorohydrin and ethylene glycol). Chemical indicator strips should be included in each batch. A validated procedure should be run with each lot of human tissue to document that sterilisation has been achieved.

A quality-control programme should demonstrate that equipment meets requirements in temperature, humidity and gas concentration for the selected period. The results of the biological indicators should be included in the batch history records.

Monitoring for the residual levels of chemicals or their breakdown products should be conducted from representative samples of the finished human tissues of each batch.

Disinfection by Chemical Agents

Iodophors, ethanol and other solvent/detergent combinations may be used as disinfectants of human bones in a validated processing procedure. The following should not be used (except for ear drums and ear ossicles) as disinfectants of human bones: mercurial, quaternary compounds, formaldehyde, beta propiolactone, glutaraldehyde and chloroform. In any instance where a chemical disinfectant or antibiotic agent is used, the package insert should identify trace residuals that may be present. Two conditions influence the effectiveness of chemical disinfectants:

- Type of Microbe:
  - G+ more susceptible to disinfectants;
  - Pseudomonands can grow in disinfectants and antiseptics;

- *M. tuberculosis* is resistant to many disinfectants;
- Endospores are the most resistant to disinfectants;
- Environment.

- Organic matter and increased temperature.

Heat

It is the most frequent and widely used of the current physical methods of microbiological control. Heat is a highly efficient means of sterilisation so long as the material to be sterilised is resistant to heat. Different types of heat application include:

- Dry heat;
- Moist heat; and
- Pasteurisation.[21]

For the use of heat as a physical method of microbiological control it is important to always consider:

- Type of heat;
- Time of application (30 minutes); and
- Temperature (100°C).[22]

It is also important to know that endospores are the most heat-resistant of all cells.

To effect sterilisation, dry heat typically requires higher temperatures than moist heat. It is also less penetrating and requires longer exposure. Nevertheless, application of dry heat is cheap and easy. The length of exposure necessary is inversely proportional to the temperature (lower temperatures require longer exposures). Note additionally that the times given are for once the indicated temperature has been achieved. This is true for all methods of disinfection and sterilisation: the clock does not begin until the material has been exposed to the antimicrobial. Incineration

[21] Pasteurisation is the application of moist heat of less-than-boiling temperatures to foods to prevent the growth of food-spoiling organisms as well as various heat-labile pathogens.
[22] Keeping at this temperature for 30 minutes kills everything except some endospores.

is another common method of dry heat sterilisation, e.g., such as the flame incineration of an inoculating loop.

Moist heat is more effective than dry heat at a given temperature or length of exposure. Moist heat is also more penetrating than dry heat. However, to achieve sterilisation employing moist heat requires rather elaborate equipment, i.e., the employment of an autoclave.[23] Just as with dry heat, temperature and length of exposure are inversely related and penetration is absolutely critical. With moist heat, penetration is even more of a problem since penetration of heat without associated penetration of moisture is simply dry heat and dry heat is less effective as an antimicrobial than moist heat; consequently, things that block moisture penetration can inhibit sterilising efficacy. Boiling water is the most common form of application of moist heat, but is not capable of killing endospores or all viruses. It is important to note that there are rare types of bacteria, which are capable of growing at high temperatures. These bacteria are classified as thermophiles and hyperthemophiles. These bacteria normally grow in unusually hot environments, including hot springs and deep-sea vents and for this reason, sterilisation by heat may not be the most efficient method to eliminate these types of bacteria. However, they are almost never found in common environments.

Other Disinfection Agents

Other agents such as ultraviolet radiation[24] or exposure to antibiotics may be used as disinfection agents. Procedures for processing such agents

[23]An autoclave is a high-pressure device used to allow the application of moist heat above the normal-atmosphere boiling point of water. Exposure to 121°C for more than 15 minutes is typically sufficient to sterilise. Again, the material must be 121°C before the clock starts. Large items, large volumes, and items that are poorly penetrated by steam may take much longer than 15 minutes to sterilise.

[24]The most lethal type of radiation is ultraviolet (UV) radiation with a wavelength of 260 nm. This is the wavelength most actively absorbed by DNA. Unfortunately, this type of radiation does not penetrate dirt, glass, water, or other substances. If a surface is dusty, then complete inactivation of all microorganisms may not occur. This type of radiation is also harmful if someone is directly exposed to it, as it may damage the skin and eyes. Due to its poor penetration, UV radiation is only useful for disinfecting outer surfaces.

should be documented and validated to ensure consistency in human tissue processing.

XIII. Storage and Quarantine of Human Tissues

Storage of Human Tissues

A maximum storage period should be determined for each type of human tissue to ensure their integrity, functionality, and sterility is maintained throughout their shelf life.[25] Factors that should be considered when establishing the expiration date for each type of human tissue include the following, as applicable:

- Method of preservation (e.g., cryopreservation, lyophilisation or dehydration) used[26];
- Storage conditions (e.g., room temperature, refrigeration and freezing);
- Packaging (e.g., ability to maintain sterility and moisture content); and
- Designated storage areas or stockrooms should be used in order to prevent damage and minimise deterioration of human tissue prior to its dispatch for clinical use.

Tissues for autologous use should be segregated from tissues for allogeneic use during storage to prevent the unintended distribution or release of autologous tissues for allogeneic use. Segregation also helps to increase the likelihood that autologous tissues receive the special handling and tracking they require, as tissues for autologous use may not have been processed according to the same standards as tissues intended for allogeneic use.

[25]The maximum storage period is considered scientifically based if it meets one or more of the following criteria: a) The storage period for specific storage conditions has been established in standards developed by recognised professional organisations, based on established practice; b) Data is available in the scientific literature to support the storage period for the specific storage conditions; and c) The storage period for the specific storage conditions has been validated by the tissue establishment.

[26]Currently accepted methods of tissue preservation include: Tissue and cell culture; hypothermic storage (refrigeration) above 0°C, but below +10°C; freezing at –40°C or below, with or without the use of cryoprotectants; freeze-drying; other dehydration methods.

Autologous tissues should be clearly labelled as such and stored separately in restricted areas, which ensures their segregation from allogeneic tissues.

Segregation may be achieved most effectively by storing allogeneic and autologous tissues in different storage equipment. If autologous and allogeneic tissues are to be stored in the same storage equipment, the storage areas for each within the storage unit should be physically separated and clearly labelled as such, in order to allow tissues intended for autologous use to be distinguished from tissues that are for allogeneic use.

Appropriate methods for authorised receipt to, and dispatch from designated storage areas or stockrooms should be specified in the documented procedures.[27]

Conditions of storage and transport should not compromise the quality of the human tissues. Equipment for the storage and transport of human tissues should be suitable for the intended use. Procedures for monitoring should be validated so that human tissue meets the specified requirements. If special storage conditions are required at any stage, these should be controlled and monitored. Human tissues ready for clinical use should be stored and issued according to documented procedures. Records should be maintained for stock reconciliation. Human tissues that have been rejected, recalled or returned should be accepted by the Quality Assurance Officer who will ensure that they are identified, recorded, and placed in separate quarantine areas.

All tissue establishments that store human tissues should ensure that any of them that are untested or for which the results of tests on donor blood samples are positive or reactive for transmissible disease agents or markers or are unavailable are segregated from all other human tissues. This means that:

- Human tissues that are untested or that are quarantined prior to the completion of testing for transmissible disease agents or markers should be stored separately;

[27] Hospitals involved in the storage of human tissues and cells (current guidance suggests 36 hours or longer) or their distribution are responsible for compliance with a code of practice adopted by the tissue establishment. This responsibility extends to the establishment of record-keeping and storage procedures to ensure the traceability of human tissues and recipients. Reports of any adverse reactions, including transmitted disease or other quality-related complications or non-compliances, should be evaluated by the hospital and reported to the tissue establishment. Hospitals should also have a documented policy for the disposal of used or unsuitable clinical materials.

- Human tissues that are found to be unsuitable for use, are unsafe, are recalled and/or tested positive or reactive for transmissible disease agents or markers should be stored separately; and
- Human tissues that have been tested and are suitable for release/distribution or use should be stored separately.

The actions taken and the final status related to each human tissue should be recorded.

Any human tissue returned to the tissue establishment should be treated as non-conforming tissue until it has satisfied a documented acceptance procedure.

Storage Temperatures

Each tissue establishment should establish acceptable temperature-range limits for the storage of human tissues at each phase of the operation, in accordance with the SOPs in force and other applicable state and/or local laws and/or regulations.

Table 4: Storage conditions for human tissues

Human tissues	Storage conditions	Temperature (°C)
Skin	Refrigerated	Between 0°C and 10°C
	Frozen, cryopreserved	–40°C or colder
	Lyophilised	Ambient[1]
Musculoskeletal	Refrigerated	Between 0°C and 10°C
	Frozen, cryopreserved and non-cryopreserved (temporary storage less than 6 months)	Between –20°C to –40°C
	Frozen, cryopreserved and non-cryopreserved (long-term storage)	–40°C or colder
	Lyophilised	Ambient[1]
Duramater	Lyophilised	Ambient[1]
Cardiovascular	Frozen, cryopreserved	–100°C or colder

Note: 1 Ambient temperature monitoring not required for lyophilised tissues.

Storage temperatures and conditions should be the same for comparable human tissues. Any exception should require written approval of the Director of the tissue establishment. The above table (AATB, 2012) could be used as reference for the establishment of storage temperatures.

Monitoring Storage Temperatures

A temperature storage monitoring system should be utilised to document temperatures and to alert tissue establishment staff when temperatures have strayed outside acceptable limits. It is recommended that low-temperature (refrigerated or frozen) storage devices and incubators should be connected to a central alarm system or each should be equipped with an audible alarm system that will sound when the temperature deviates from the acceptable storage range. The alarm system should be connected to an emergency power source. Continuous recording and daily review of temperature data are recommended.

Procedures should be in place for reviewing temperature data. Documentation of such review should be indicated with the reviewer's initials and the date. If temperature recording charts are used, they should be initialled and dated when placed on and removed from the storage unit. If storage utilises liquid nitrogen, its levels of temperature should be monitored and documented at an interval specified in the SOPs in force.

Tissue establishments should provide specific instructions on corrective actions to be taken when temperatures fall outside the established temperature limits.

Storage of Unprocessed, Frozen and Cryopreserved Human Tissues

Procedures for storing human tissues that have not been processed or preserved, and frozen and cryopreserved human tissues to ensure graft safety and function should be written.

Unprocessed human tissues (e.g., small fragments of particular cartilage and skin) may be aseptically procured in an operating room and refrigerated at 4°C or in accordance with written procedures. Unprocessed human tissues should not be used in a patient until donor blood testing is completed according to the code of practice and SOPs in force, available bacteriologic results are acceptable, and donor suitability has been approved by the Director of the tissue establishment.

After aseptic procurement in the operating room, processed frozen or cryopreserved musculoskeletal human tissues should be stored at temperatures of –40°C or colder within 24 hours of procurement. Temporary storage of processed frozen or cryopreserved musculoskeletal human tissues between –20°C and –40°C is limited to 6 months total, and human tissues stored at this temperature range should then be transferred to –40°C or colder, used or discarded.

Frozen or cryopreserved human skin should be stored at ultra-low (–40°C or colder) temperatures. A cryopreservative solution (e.g., DMSO or glycerol) is usually added to treat the human tissue prior to freezing. Documentation of the concentration of cryoprotectants and nutrients or isotonic solutions in the cryopreservative solution should be maintained.

Properly packaged specimens are frozen by placing the specimens below –40°C or may be subjected to control rate freezing using a computer-assisted liquid nitrogen freezing device.

If a programmed control-rate freezing method is used, a record of the freezing profile should be evaluated, approved, and recorded.

Expiration dates of frozen and frozen cryopreserved human tissues should not exceed 5 years from the date of processing, unless a longer expiration date has been validated and approved by the Director of the tissue establishment after consulting the Advisory Board.

Storage of Lyophilised or Dehydrated Human Tissues

Lyophilised or dehydrated human tissues should be stored at ambient temperature or lower. The use of simple dehydration (evaporation) of human tissues as a means of preservation should be controlled in a manner similar to that for freeze-drying. Temperatures of simple dehydration should be below 60°C. Each dehydration cycle should be monitored for temperature during operation. Following dehydration, representative samples should be tested for residual moisture.

Expiration dates of lyophilised or dehydrated human tissues should not exceed 5 years from the date of processing, unless a longer expiry date has been validated and approved by the Director of the tissue establishment after consulting the Advisory Board.

Storage of Refrigerated Human Tissues

Procedures for storing refrigerated musculoskeletal human tissues to assure tissue viability should be written. Refrigerated musculoskeletal human tissues should be retrieved aseptically and placed in an isotonic or nutrient medium with suitable antibiotics between 0°C and 10°C. If any additional processing of refrigerated musculoskeletal human tissues is necessary, the total wet ice/refrigeration time should be no longer than 5 days from retrieval. Refrigerated human skin should be stored between 0°C and 10°C in a refrigeration system that is monitored, with a permanent record made of the temperature.

Storage Temperature Records

Documentation that the human tissues were continuously maintained at the required storage temperatures should be maintained. Refrigerated skin may be returned to the inventory, if it has been maintained between 0°C and 10°C in a closed container.

Storage of Frozen and Cryopreserved Human Tissues

The expiration time of refrigerated musculoskeletal human tissues should be 5 days from the date of recovery or as established in the SOPs in force, using a validated method for determining expiration dating. Human skin should be stored refrigerated for no longer than 14 days.

Emergency Transfers

Policies and procedures should be developed for the emergency transfer of human tissues to an alternative designated storage facility and for alternative monitoring methods in the event of mechanical failure or loss of coolant. These should include specification of tolerance limits or temperatures and time limits after which the initiation of the emergency transfer is required. Actions to be taken when limits have been exceeded should also be specified in the SOPs in force.

Storage of Food and/or Liquids for Human Consumption

Mechanical storage appliances used for storing human tissues, reagents, media, refrigerants or other laboratory solutions should not be utilised for the storage of food and/or liquids for human consumption and should be marked accordingly.

Storage Expiration Date/Storage Period

The maximum storage period for a group of human tissues should be appropriate to the type of human tissues, its packaging and processing, as well as to its intended application. Expiration dates should be qualified to demonstrate that the packaging is suitable to maintain product integrity (e.g., sterility, moisture content, etc.) for the entire shelf life. The implanting physician should be informed of any expiration dates related to the human tissues that are going to be transplanted.

Each tissue establishment should determine a maximum storage period allowable for grafts to be distributed. Limitations imposed by packaging or by anticipating untoward effects of long-term storage on human tissue characteristics related to function, should be taken into account.

Storage of Human Tissues Whose Test Results are Positive

Autologous tissues, for which a donor sample tests positive or reactive for infectious diseases, should be appropriately segregated during storage. The Director of the tissue establishment must establish procedures for storage of human tissues from donors whose test results are positive or repeatedly reactive.

Human Tissues in Transit Storage Environment

Maintenance of defined environmental conditions during transit of human tissues should be required. Specific environmental conditions should be in accordance with the SOPs in force, and applied state and/or local laws and/or regulations.

Stock Rotation

Reagents and supplies with expiration dates or production dates should be stored in a manner to facilitate inventory rotation. Supply and reagent inventories not bearing expiration or production dates should be labelled with the date of acquisition and stored in a manner as to facilitate inventory rotation. Older reagents and supplies should be used first.

Expired reagents and supplies should not be used for human tissues intended for transplantation. Reagents should be stored in accordance with the manufacturer's instructions.

Quarantine of Human Tissues

Quarantine process segregates human tissues that have not met the screening and testing requirements from those that have, and prevents them from being used in transplantation or distributed for research or other purposes. In addition, human tissues that are implicated in any error, accident or adverse reaction investigation should also be quarantined until the results of the investigation have determined that the human tissues are safe for transplantation or can be used for other medical purposes or should be disposed.

In cases where human tissues donated by living donors is going to be stored, the human tissues should be held in quarantine for at least 180 days, at which time the donors should be retested for the following infectious disease markers before the tissues are released:

- Anti-HIV-1 and anti-HIV-2;
- Anti-HBc, IgG, and IgM;
- Antibodies to hepatitis C virus (anti-HCV); and
- Anti-HTLV-I and anti-HTLV-II for viable, leukocyte-rich tissues.[28]

In the case of fetal or infant donors, surrogate testing may be required after the donated human tissues have been quarantined for at least 180

[28] Human tissues that are not considered leukocyte-rich include, among others, bone, cartilage, corneas, ligaments, sclera, skin, and tendons.

days. This means that testing should be done using a specimen obtained from the birth mother instead of the foetal or infant donor. Since surrogate testing is intended to address vertical transmission of infectious agents from the birth mother to a donor who is less than 18 months or who donated human tissues within the 12 months beyond breastfeeding, the need for surrogate testing will be determined by the age of the donor at the time of donation. For example, if a donor was 2 months at the time of donation, surrogate testing will be required after the 180 day quarantine period, because the donor will still be less than 18 months. However, if the donor is 14 months at the time of donation, surrogate testing will not be required after the 180 day quarantine period, because the donor will no longer be less than 18 months.

If the initial testing performed on the living donor blood specimen included NAT for HIV-1 and HCV, 180 day quarantine and testing of a repeat blood sample is not required.

Quarantine Storage Areas

Quarantine human tissue storage areas, including storage areas within freezers, refrigerators or other human tissue storage units, should be physically separated and clearly labelled to distinguish quarantine human tissues from human tissues not suitable for transplant and from human tissues available for distribution.

Situations Requiring Quarantine

Human tissues should be quarantined until they are either determined to be suitable for transplantation or appropriately categorised. All human tissues should be quarantined until the following criteria for donor suitability are satisfied:

- All required infectious disease testing has been completed, reviewed by the Medical Director/Consultant, and found to be negative or non-reactive; and
- Donor screening has been completed, reviewed by the Medical Director/Consultant, and determined to indicate freedom from risk factors for and clinical evidence of HIV, hepatitis B, and/or hepatitis C infection.

Human tissues of donors known to be reactive on tests for anti-HIV-1, anti-HIV-2, anti-HTLV-I, anti-HTLV-II, anti-HCV or HBsAg should be stored in a physically separated area clearly identified from human tissues of seronegative donors.

The release of such human tissues should require the informed consent of the recipient and the treating physician as well as the approval of the Director and Medical Director/ Consultant of the tissue establishment.

Human tissues should be quarantined at any phase of the operation when its release could affect its safety, effectiveness or quality, and subsequently, the health of the recipient. The following human tissues should be quarantined:

- Retrieved human tissues that are pending completion of processing, packaging, preservation or labelling, and final-release-approval signature;
- Human tissues retrieved from donors not meeting established donor suitability criteria, including unacceptable test results;
- Human tissues involved in a recall pending investigation, documentation, and resolution;
- Human tissues failing to meet technical or quality assurance specifications;
- Human tissues pending discard as medical waste; and
- Human tissues returned by a consignee, pending evaluation.

Labelling Quarantined Human Tissues

All human tissues processed or shipped prior to determination of donor suitability should be under quarantine.

Such tissues should be accompanied by records assuring identification of the donor and indicating that the human tissues have not been determined to be suitable for transplantation. Human tissues determined to be unsuitable for transplantation and intended for release for other purposes should be identified accordingly.

Quarantine Records

Quarantine records for human tissues quarantined post-release should indicate the reason for quarantine and the final outcome of the human tissues. Release dates or disposal dates should be indicated as well.

XIV. Packaging, Labelling and Transportation

Package Insert

Human tissues deemed suitable for transplantation should be accompanied by a summary of records documenting the fact that all required disease screenings and testing has been completed, specifying that the results have been reviewed and accepted by the person responsible. A package insert containing instructions for proper storage and thawing, where appropriate, should accompany all human tissues, covering graft preparation, handling and reconstitution where appropriate. Specific instructions should be enclosed for material requiring special handling.

Package Insert Requirements

Inserts should contain the following information, if applicable:

- A statement limiting use to specific health professionals;
- A statement that the human tissues is intended for use in one patient on a single occasion only;
- Indications and contraindications for use of the human tissues;
- Appropriate warnings and a list of possible significant adverse reactions;
- Instructions for opening the package and/or container, and for reconstitution;
- The expiry time, if applicable, of human tissues following reconstitution;
- Instructions for preparation of human tissues for transplantation;
- A statement that the human tissue was prepared from a donor who was non-reactive or acceptable when tested for the mandated microbiological tests, verifying that appropriate and licensed tests were used;
- A statement for non-sterilised material: "This human tissue may transmit infectious agents";
- A statement, if applicable, that the human tissues may not be sterilised or re-sterilised;
- Recommended storage conditions for the human tissues;
- A statement that it is the responsibility of the end user to maintain the human tissues in appropriate storage conditions prior to transplantation;
- Special instructions for each particular human tissue, for example, "do not freeze";

- The presence of known sensitising substances in the human tissues;
- The type and calculated amounts of antibiotics and preservatives added during processing;
- A statement that adverse reactions potentially attributable to the human tissues should be reported promptly to the tissue establishment; and
- A statement that it is the responsibility of the recipient hospital or other material storage and distribution facility or clinician, to maintain recipient records for tissue tracking post-transplantation.

Packing

Packaging and marking processes, including materials used, should conform to the specified requirements.

All tissue establishments should ensure that the packaging materials used are capable of maintaining the integrity of the human tissue. The documented evidence should be available upon request. Only packaging materials assessed and released by the Quality Assurance Officer or by a designated alternate should be used in the packaging of the human tissue. Materials that are outdated or rejected should be adequately segregated until their disposal, which should be recorded. All packaging materials must be visually examined for damage before being used.

Upon receipt, all packaging materials should be examined and/or tested as required against the specifications described on the certificate of analysis, the packaging documents or the manufacturer's instructions, as appropriate.

Packaging procedures should be established and maintained by the tissue establishment to ensure that:

- The human tissue is presented in a container designed to maintain quality and prevent contamination;
- The human tissue is capable of being presented in an aseptic manner, if its use so requires;
- The package clearly reveals whether it has been opened;
- The tissue establishment records the identity of persons who perform the final labelling operation; and
- The suitability of packaging and labels for transport and storage has been validated.

Labelling

There shall be written procedures designed and followed to ensure that correct labels, labelling and packaging materials are used. Each labelling phase for all human tissues should be documented. Material should be labelled for identification and tracking during all phases of procurement, processing, preservation and distribution of the human tissues. Use of a unique donor identification number should be incorporated into the tissue identification label to facilitate donor recipient tracking. Labelling should be clear, legible and indelible. For autologous or directed donations, the name and/or identifier of the intended recipient, if known, should be included. Unit labels and/or package inserts should be labelled with:

- The full name of the tissue establishment(s), responsible for determining donor suitability, processing and distribution as relevant, and the address of the establishment determining donor suitability;
- A description of the contents, including size, number and amount or volume of human tissues;
- A batch/lot/serial number or human tissue identification number;
- The date of donation;
- Advice on handling and any hazards that might occur in use;
- Sterilisation or inactivation procedure used, if applicable;
- Preservative and/or method of preservation used and its concentration, if applicable;
- Potential residuals of added processing agents/solutions;
- Results of screening tests performed and labelled with the warning: "This product may transmit infectious agents";
- Directions for opening and aseptic presentation, where necessary;
- An expiry date for human tissues that have a determined shelf life;
- A statement that each package is for single patient use only;
- Directed tissues intended for autologous use should be prominently labelled "For autologous use only" and the donor/recipient's name identification provided;
- Each human tissue intended for direct allogeneic use should be prominently labelled "For use by intended recipient only" and the recipient's identification provided; and
- Any necessary instructions for storage.

The tissue label applied by the tissue establishment should not be removed, altered or obscured. Where it is impractical to label the unit container with this information, it should be included in the package insert.

However, all unit labels should at least include a description of the contents, (including size, number or volume, where relevant), the full name and address of the tissue establishment, a batch/lot/serial number and an expiry date for finished human tissues that have a determined shelf life. Accompanying documentation should contain all the information described for container labelling and the following additional information:

- Origin of human tissue (country of procurement);
- The nature and results of biological tests performed on the donor using appropriate and licensed tests;
- Processing methods used and results of sterility tests or inactivation controls;
- Special instructions indicated by the particular human tissue for storage or implantation. Human tissue that is to be reconstituted at or prior to the time of use, should include information on the conditions, under which such human tissue should be stored and reconstituted prior to implantation;
- Indications and contraindications for the use of each human tissue, when necessary; and
- A statement that each human tissue should be used for a single patient only.

Integrity and Sterility of the Containers

Packaging should be designed to ensure tissue integrity and prevent contamination of the contents of the final end-user. The packaging materials should also be compatible with the characteristics of the human tissue in order to prevent any interactions, which may cause the package to degrade or chemicals from the packaging to be absorbed by the human tissue. Sterilised containers should be handled in a manner to preclude contamination.

Visual Inspection of the Containers

Each container should be examined visually for damage, impurities, defects, broken seals or evidence of contamination, which could compromise the quality, integrity or safety of the human tissues prior to use and immediately after filling.

When a visual inspection through the container is possible, a sufficient area of the container should remain uncovered to permit inspection of the contents.

Containers not meeting specifications should not be used for the transportation of human tissues.

Physical Properties of the Containers

The container should maintain its integrity, withstand sterilisation and storage conditions, not produce toxic residues during storage, and maintain human tissue integrity and quality for the labelled shelf life.

The type of human tissue container may vary with the type of human tissue and processing methods used. They should maintain the human tissue sterility and integrity, withstand the sterilisation and storage methods utilised and avoid the production of toxic residues. They should conform to applicable state and/or local laws and/or regulations.

Each human tissue container should be examined visually for damage or evidence of contamination before and after processing and prior to its dispatch.

Containers should not interfere with the effective use of appropriate agents applied to sterilise or disinfect the human tissues.

Final packaging containers should be adequate for use at defined storage temperatures and documented to remain stable and impervious to microbial particles under normal environmental conditions at the specified temperature and throughout the recommended thawing regimen.

Validation and Expiration of the Container

If human tissues to be shipped require specific environmental conditions other than ambient temperature, the capability of the transport container to maintain the required environmental conditions should be demonstrated and documented in a validation study.

The length of time that these conditions can be maintained by the transport container, assuming normal handling, should also be determined and documented. Expiration dates of the transport container should be noted on the outside of the transport container.

Residual Levels in Packaging

If ethylene oxide is used for sterilisation, processing or packaging of components that come in contact with the human tissue (e.g., disinfection jars or packaging pouches), residues of ethylene oxide, ethylene glycol, and ethylene chlorohydrin should be evaluated.

Final Inspection

All packages should be subjected to a final inspection to ensure that the containers are intact, the labels are accurate, the package insert is present, and the final package is appropriate for the type and requirements of the human tissue being shipped.

The exterior of the transport container should be inspected to verify that the name, address and telephone number of the distributing facility and the name and telephone number of the end-user are present. Verification of any hazardous materials, type of refrigerant used, transport (shipping) expiration date if applicable, and prominent identification as human tissue, should be clearly visible. These inspections should be documented, including identification of staff conducting the inspections.

Transportation

The mode of transportation selected should be determined by any special shipping and handling requirements of the human tissues and/or shipping refrigerants, by shipping restrictions of commercial carriers, and the urgency of the request for human tissues.[29]

Transport and Delivery

All tissue establishments must arrange for the protection of the quality of human tissues after the final inspection and test have been carried out.

[29]To manage the huge amount of samples and share them with research centres worldwide, all tissue establishments need to have safe and transparent protocols for shipment as well as proper accompanying documentation for the handling and management of these precious and sensitive specimens (Ravid, 2008).

Where contractually specified, this should be extended to include delivery to the destination. The name and address of the shipping package consignee should be included in the quality records. All tissue establishments should document its policy for the acceptance or rejection of unused human tissues returned to the tissue establishment. Users should be clearly informed of this policy. All tissue establishments should require that any recognised intermediary maintains records of distribution available for inspection.

Quality Control of Environmental Conditions

If human tissues to be shipped require specific environmental conditions other than ambient temperature, quality control monitoring of the shipping packaging must be performed according to the SOPs in force to verify maintenance of the required environmental conditions. These quality control checks should be documented.

Quarantine

Human tissues should be stored under quarantine until the tissues are determined to be suitable for transplantation. All human tissues should be under quarantine until donor screening tests have been completed and reviewed by the person responsible within the tissue establishment and found to be acceptable. Materials known to be or suspected of being infected should preferably be stored in separate refrigerators or freezers or in liquid nitrogen containers.

Receipt of New Shipments

Containers should be stored under quarantine until the containers have been tested, sampled or examined, as appropriate, and released for use.

XV. Monitoring Systems

Audits

Audits are vital aspects of tissue banking to take stock, ensure that quality processes are being implemented and documents are being appropriately maintained, identify areas for potential growth, and address recurring problems. All stages of human tissue — recovery or collection, processing, sterilisation, preservation, packaging, storage, distribution and transplantation — should be audited.

An optimal audit is one that is routinely performed on-site by individuals qualified to evaluate acceptable adherence to the code of practice and SOPs in force and includes, but is not limited to, verifying that:

- All documentation relating to a donor is complete and initialed by the individuals completing the forms;
- Equipment has undergone performance validation and is being used correctly;
- Recoveries are performed in a clean or aseptic environment;
- Serological tests are performed with licensed tests and licensed test kits approved for deceased persons testing, when available;
- Precautions are taken to prevent pooling of human tissue from multiple donors or cross-contamination between donors during recovery and transportation to the processor;
- Tissue establishment staff receives orientation and continuing education regarding the SOPs in force, technical training, quality-control protocol training, and computer training;
- Human tissue is packaged and shipped according to the criteria stated in the SOPs in force; and
- Human tissue that has been released for clinical use is being stored and tracked according to the SOPs in force.

Internal audits should be conducted by the Quality Assurance Officer or qualified personnel that do not have direct responsibility for the processes being audited. Focused audits should be conducted to monitor controlled access areas and when problems with quality have been identified.

The planning, implementation and monitoring of internal quality audits should be performed according to documented procedures.

National competent health care authorities should organise on a regular basis external audit and the Director of the tissue establishment should also carry out appropriate internal audits in order to ensure compliance with the requirements included in the code of practice in force.

National competent health care authorities should also ensure that appropriate internal control measures are in place for the procurement of human tissues. External and internal audits should be organised and control measures should be carried out by the national competent health care authorities and the Quality Assurance Officer on a regular basis. The interval between two external audits shall not exceed two years. Such external audits should be carried out by officials representing the national competent health care authority. These officers should be empowered:

- To audit tissue establishment and other related facilities; and
- To evaluate and verify the procedures and activities carried out in the tissue establishment and other related facilities;

Audits should include examination of all records and processes, and their compliance with the SOPs in force. Audit reports should contain all the observations made during the inspection along with the dates and, where applicable, recommendations for corrective measures within specified time frames. Statements about the actions that are subsequently taken should also be recorded along with the dates by the tissue establishment staff responsible for the systems audited, and these must be reviewed by the Director of the tissue establishment. The results with dates of re-audits must be documented.

The type and frequency of adverse incidents, complaints and the effectiveness of corrective and preventive actions must be reviewed by the Director of the tissue establishment to ensure that the quality system is effective and suitable. The national competent health care authorities and the Director of the tissue establishment should organise audits and adopt additional internal control measures as appropriate whenever there is any serious adverse reaction or serious adverse event detected or reported.

Corrective and Preventive Actions

In the event of a non-conformance, corrective actions should include a review of the causes of the non-conformance and development of established procedures to prevent recurrence.

All corrective and preventive actions should be recorded in existing SOPs in force and implemented. The procedures for corrective actions must cover:

- Effective handling of reported adverse incidents and reports of other non-conformities;
- Investigation of the cause of non-conformities relating to human tissues, processes and the quality system;
- Reviewing and recording the results of the investigation;
- Specification of the corrective actions to eliminate the cause of the non-conformities; and
- Application of controls to ensure that corrective actions are taken and are effective.

Non-conforming Human Tissues

To prevent the unintended use of non-conforming human tissues, documented procedures should be established and monitored to provide for identification, evaluation, segregation, disposal of non-conforming human tissues and notification of the Quality Assurance and Processing Officers in the tissue establishment.

The responsibility for the review and approval for the distribution of non-conforming human tissues for research purposes should be defined and reviewed in accordance with documented procedures. Non-conforming human tissues may be:

- Accepted with or without reprocessing;
- Regraded for alternative applications;
- Rejected or disposed of as clinical waste; and
- Reprocessed to meet the specified requirements.

The reprocessing of non-conforming human tissues should be exceptional. It should only be allowed if the final quality is not affected, if specifications are met, if it is done in accordance with authorised procedure, and after a risk assessment. Records must be kept of the reprocessing of such type of human tissue.

Complaints

All feedback information, including reported complaints and details of returned human tissues must be documented, investigated, analysed, collated and communicated in accordance with defined procedures by a designated person within the tissue establishment. Complaints should be classified according to whether they have deviated from the SOPs in force or prevailing laws and regulations (error) or whether they entail occurrences outside the scope of the SOPs in force (accident) or whether they involve an unintended and undesirable response after transplantation in the recipient (adverse event). If the error or accident has medical consequences or will affect the safe use of the human tissue, the Medical Director/Consultant should review and evaluate the incident and recommend actions. If associated human tissue may be affected, such associated tissue should be located and quarantined until the incident is resolved. If necessary, actions may involve a recall of human tissues already distributed.

If it is deemed unnecessary for any complaint to be followed by corrective actions, the reasons and the name of the individual responsible for the decision should be recorded. When the investigation determines that activities at other premises or third parties played a part in the complaint, a summary of the original complaint and the copy of the outcome report should be sent to those premises. Consideration should be given to amending the agreement or contract as necessary.

When an investigation is made, a record of the investigation should include at least:

- The date the complaint was received;
- The name and unique identifier of the human tissue;
- The name and contact details of the complainant;
- The nature and details of the complaint;
- The details of the investigation with the dates and results;
- The corrective actions taken; and
- The communication with the complainant.

Adverse Events

National competent health care authorities should ensure that all tissue establishments have in place a system to report, investigate, register and transmit information about serious adverse events and reactions, which may influence the quality and safety of human tissues and which may be attributed to the procurement, testing, processing, storage, and distribution of these tissues, as well as any serious adverse reaction observed during or after clinical application, which may be linked to the quality and safety of the human tissues distributed by the tissue establishment.

All hospitals and other medical facilities using human tissues should report any relevant information on tissue establishment engaged in the donation, procurement, testing, processing, storage, and distribution of human tissues in order to facilitate traceability and ensure quality and safety control. Reports of adverse events should be evaluated by the institution where the human tissue was used and reported immediately to the tissue establishment.

All adverse events should be reviewed by the Medical Director/Consultant of the tissue establishment who should determine the impact and the manner of resolution of these adverse events. The Director of the tissue establishment should take responsibility for the implementation of the appropriate actions, in accordance with state and/or local laws and/or regulations. All actions taken should be documented. If the investigation indicates that an adverse event was the result of an error or accident, procedures for errors and accidents must be followed.

When donor-to-recipient disease transmission through human tissues use is discovered, all facilities involved in the procurement and distribution of the human tissues from the infected donor should be notified without delay in accordance with state and/or local laws and/or regulations on confidentiality. Those notified include, but are not restricted to, the national competent health care authorities, organ procurement organisations and tissue establishments, retrieval centres, distribution centres and the transplantation physician(s). If clinically relevant, the physician must be informed.

Written reports of the investigation of adverse events, including conclusions, follow-up and corrective actions should be prepared and maintained by the tissue establishment in an adverse event file.

An accreditation system for all tissue establishments and a national system for notification of adverse events and reactions linked to the procurement, testing, processing, preservation, storage, and distribution of human tissues should be established by the national competent health care authorities in all countries. Each tissue establishment should ensure that an accurate, rapid and verifiable procedure is in place, which will enable it to recall from distribution any human tissue, which may be related to an adverse event or reaction.

Return of Human Tissues

All tissue establishments should adopt a policy authorising or prohibiting the return of human tissues in its original unopened container. If returns are permitted, the integrity of the container, package, and labelling should be examined for evidence of contamination or tampering. If there is any evidence of contamination, tampering, mishandling or failure to maintain required storage temperatures, human tissues should not be returned to the distribution inventory. Information pertaining to the return of human tissues should be recorded in the tissue records as follows:

- Documentation of package and/or container examination;
- Documentation of end-user handling, storage (including temperature records) and transport conditions;
- Reason for the return;
- Suitability of the returned human tissues for transplantation; and
- Date and name of the tissue establishment staff authorised to evaluate and determine the suitability for transplantation of the human tissues.

Recalls

All tissue establishments should have specific written policies and procedures for the treatment of a recall. These procedures should cover:

- The system to prevent distribution of the affected batches (or donations from the same affected donor);
- The method of communicating recall and advisory notices to all relevant parties, including other tissue establishments that may have processed and stored human tissues from the same affected donor;
- The records to be maintained;

- The reconciliation of returned human tissues;
- The storage and quarantine of undistributed and recalled human tissues; and
- The regulatory authorities to be informed.

The most effective means of improving the recall system would be the introduction of a globally unique donation identification number that is used on all human tissues from a single donor. Such an identifier provides a rapid alerting tool that can be used to help prevent the use of compromised tissues. When deemed appropriate, an alert could be issued to the transplant community to suspend the use of all or a specific supplier subset of human tissues bearing the specified unique identifier. Globally unique identification also strengthens the traceability trail in any single points of failure in the traceability chain and any failure is far more likely to be overcome, if the reference number used in every organisation is the same. Moreover, if the unique identifier can identify the assigning tissue establishment responsible for procurement, a shortcut exists from the recipient back to the donor allowing much more rapid tracing (Ashford, 2010).

Circumstances Requiring Recall

A recall may be instigated as a result of a complaint, an adverse event or as a result of late information received that the donor did not meet the inclusion and exclusion criteria. Human tissues that were released to distributable inventory or supplied to an end-user and subsequently determined to be unsuitable for transplantation should be recalled.

Notification Responsibilities

Upon discovery of the need for a recall, the tissue establishment should promptly notify all entities to which affected human tissues were distributed or dispensed and the recovery agency, if applicable. A person should be nominated to initiate and coordinate the procedures for recall.

Handling of Human Tissue Recalled

All human tissues not already transplanted, which are subject to recall, should be located and quarantined pending resolution of the recall. Recalled human tissues must be identified, stored, and quarantined whilst awaiting a decision.

Recall of Transplanted Human Tissues

If the human tissue recalled has been transplanted or used for research, the subsequent investigation, in-house action, and notification of end-users or recipients should be handled as a potential adverse event and investigated accordingly.

Recall Records

The recall process must be recorded and a final report issued, including reconciliation between the number of finished human tissues originally delivered and subsequently recovered. All recall records should be retained for at least 10 years beyond the date of distribution or the date of transplantation whichever is later. The recall file should include the following information:

- Events necessitating the recall;
- Measures taken to recall human tissues;
- Documentation of all communications related to the recall (i.e., phone calls and/or written correspondence and notices sent);
- Quarantine details;
- The final destination of human tissues recalled (transplantation, research or disposal);
- Corrective actions recommended and implemented; and
- Review of corrective actions by the Director of the tissue establishment or the Medical Director/Consultant, if the recall is of a medical nature.

XVI. Documentation

Record Keeping

All tissue establishments should keep a record of their activities, including the types and quantities of human tissues procured, tested, preserved, processed, sterilised, stored and distributed or otherwise disposed of, and on the origin and destination of the human tissues intended for transplantation or research.[30] Records should include the following information:

- Number of human tissue donors;
- Listing of all human tissues ordered, stored, and used;
- The names and addresses of the organisations, institutions or persons to whom the human tissues were supplied;
- Informed consent documents;
- Donor suitability assessment criteria;
- The number of human tissues recovered, processed, sterilised, preserved, stored, quarantined, released, and distributed;
- Testing record review;
- Ordering and receipt of human tissues acquired from other sources;
- Package integrity upon receipt;
- Transport temperature controlled and acceptable;
- Source facility and unique identifier of each human tissue;
- Instructions/procedures for reconstitution;
- Identity of personnel preparing, accepting, and issuing human tissues;
- Dates and times of preparing, accepting, and issuing human tissues;
- Documentation in the recipient's health record of the unique identifier of each human tissue;
- Quality management records;
- The number of human tissue donations, which were condemned or discarded and the reason for which they were condemned or discarded;
- The nature and number of human tissue donations that gave results;
- Indicative of microbial contamination and/or infectious disease;
- Recall criteria and procedures;
- The number of adverse events reported; and
- Disposal of human tissues.

[30] Records are a critical component of any quality system. They are documented evidence of compliance, and should be maintained concurrently with the performance of each significant step in the processing, importation, storage, distribution (including exceptional distribution), transplantation and investigation of error and accident and adverse reaction of each human tissue so that all steps can be clearly associated with the person, time/date and location of such activities.

For human tissues obtained from outside tissue establishments, copies of pertinent records should be forwarded to the source facility. Documentation assists in clinical evaluation and in tracking recipients, if an adverse event is identified.

The Director of the tissue establishment should submit to the national competent health care authorities an annual report on these activities. This report should be publicly accessible by all interested parties.

The national competent health care authorities should establish and maintain a publicly accessible register of tissue establishments specifying the activities for which they have been accredited, designated, authorised or licensed.

National competent health care authorities should also establish a network linking the national tissue establishment registered.

Records established by tissue establishments should be confidential, accurate, complete, legible, and indelible. All human tissue donors, processing, storage, and distribution records should be maintained for 10 years beyond the date of distribution, date of transplantation or expiry date, whichever is later or longer, if required, by state and/or local laws and/or regulations. Records should be maintained in a manner to preserve their completeness and accuracy over time.

Records established by tissue establishments should hold all information that identifies the origins of the human tissues and demonstrates that each human tissue meets all the quality requirements included in the code of practice and SOPs in force. Records should show that all the required processing steps and all quality-control tests have been performed correctly by trained staff and that the human tissues have only been released for use after the correct authorisation has been given by the Director of the tissue establishment.

Records should also demonstrate correct handling and storage of human tissues and track the final status of the tissues, whether transplanted, discarded or used for research. The use and storage of records should be controlled.

All tissue establishments should keep records with respect to human tissues that it processes. These records should contain at least all of the following information:

- The donor identification code;
- Documentation showing completion of the donor suitability assessment;

- A description of the human tissues retrieved from the donor;
- If applicable, the name of any tissue establishment from which it received a donor referral or to which it made a donor referral;
- The name of the retrieval establishment;
- Documentation of all processing activities;
- The notice of exceptional distribution, if any; and
- Documentation of any reported errors, accidents, and adverse reactions and their investigation, if any, in connection with human tissues retrieved from the donor that it banked or distributed and any corrective action taken.

Traceability

Policy makers are now recognising the importance of traceability of all human tissues recovered. In the most recent version of the World Health Organisation's Guiding Principles on Organ and Tissue Transplantation (World Health Organisation, 2010), guiding principle 10 states that: "The level of safety, efficacy and quality of human cells, tissues and organs for transplantation, as health products of an exceptional nature, must be maintained and optimised on an ongoing basis. This requires implementation of quality systems including traceability and vigilance, with adverse events and reactions reported, both nationally and for export human products." Within European Directive 2004/EC/23 there is a responsibility placed on Member States to ensure that "all tissues and cells procured, processed, stored or distributed on their territory can be traced from the donor to the recipient and vice versa. This traceability shall also apply to all relevant data relating to products and materials coming into contact with these tissues and cells".

Procedures for traceability of human tissues should be established, documented and maintained by the tissue establishment. These procedures should define the extent of traceability of human tissues and facilitate corrective actions in case of adverse events.

Traceability of human tissues should include all components, materials used, and records of the environmental conditions. There should be an effective system[31] that enables the traceability of human tissues between

[31] For the traceability of human tissues, the tissue establishment should put in place a coding system. A coding system is a short means of representing textual information (e.g., a

the donor, the finished human tissues and the identification of the recipient. The receiving hospital should maintain internal records on the finished human tissues, which ensures the continuity of a two-way audit trail. All tissue establishments should maintain records, which document the destination of distributed human tissues: implantation (date, surgeon, and recipient identification), destruction (date and place) and of any adverse event reports.

Each donor should be assigned a unique donor identification number to facilitate tracing of the human tissues from the donor and the final disposition of each human tissue derived from the donor.[32] At the time of collection, the collection container should be labelled with the date and time of collection or retrieval and the donor's identification or, in the case of client depositors, his/her name.

In case of human tissues for research activities, the tissue establishment should act as a custodian of the human tissues (and their derivatives such as cells, RNA, and DNA extracts) and there is no ownership. At the same

---

product description), which can prevent meaning shift between languages. Defined structures in codes permit computer processing thereby reducing human error. However, human interpretability may also be desirable, for example human interpretability in labelling is desirable to negate the requirement for computer readers at all stages from donor to recipient. A coding management system manages the relationship between coded and textual representations and is typically the responsibility of an independent organisation in many countries. Coding management can be undertaken 'in house', or may be operated independently on a not-for-profit basis. A tissue or cell coding system underpins traceability by having unique identification of material. This is a combination of description of the product and the tissue establishment, plus processing/graft information. This facilitates product exchange, stock control, integration of information in hospitals, and analysis of tissue graft transplant outcome data. It can overcome language barriers, support regulatory and ethical control, communication between software systems (including that embedded in testing equipment) and support reporting requirements established by state and/or local laws and/or regulations (Reynolds *et al.*, 2010).

[32] A single human tissue product may pass through several different organisations on its journey from donor to recipient. These may all be in the same country and within the purview of a single regulatory authority or may span multiple countries and regulators. Adding to the complexity is the fact that there is generally no unique identification of human tissues from a single donation event; hence the organ procurement organisation will use one identifier, the eye bank a second and the tissue establishment a third. A lack of cross referencing between the procurement organisation identifiers means there is no formal traceability across the different types of donation in this case, organs, eyes and musculoskeletal tissues (Ashford, 2010).

time, the tissue establishment should accompany the human tissues with all available clinical/genetic/pathological data in an anonymised form for traceability purposes.

Human tissue units should be assigned the same tissue identification number only if they are identical and processed as a lot.

National competent health care authorities should ensure the traceability of human tissues from the donor to the recipient and vice-versa as well of all relevant data relating to products and materials coming into contact with these tissues by adopting an adequate system. For this reason, human tissues and all relevant data should be identified by a unique identifier, which correlates with the donor identifier. The unique tissue identifier should be used in all records that track the manipulation and storage of the human tissues from the time of donation to transplantation, research or disposal. Records should permit tracing of human tissues from the donor to recipient.

Traceability should be enforced through accurate substance, donor, recipient, tissue establishment and laboratory identification procedures as well as record maintenance and an appropriate labelling system.

All tissue establishments should keep the data necessary to ensure traceability of human tissues at all stages. Data required for full traceability of the human tissues should be kept for a minimum of 10 years after clinical use. Data storage may also be in electronic form.[33]

Despite all efforts made by different countries and international organisations and professional associations, traceability remains poorly understood and inadequately controlled in many countries, and does not provide the necessary responsiveness, reliability and longevity to ensure patient safety. There are three key reasons for this:

- There is a lack of appreciation of the complexity of the information trail;

[33]The ability to share coded data between different donor sectors in the future may help with risk prevention measures and provide clearer indications of donor suitability (for example potential benefits of being able to defer an unsuitable high-risk donor from all potential donated material pools). It may also reduce duplication (multiple manual entry of donor data on separate systems), and ensure better recall management (because a donor or processing methodology is more easily identifiable) (Reynolds *et al.*, 2010).

- Traceability tends to be viewed in a fragmented rather than holistic manner with the assumption that joining together the links at the time of information retrieval will result in a full traceability chain; and
- Traceability data tend to be regarded as static rather than dynamic with the assumption that if the traceability path is intact today it will be so in the future (Ashford, 2010).

Contract Records

When two or more tissue establishments participate in human tissue procurement, processing, storage or distribution functions, the relationships and responsibilities of each should be documented and should comply with relevant scientific and quality professional standards by all parties. All tissue establishments should perform on-site audits of contract laboratories to ensure their compliance with relevant scientific and professional standards, technical manuals, and the tissue establishment's own requirements.

Records should include identification and evaluation of the donor, blood testing and micro-biological evaluation of the donor, conditions under which the human tissue is procured, processed, sterilised, tested and stored, and its final destination.

Records should indicate the dates and the identity of the tissue establishment staff involved in each significant step in the operation.

Distribution Records

Distribution records should be maintained by all tissue establishments that ship human tissues to other entities. These records should be designed to permit human tissues to be traced from the donor to an end-user and from an end-user back to the donor. Human tissue distribution records should include:

- Date of order placement;
- Name and address of the end-user;
- Type and quantity of human tissues ordered;
- Information pertaining to human tissues shipped including:
    - o Identification number(s) of human tissues;
    - o Collection and/or expiration date of the human tissues;

  - o Date of shipment;
  - o Type and amount of refrigerant, if any, used for shipment;

- Mode of transportation and/or courier;
- Name of the staff member filling the order; and
- Identifying information, if available, about the intended recipient.

All tissue establishments should establish recipient follow-up data-collection protocols.

Inventory

A record of unprocessed, processed, quarantined and distributed human tissues should be maintained for a period to be established by the Director of the tissue establishment. If there is any evidence of contamination, tampering, mishandling or failure to maintain required storage and/or transportation temperatures, then human tissues should not be returned to the inventory.

Reports of Adverse Events and Noncompliance

An adverse events file should be maintained including any non-compliance. The file should contain all reports presented on adverse events and non-compliance for the period established in the SOPs in force. The report should describe the incident, the investigation, corrective actions taken, and any follow-up activities required.

Computer Records

If a computerised recordkeeping system is used, there should be a system to ensure the authenticity, integrity, and confidentiality of all records and the ability to generate true paper copies.[34]

A schematic plan or flow diagram for software should be available to evaluate the capability of the system to prevent inaccurate input or output

---

[34] An extensive information technology component is essential to tie all factors together, including a user-friendly database and automated processing, storage and retrieval, samples coding and web-based monitored shipment and tracking (Ravid, 2008).

of data and programming errors. A description of the system, its function and specified requirements should be documented.

Appropriate controls should be in place to ensure access to only authorised personnel and permit changes in master production and control records by authorised personnel only. The system should record the identity of persons entering or confirming critical data.

The introduction of computerised systems into processing practices, including storage, distribution and quality control does not alter the need to comply with the requirements included in the code of practice in force. The same criteria and standards apply to other records also.

Alterations to the system or programme should be made only in accordance with defined procedures. When the release of finished batches of human tissues is conducted by computerised systems, they should identify and record the person releasing the batches. Alternative management systems should be available to cope with failures in computerised systems.

Other Records

Records should be maintained for each piece of equipment, which could affect the quality and the safety of the human tissues, processed by the tissue establishment. These records should include, among others, the following data:

- Identity of the equipment;
- Serial number or other unique identifier;
- Manufacturer's name and contact information;
- The date when the equipment was received, put into service, and if applicable, out of service;
- Manufacturer's instructions, if available, or reference to their retention;
- Equipment performance records that confirm the equipment's suitability for use (equipment qualification), including calibration and/or verification records (which should incorporate such information as dates of tests, test results, adjustments made, acceptance criteria, and frequency of checks);
- Schedules of completed and anticipated maintenance activities;
- Any damage, malfunction, modification or repair of the equipment;

- Usage log sheet; and
- Records of recall.

These records should be readily available for the lifespan of the equipment and should be kept for one year after the expiry date of the last product processed by this equipment. Each item of equipment should be uniquely labelled, marked or otherwise identified.

All tissue establishments should have records, which indicate that all laboratory testing of transmissible disease markers are performed in accordance with the corresponding test kit manufacturer's instructions. Where applicable, records of written agreement between the tissue establishment and any testing laboratory should be in place to provide relevant information, including:

- The appropriate tests to be performed for each sample;
- A stipulation that the laboratory is to follow the manufacturer's instructions and perform the tests within the limits and time frames suggested by the manufacturer;
- A stipulation that the test kits used to test donors for transmissible disease agents or markers should comply with the code of practice in force;
- Testing validation data;
- The method of reporting results to the tissue establishment and an interpretation of the results; and
- Names and titles of personnel responsible for the review and release of testing results.

Records of all test kits used during the processing should include, but are not limited to:

- The name of the test kit;
- The lot number;
- The name, lot number and expiry date of the solutions and reagents used;
- The expiry date;
- Catalogue number;

- The name of the manufacturer;
- Testing validation data; and
- Records of recall, if applicable.

For testing laboratories, detailed testing records and logs, including quality controls, calibration, maintenance and other supporting documents, are to be made readily accessible to the source establishment.

Records should be maintained for each critical supply item that could affect the quality and the safety of the human tissue. These records should include, among others, the following information:

- Identity of the supply, including type and lot number;
- Manufacturer's name and the contact information;
- Expiration date, if applicable;
- Manufacturer's instructions, if available;
- Records to demonstrate that non-disposable instruments used in the processing are cleaned, disinfected and/or sterilised to prevent contamination and cross-contamination according to written procedures; and
- Records showing that sterile single-use instruments have been inspected for sterility prior to use, and giving the name of the person that did the verification.

Where applicable, records of written agreement between the tissue establishment and the retrieval establishment should be maintained to provide relevant information such as the roles and responsibilities of the parties involved. The written agreement should also include an attestation that they are in compliance with the code of practice and SOPs in force.

XVII. Education and Training

All tissue establishments that distribute human tissues should have sufficient qualified staff with the necessary experience to perform their respective tasks within the tissue establishment and should also have a system for the orientation and training, both initial and ongoing, of the staff and for the evaluation of their competency.

The Director of the tissue establishment should ensure that initial and ongoing educational opportunities are provided to meet the needs of personnel who perform different tasks within the tissue establishment. Regulations and standards affecting tissue establishment activities are evolving. Initial education provides a baseline to support a beginning level of job performance. Ongoing education offers personnel an opportunity to enhance skills and learn about changes in regulations and standards in force. An introduction and review of tissue banking ethics, policies and procedures should be included in the orientation and ongoing education of personnel to assist them in the development of knowledge, skills, and attitudes that positively affect patient outcomes. The Director of the tissue establishment should also ensure that the tissue establishment staff are competent to perform the tasks assigned to them within the tissue establishment. Competency assurance is essential because errors may cause breaches in regulations, compromise the integrity or function of the human tissue, contaminate it, and/or lead to negative outcomes of transplantation.

Training programmes should be available prior to the implementation of a new procedure or any revision of an existing procedure, and the effectiveness of the programmes shall be assessed by regular competency evaluation. The assessment of competency may include:

- Direct observation of performance;
- Monitoring of recording and reporting;
- Written tests to assess problem-solving skills;
- Assessment of knowledge of operating procedures and theory; and
- Performing routine testing, assessment of performance in proficiency tests.

Records of the qualifications, training and continuing competency of individuals should be maintained.

The educational and training requirements for each member of the tissue establishment staff should be determined and specified by the Director of the tissue establishment to ensure that all processes applied to human tissues that may affect quality are being carried out by trained staff in accordance with the documented procedures. There should be regular and formal appraisal of technical and QA staff competency and familiarity with current regulations and codes adopted by the tissue establishment.

Procedures should be established and maintained for identifying training needs and providing training for all tissue establishment staff that perform activities affecting quality (e.g., donor suitability, tissue recovery, storage and transport), including contracted staff or service providers with whom the tissue establishment has a contract.

Personnel who carries out or supervise specialised tasks should have the appropriate education, training and/or experience that cover regulations, policies, processes and process controls pertaining to the assigned task. Staff engaged in verification and validation activities should be educated on the errors and accidents that may occur.

All personnel who are required to work under special environmental conditions, or who perform special processes or functions, should be appropriately trained or supervised by qualified staff. Members of the tissue establishment staff who occasionally work in processing areas should also be appropriately trained.

Training and retraining should be in accordance with approved programmes. All tissue establishment staff should be made aware of the consequences at all levels of non-compliance with SOPs, and the possible serious medical consequences to recipients of unsafe human tissues resulting from the improper performance of their specific jobs.

Training and education should include as applicable, the orientation of new employees; requirements for quality, good laboratory practice, implementation of the SOPs in force, code of ethics and code of practice adopted; effective use of electronic systems; appropriate continuing professional development through workshops, clinical meetings, training courses, seminars, and conferences, among others.

Training should ensure that staff are able to perform correctly and independently, among others, the following duties:

- Screening of potential donors, when applicable;
- Performing blood investigations and culture tests;
- Procuring human tissues;
- Processing of human tissues;

- Sterilising/disinfecting human tissues[35];
- Preparing documents;
- Storing human tissues;
- Distributing human tissues; and
- Promoting public and professional awareness of human tissue donation and transplantation;

There are several modalities that can be used for training of tissue establishment staff and medical personnel. The Director of the tissue establishment, in consultation with the national competent health care authorities, should select the most appropriate training modality. These include, but are not restricted to:

- In-house training course;
- National courses;
- Course organised by professional bodies;
- Regional and international training courses organised by other countries;
- National and international distance-learning training courses; and
- Internet training courses.

If the internet training course modality is selected, the following elements should be considered:

- Determination of the number and type of servers that should be used to ensure stable and continuing communication between the registered students, and the different external consultants supporting the course;
- Integration of the servers with local networks, backup procedures, technical support and firewalls, among others;
- Identification of the different software that need to be purchased to ensure the effective use of the internet to carry out the training programme;
- Selection of the teaching materials to be used after the necessary adaptations of these materials for this type of training modality;
- Integration of the teaching materials with local administrative systems, such as students' records, course records, etc.;

[35]Excepting those cases in which the ionising radiation technique is used for the sterilisation of the human tissues.

- Identification of the access to be given to the registered students to the different teaching materials available in the course; and
- Identification of a library of tools in building student support environments.

For the implementation of an internet training course, students should have access to computers to avail of teaching materials, receive assignments, engage in discussions and take examinations; a tissue establishment duly recognised to assist the students in their practical work; and appropriate communication lines with the Director and professors of the course.

All training activities should be documented and records maintained up to date and evaluated regularly. Training records should include the following information:

- Job specifications with appropriate training;
- Training received by new staff;
- Training of staff in new tasks;
- Review and training prior to implementation of new and/or revised SOPs/codes adopted by the tissue establishment;
- Regular training in safety procedures; and
- Participation in workshops, seminars, meetings or other continuing education programmes.

Upon termination of employment, training records should be retained as required by law or as determined by the Advisory Committee.

Chapter VI

Role of Governments, the World Health Organization, the International Atomic Energy Agency and Regional Professional Associations in the Promotion of Ethics in Tissue Banking

According to the WHO (2003), ethical practice of transplantation requires setting barriers, defining abuses and the identification of disciplinary measures to be applied in case of non-compliance with ethical principles. Safety for both donors and recipients is an essential factor in human tissue transplantation.

It is important that countries provide the oversight of all transplant activities, with national competent health care authorities ensuring the adoption of appropriate legislations, regulations and standards, particularly the adoption of a code of ethics and a code of practice by all tissue establishments operating in the country. The adoption of ethical principles, a code of ethics and a code of practice are essential elements in order to promote high standards in human tissue transplantation. These ethical principles and the codes of ethics and practice should deal with the issue of access to transplantation, quality and safety, and to include a rational and cost-effective use of transplantation, among others. The WHO, the IAEA and regional/international professional associations already established in the field of tissue banking can facilitate the formulation of global principles, keeping in mind the regional and cultural diversity. The main roles of these organisations are indicated in the following sections.

Governments

The primary role of governments in the field of ethics in tissue banking is:

- To establish a legal framework within which transplant services can operate, monitor and report, and ensure that specific mechanisms are in place for regulating the various elements required for an effective transplant service, including traceability and standards. The legal framework should include a transplant law, the circumstances in which human tissues can be retrieved, the consent or authorisation needed, death certification and the regulation of health care service providers or other bodies involved in transplant services;
- To put in place mechanisms for the protection of donors and recipients. This should ensure rapid investigation of any untoward incidents occurring in relation to the transplantation services, so that timely corrective and preventive actions can be taken;
- To designate and approve a non-commercial national or international body responsible for the allocation and distribution of human tissues;
- To set up a system of authorisation and inspection of procurement organisations and tissue establishments in order to ensure the safety of the donors and the recipients;
- To promote the development of a system for the altruistic voluntary non-remunerated donation of human tissues, and to increase public awareness and understanding of the benefits of the voluntary non-remunerated provision of human tissues from deceased and living donors. For this reason, governments should oppose the seeking of financial gain or comparable advantage in transactions involving human body parts, and should encourage health care professionals to notify to the relevant national competent health care authorities when they become aware of such practices in accordance with national capacities and legislations;
- To promote a system of transparency, equitable allocation of human tissues, guided by clinical criteria and ethical norms, as well as equitable access to transplantation services in accordance with national capacities;
- To improve the safety and efficacy of donation and transplantation services by promoting international best practices and to strengthen

national and international authorities and/or capacities to provide oversight, organisation and coordination of donation and transplantation activities. Special attention should be given to maximising donation from deceased donors and to the protection of the health and welfare of living donors with appropriate health care services and long-term follow-up;

- To collaborate in collecting data including adverse events and reactions on the practices, safety, quality, efficacy, epidemiology and ethics of donation and transplantation and to encourage the implementation of globally consistent coding systems for human tissues in order to facilitate national and international traceability of materials of human origin for transplantation;
- To promote regional and international cooperation between different tissue establishments and transplantation institutions. Regional and international cooperation is necessary to increase the chances of providing human tissues for patients in life-threatening situations. For these reasons, governments should ensure that there is good cooperation between their allocation organisations and those set up in other countries in charge of human tissue transplant;
- To promote the elaboration of an internationally accepted unified coding system as well as common product names and definitions for unique product identification to identify human tissues used in transplantation for traceability purposes;
- To promote collaboration and consultation between regulatory and health care authorities as well as with the scientific and professional associations already established with the purpose of ensuring the compatibility of the different regulatory systems;
- To promote the development of global systems of vigilance and surveillance to ensuring optimal medical practice in the field of tissue banking;
- To support the establishment of a limited number of regional tissue processing centres for the purpose of providing high-quality sterile human tissues in special situations to specific tissue establishments, when necessary;
- To promote a closed cooperation between tissue establishments and organ transplant organisations at the national level and the establishment of a National Transplant Office to coordinate this cooperation.

World Health Organization

The main actions that WHO can promote in the field of ethics in tissue banking are the following:

- Encouraging the development of transplantation therapies in WHO member states in an ethically appropriate manner;
- Working with national governments to developing agreements on minimum datasets needed to support evidence-based transplants and allocation policies;
- Supporting a programme on human tissue transplantation at WHO and establishing a WHO Expert Advisory Panel for human tissue transplantation;
- Facilitating in collaboration with other relevant international authorities the development of a core of technical and ethical standards for the management of the safety, quality and efficacy of human tissue for transplantation, including the adoption of a code of ethics and a code of practice by all of its member states;
- Encouraging WHO member states to develop a legal framework, a national policy, a code of ethics and a code of practice on tissue transplantation activities;
- Providing support to WHO member states and non-governmental organisations in order to eliminate trafficking in material of human origin;
- Promoting the establishment of an international network of tissue establishments in order to collect the relevant information related to tissue procurement, processing and transplantation in all countries in all regions[1];

[1] A global database on human tissue procurement, processing and transplantation is achievable through a multinational effort promoted by WHO and supported by governments and professional associations. Such a database should have central coordination, periodic reports, space and time comparison and credibility. Credibility can be established by ensuring that accredited bodies complete questionnaires, requiring peer review of reports, recognising all institutions and banning smoothing factors on reports. The database should be freely accessible to all and can support the global development of transplants of organs and tissues. Existing national and regional experience in surveillance of therapeutic

- Facilitating alliances between national transplant organisations in WHO member states with the aim of promoting cooperation at legal, ethical and technical levels;
- Promoting the highest possible cooperation among WHO member states in the field of tissue banking;
- Promoting the highest possible cooperation among different professional associations already established in the field of tissue banking in different regions;
- Facilitating communication between regulators and providers on the international circulation of human tissues for transplantation;
- Collecting data on the extent of paid tissue donation;
- Creating a global map of the known infectious risks and the safety measures that are applied to donors and donations in different countries and regions of the world;
- Helping WHO member states develop capacity for national regulatory approaches to quality and safety;
- Encouraging the measurement of the donor outcomes for living donors in different clinical environments, through collaborative global data collections;
- Encouraging countries to support the consensus on basic principles of xenotransplantation[2] safety and oversight, which are as follows:
    - Defining the nomenclature for different types of xenotransplantation;
    - Identifying countries in which xenotransplantation occurs;
    - Supporting the approach that regulations should be in place in all countries in which clinical trials of xenotransplantation occur;

---

products of human origin should be consolidated, shared and expanded towards encompassing global activity.

[2]Xenotransplantation represents a potential opportunity to ensure a constant supply of tissues for transplantation. However, the scientific hurdles to successful xenotransplantation in humans currently mean that it should only be undertaken under strict clinical trial conditions. There are substantial potential risks to human health from the transmission of xenogeneic infectious agents through xenotransplantation. Careful international monitoring of these clinical trials and of each subject is thus essential to ensuring the safety not only of subjects, but also of their families and the broader human population. These issues transcend currently accepted norms of subject consent and medical responsibility for monitoring of the consequences of xenotransplantation.

  - Developing general recommendations for obtaining informed consent in situations that may represent a risk to the general public and in which individual rights and the public good may come into conflict;
  - Fostering agreement between WHO member states to control the transfer of tissues for xenotransplantation; and
  - Implementing an international xenotransplants surveillance system.
- Rewriting and updating the Guiding Principles, published by WHO in 1991, especially concerning:
  - Measures to ensure safe and voluntary altruistic donations from living donors; and
  - Financial transactions and coercion.
- Promoting regional educational strategies for hospital coordinators and health care professionals;
- Promoting and improving research, education, training, and clinical use of human tissues;
- Identifying and disseminating relevant information on successful models of transplantation that use local resources and cultural norms. It is important to stress that success will not come from the provision of isolated components of support, but should involve the comprehensive support of individuals and programmes extending throughout legal, social and clinical aspects of transplant programmes;
- Promoting the elaboration of an internationally accepted unified coding system to identify human tissues used in transplantation for traceability purposes[3];

[3]The American Association of Tissue Banks (AATB), in collaboration with ICCBBA has established a North American Tissue Technical Advisory Group (NATTAG) to advice on the use of the ISBT 128 information system. Both AATB and ICCBBA recognise the importance of international consistency, and have thus invited EATB to participate in the work of this group, with a view to further developing the terminology to satisfy global needs. A first draft of the terminology has been released for public comment. The development of a global terminology is a major challenge, but brings with it the potential to improve patient safety. Building strong international support for this project is essential to ensuring its future success.

- Promoting the development of global systems of vigilance and surveillance for ensuring optimal medical practice in the field of tissue banking;
- To support the establishment of a limited number of regional tissue processing centres for the purpose of providing high-quality sterile human tissues in special situations to specific tissue establishments, when necessary; and
- To promote a closed cooperation between tissue establishments and organ transplant organisations at national level and the establishment a National Transplant Office to coordinate this cooperation.

International Atomic Energy Agency

The main actions that the IAEA can promote in the field of ethics in tissue banking are the following:

- Promoting, supporting and improving research, education, and training in the use of the ionising radiation technique for the sterilisation of human tissues;[4]
- Reviewing the IAEA Radiation Sterilisation of Tissue Allografts: Requirements for Validation and Routine Control. A Code of Practice,

[4]The IAEA should support the realisation of safety and optimisation of radiation sterilisation of human tissue studies, particularly on functional properties of irradiated human tissues. To assure safety of patients receiving tissue allografts during surgical treatment, several decontamination or sterilisation procedures are implemented during the processing. Irradiation of tissue allografts is one of the developed and widely used methods for sterilisation in the world, which have been promoted by the IAEA during the past 40 years. Gamma rays, X-rays, and electron beams have been used with doses ranging from 15 to 80 kGy. Controversies exist regarding the optimal dose for sterilisation since radiation can evoke numerous changes in human tissues structure resulting in its change in functionality. The major aim in the study is to facilitate research and disseminate the results in IAEA member states on the radiation-induced effects on tissue grafts processed and preserved by different methods. The newly acquired knowledge established from harmonised research methodologies will be useful in providing high quality tissue allografts and will provide the necessary inputs to the process of reviewing the current text of the IAEA Radiation Sterilisation of Tissue Allografts: Requirements for Validation and Routine Control. A Code of Practice.

adopted by the IAEA in 2007, takes into account papers that have been published on the subject;

- Promoting the adoption by all WHO and IAEA member states of a code of ethics and a code of practice taking as reference the model proposals that have been included in chapters 3 and 5;
- Supporting the implementation of an interregional project with the purpose of strengthening the capacity for national regulatory authorities in the field of quality and safety;
- Promoting the establishment of an international network of tissue establishments in order to collect the relevant information related to human tissue procurement, processing and transplantation in all countries in all regions, particularly the use of the ionising radiation technique for human tissue sterilisation;
- Promoting the highest possible cooperation among IAEA member states in the use of the ionising radiation technique for the sterilisation of human tissues;
- Promoting the highest possible cooperation among different regional and national professional associations already established in the field of tissue banking in the use of the ionising radiation technique for the sterilisation of human tissues;
- Promoting the development of global systems of vigilance and surveillance to ensuring optimal medical practice in the field of tissue banking;
- Supporting the establishment of a limited number of regional tissue processing centres for the purpose of providing high-quality sterile human tissues in special situation to specific tissue establishments, when necessary; and
- Promoting a close cooperation between tissue establishments and organ transplant organisations at the national level and the establishment a National Transplant Office to coordinate this cooperation.

Regional Professional Associations

The main actions that regional professional associations such as American Association of Tissue Banks, European Association of Tissue Banks,

Asia-Pacific Association of Surgical Tissue Banking and Latin American Association of Tissue Banks (Asociacion Latinoamericana Bancos de Tejidos) can bring about in the field of ethics in tissue banking are the following:

- Promoting and improving research, education, and training in the use of the best technique for the sterilisation of human tissues;
- Encouraging the development of transplantation therapies in an ethical manner in participating institutions;
- Promoting the development of a core of technical and ethical standards for the management of safety, quality and efficacy of human tissues for transplantation that can serve as a model for participant tissue establishments;
- Encouraging participant tissue establishments to develop and adopt a legal framework, a national policy, a code of ethics and a code of practice on human tissue transplantation activities, especially ensuring coordination of the procurement of human tissue from deceased donors;
- Promoting the establishment of an international network of tissue establishments in order to collect the relevant information related to human tissue procurement, processing and transplantation in all tissue establishments located in all countries in all regions;
- Facilitating alliances between national transplantation organisations and the promotion of the cooperation at legal, ethical and technical levels;
- Promoting the highest possible cooperation among different regional and national professional associations already established in the field of tissue banking in different regions and between these associations and regulatory and national competent health care authorities;
- Promoting regional educational strategies for hospital coordinators and health care professionals;
- Promoting and improving research, education, training and clinical use of human tissues;
- Identifying and disseminating relevant information on successful models of transplantation that use local resources and cultural norms;
- Promoting the elaboration of an internationally accepted unified coding system to identify human tissues used in transplantation for traceability purposes;

- Promoting the development of global systems of vigilance and surveillance for ensuring optimal medical practice in the field of tissue banking;
- Supporting the establishment of a limited number of regional tissue processing centres for the purpose of providing high-quality sterile human tissues in special situations to specific tissue establishments, when necessary; and
- Promoting a closed cooperation between tissue establishments and organ transplant organisations at the national level and the establishment of a National Transplant Office to coordinate this cooperation.

Chapter VII

Conclusions

The use of human tissues in certain medical treatments and in scientific medical research has increased in a variety of ways in the past years. Transplantation of human tissues is now an effective therapy across a wide range of both fatal and non-fatal diseases in many countries from all regions. The majority of transplants involve certain types of organs, but demand for skin for treatment of burns has also increased. There is a growing global problem of a demand for different types of human tissues, which now exceed the available supply due to an increase in their use in many countries.

Several problems exist in banking and the transplanting of human tissues. One of these problems is the potential for viral or bacterial disease transmission. This problem is of great concern to clinicians and patients and is one of the limiting factors confounding the widespread adoption of allograft bone and soft human tissues in certain medical treatments. Another problem that exists, despite the potential for the transfer of infections through the transplant of allografts, is the absence of national laws for quality and safety in most countries, including European countries and the USA.

Undoubtedly, the use of allograft tissues will increase in the coming years, and for this reason the safety of human tissues will continue to be a critical issue in several countries. Due to these foreseeable increases, there is a need for standardisation of the current diversity in human tissue definitions, and quality and safety practices, for the harmonising of national laws in force in different countries in the field of tissue banking and transplantation, and for the establishment of global networking and cooperation among different tissue establishments.

The success rates for transplantation of human tissues, which do not require immunosuppression, have also ensured that such procedures are frequently the treatment of choice in the respective therapeutic areas in a group of developed and developing countries. It is, however, clear that ethically unacceptable practices occur in a number of countries and this situation should be eliminated.

At the same time, society demands general respect for the human body and its parts and, for this reason, human tissues should not be used at will or abused.

Wherever tissues are removed from human beings, and possibly transplanted into other human beings, the activities involved in the collection and use of such tissues should be subject to ethical requirements intended to safeguard respect for human beings, their dignity and autonomy, and for the common good. In all cases, the donation, procurement, testing, processing, preservation, sterilisation, storage and distribution of human tissues intended for human applications should comply with high standards of quality and safety in order to ensure a high level of health protection to donors and recipients of human tissues in all states.

Activities of procurement of human tissues as well as activities carried out by tissue establishments require authorisation. This authorisation should be subject to compliance with basic ethical principles and with health safety standards, which themselves are an ethical imperative. For this reason, human tissue donation should not be practised unless there is no feasible alternative and means are in place to effectively protect the donor's health and safety. Tissue establishments have an eminent responsibility to supervise the implementation of these regulations and ethical principles. They should refuse to accept those human tissues the procurement procedures of which do not satisfy ethical principles and safety regulations.

There is an important and urgent need to consider, clarify and, where necessary, strengthen the ethical and legal framework within which the clinical and research uses of human tissues take place. The ethical issues relate directly to the core of respect for human beings, namely that they and their bodies should not be injured and that nothing should be done to them and their bodies without their explicit consent. The limitations of the existing framework of legal and professional regulations point to the conclusion that a coherent approach is needed to any further regulation.

Governments should take all necessary measures to ensure that any promotion and publicity activities in support of the donation of human tissues comply with the guidelines or legislative provisions laid down by the state and/or local laws and/or regulations. Such guidelines or legislative provisions should include appropriate restrictions or prohibitions on advertising the need for, or availability of, human tissues with a view to offering or seeking financial gain or comparable advantage.

The success rates for transplantation of human tissues have ensured that processed human tissues can be used more frequently in specific medical treatments without increasing the risk of the recipients. To avoid the improper uses of the human tissues procured by a tissue establishment, it is necessary to promote and adopt certain ethical principles to be observed by the operators and medical staff during the procurement, processing, storage, distribution and use of human tissues. The purpose of observing ethical principles is to avoid not only the abuse and unethical practices in tissue banking, but also the violation of specific regulations in force in the country.

As one donor may yield several tissue transplant products, which could be used later in certain medical treatments or research activities, there is a need for safety measures in the procurement, processing, storage, distribution, and use of human tissues. Any misconduct during these processes could lead to dire consequences. For this reason, each state should set itself the target to guarantee to its citizens high and ethical standards in all health care activities, particularly in the area of tissue banking. This protection must extend to all tissue donors and recipients, as well as to all health care professionals and technicians that are involved in the procurement, processing, distribution and use of human tissues in certain medical treatments or in specific research activities.

At present, the international community cannot be assured that the quality and, in particular, the safety of human tissues for transplants, is properly guaranteed in all countries and regions. There are at least four main reasons for this. One is the shortcomings of international and regional ethical rules and standards in tissue banking. The second is the lack of national ethical rules and standards in force in various countries. The third is the lack of proper regulatory oversight in the field of tissue banking in several countries. The fourth is the lack of harmonisation of existing ethical regulations and standards. Addressing these problems should be one of the highest priorities for the tissue banking community during the coming years.

Lastly, it is important to highlight the following: ethical practice of transplantation requires setting barriers, defining abuses and the identification of disciplinary measures to be applied in case of non-compliance with ethical principles. Safety for both donors and recipients is an essential factor in human tissue transplantation.

Bibliography

A Code of Practice for Tissue Banks (2001). UK Department of Health.

Ashford, Paul (2010). Traceability. *Cell Tissue Bank* DOI 10.1007/s10561-010-9195-3. Springer.

Basic Standards for Operating a Human Tissue Bank. Japanese Society of Tissue *Transplantation* (JSTT).

Bauer, K., Taub, S. and Parsi, K. (2004). Ethical issues in tissue banking for research: A brief review of existing organisational policies. *Theoretical Medicine Bioethics*.

Brychta, P. (2002). EATB. Standards for banking of biologic skin substitutes (BSS). *Cell and Tissue Banking*, 3: 59–71.

Buck, B.E. and Malinin, T.I. (1994). Human bone and tissue allografts. Preparation and safety. *Clin. Orthop. Relat. Res.*, 303: 8–17.

Centers for Disease Control and Prevention (CDC) (2002). Allograft-associated bacterial infections — United States. *MMWR. Morb. Mortal Wkly. Rep.*, 51: 207–210.

Clinical Trials Directive (2001). Directive 2001/20/EC of 4 April 2001 of the European Parliament and of the Council.

Code of Ethical Principles and Conduct (2001). PAHO Directing Council (CD46/28), Washington DC, USA.

Code of Practice for the Acquisition, Storage and Use of Human Biological Material for Research (2011). Tissue Governance Manager Version 3.0. 11th January 2011. Approved by the Tissue Bank Governance Committee. Brighton and Sussex Medical School and Brighton and Sussex University Hospitals.

Chan, T.C. (2003). Guidelines for Health Care Institutions Providing Tissue Banking. Licensing and Accreditation Branch, Ministry of Health, Singapore.

Davenport, J. (1997). Ethical Principles in Clinical Practices. *The Permanente Journal*, Portland, USA.

Dermont, E. (2005). Study Report: Percentage of Donors Discarded Due to Autopsy Findings (Internal report). Tampa, Florida LifeLink Tissue Bank.

Directive 2004/23/EC of the European Parliament and of the Council on Setting Standards of Quality and Safety for the Donation, Procurement, Testing, Processing, Preservation, Storage and Distribution of Human Tissues and Cells (2004). The European Parliament and the Council. PE-CONS 3628/04. Strasbourg.

Dodd, R.Y., Notari, E.P. IV and Stramer, S.L. (2002). Current prevalence and incidence of infectious disease markers and estimated window-period risk in the American Red Cross blood donor population. *Transfusion*, 42: 975–979.

Ethics, access and safety in tissue and organ transplantation: Issues of global concern (2003). WHO report. World Health Organization, Madrid, Spain.

Ethical principles for medical research involving human subjects (2000). Declaration of Helsinki, World Medical Association, Adopted by the 18th WMA General Assembly Helsinki, Finland, June 1964 and amended by the 29th WMA General Assembly, Tokyo, Japan, October 1975, 35th WMA General Assembly, Venice, Italy, October 1983, 41st WMA General Assembly, Hong Kong, September 1989, 48th WMA General Assembly, Somerset West, Republic of South Africa, October 1996, and the 52nd WMA General Assembly, Edinburgh, Scotland, October 2000.

Ethical Principles for Medical Research Involving Human Subjects (2008). World Medical Association Declaration of Helsinki. 59th WMA General Assembly, Seoul, October 2008.

Ethics, access and safety in tissue and organ transplantation: Issues of global concern (2003). WHO's report. World Health Organization, Madrid, Spain.

Ethical principles and guidelines for the protection of human subjects of research (1979). The Belmont Report. The National Commission for the Protection of Human Subjects of Biomedical and Behavioral Research, Department of Health, Education, and Welfare, USA.

Ethics and the exchange, sale of and profit from products derived from human tissue (2009). National Health and Medical Research Council, Canberra, Australia.

Finegold, S.M., Attebery, H.R. and Sutter, V.L. (1974). Effect of diet on human fecal flora: Comparison of Japanese and American diets. *Am. J. Clin. Nutr.* 27: 1456–1569.

Gassner, U.M. (2007). Legal aspects of tissue banking. *Pathobiology*, 74(4): 270–274.

Greenwald, S.A., Boden, S.D., Goldberg, V.M., Khan, Y., Laurencin, C.T. and Rosier R.N. (2002). Bone-graft substitutes: Facts, fictions and applications. In: American Academy of Orthopaedic Surgeons 69th annual meeting, Dallas, Texas, USA.

Gillet, G. (2007). The use of human tissue. *J. of Bioethical Inquiry*, 4: 119–127.

Gilman, S.C. (2005). Ethics, Codes and Codes of Conduct as Tools for Promoting an Ethical and Professional Public Service. Comparative Successes and Lessons. Prepared for the PREM, the World Bank. Washington, DC, USA.

Gocke, D.J. (2005). Tissue donor selection and safety. *Clin. Orthop. Relat. Res.* 435: 17–21.

Guidance Document for Cell, Tissue and Organ Establishments: Safety of Human Cells, Tissues and Organs for Transplantation (2009). Health Canada Publication. Ministry of Health, Canada.

Guiding principles on human cell, tissue and organ transplantation (2010). World Health Organization. <http://www.who.int/transplantation/Guiding_Principles_Transplantation WHA63.22en.pdf.> Accessed 12 July 2010.

Hackett, K. (2001). Tissue donation, tissue bank 2001 report. Halifax, Canada. 2001.

Hirn, M.Y., Salmela, P.M. and Vuento, R.E. (2001). High-pressure saline washing of allografts reduces bacterial contamination. *Acta. Orthop. Scand.*, 72: 83–85.

Human tissue: Ethical and legal issue (1995). Nuffield Council of Bioethics. Pathobiology J.. 1995.

Human organ and tissue transplantation (2002). Resolution WHA 63.22 of the Sixty-Third World Health Assembly. Cell Tissue Bank (2010) 11: 411–412, DOI 10.1007/s10561-010-9227-z. 2010.

Human Tissue Research (2002). Consultation Paper. The Bioethics Advisory Committee. Singapore HGS-CP.1/2001-PC1-1.1 PC1 – 3.0. February 2002.

IAEA Code of Practice for the Radiation Sterilisation of Tissue Allografts. Requirements for Validation and Routine Control (2007). IAEA, Vienna, Austria.

Indech, B. (2000). The international harmonization of human tissue regulation: Regulatory control over human tissue use and tissue banking in select countries and the current state of international harmonization efforts. *Food and Drug Law Journal*, 55(3): 343–372.

Informed Consent in Tissue Donation: Expectations and Realities (2001). Department of Health and Human Services. OEI-01-00-00440. Boston, USA.

International Ethical Guidelines for Epidemiological Studies (2008). Council for International Organisations of Medical Sciences (CIOMS) in collaboration with the World Health Organization (WHO). CIOMS, Geneva. Switzerland.

Kevin, A. and Sandie, M. (2011). Ethical tissue: A not-for-profit model for human tissue supply. *Cell and Tissue Banking,* 12: 9–10.

Kostiak, P.E. (2000). The evolution of quality systems in human bone banking: The U.S. experience. *Cell and Tissue Banking*, 1: 155–160.

Little, M.P. (2003). Risks associated with ionizing radiation. *British Medical Bulletin*, 68: 259–275.

Miller, S. (2002). Model Code of Ethical Principles. Paper presented for the Professional Standards Council, June, P.S.C., Sydney.

Morales Pedraza, J. and Herson, M.R. (2011). The importance of ethics in the field of human tissue banking. *Cell and Tissue Banking*, 13(1): 103–117.

Morales Pedraza, J. (2012). The Use of the Ionizing Radiation Technique for Tissue Sterilization: The International Atomic Energy Agency (IAEA) Experience. Nova Science Publishers, Inc., New York. USA.

Morales Pedraza, J. (2012). A model of a code of ethics for tissue banks operating in developing countries. *Cell and Tissue Banking*, 13(4): 607–622.

Morales Pedraza, J. and Gajiwala, A.L. (2012). A model code of practice for tissue banks. *IJOE*, 8(1–2).

Morales Pedraza, J. (2009). Elements for Effective Management of a Business Corporation Crisis Situation. In: Crisis Management. Patrick Alvintzi *et al.* (eds.). Nova Science Publishers, Inc. New York, USA.

Nelkin, D. and Andrews, L. (1998). Homo economicus: The commercialisation of body tissue in the age of biotechnology. Hastings Center Rep. 28(5): 30–39.

Operational Guidelines for Ethics Committees That Review Biomedical Research (2000).TDR/PRD/ETHICS/2000.1.WHO, Geneva, Switzerland.

Oversight of Tissue Banking (2001). Department of Health and Human Services, Office of Inspector General, USA.

IAEA International Standards for Tissue Banks. *Advances in Tissue Banking*, Vol. 7. editor Glyn O. Phillips (2003). World Scientific Publishing.

Pierscionek, B.K. (2011). The current limitations on tissue banking from an academic perspective. *Cell and Tissue Banking*, 12: 23–24.

Pruss, A., Göbel, U.B. and Pauli, G. (2003). Peracetic acid-ethanol treatment of allogeneic a vital bone tissue transplants — a reliable sterilisation method. *Ann. Transplant.* 8: 34–42.

Pruss, A., Perka, C. and Degenhardt, P. (2002a). Clinical efficacy and compatibility of allogeneic avital tissue transplants sterilised with a peracetic acid/ethanol mixture. *Cell and Tissue Banking*, 3: 235–243.

Pruss, A., Kao, M., Gohs, U., Koscielny, J., von Versen, R. and Pauli, G. (2002b). Effects of gamma irradiation on human cortical bone transplants contaminated with enveloped and non-enveloped viruses. *Biologicals*, 30: 125–133.

Quintana-Trias, M.O. (1998). Ethical aspects of human tissue banking. Opinion of the European Group on Ethics in Science and New Technologies No. 11, 21 July 1998, EU Commission Working Document.

Ravid, R. (2008). Standard Operating Procedures, ethical and legal regulations in BTB (Brain/Tissue/Bio) banking: What is still missing? *Cell and Tissue Banking*, 9: 121–137.

Recommendations REC-RCIDT-2007 (7) and 2008 (8). Ibero-American Donation and Transplant Council.

Recommendation Rec RCIDT 2007 (7) on guides for the quality and safety of cells and tissues of human origin for transplantation. Ibero-American Donation and Transplant Council.

Recommendation Rec RCIDT 2007 (8) on donation and transplantation of organs, tissues and cells. Ibero-American Donation and Transplant Council.

Reynolds, M., Warwick, R.M., Poniatowski, S. and Trias, E. (2010). European coding system for tissues and cells: A challenge unmet? *Cell and Tissue Banking*, 11(4): 353–364.

Sanders, L.M., Giudice, L., and Raffin, T.A. (1993). Ethics of Fetal Tissue Transplantation. *The Western Journal of Medicine*, 159 (3): 400–407.

Silva, M.C. and Ludwick, R. (1999). Interstate Nursing Practice and Regulation: Ethical Issues for the 21st Century. *Online Journal of Issues in Nursing*, 4 (2). Available at: <www.nursingworld.org//MainMenuCategories/ANAMarketplace/ANAPeriodicals/OJIN/TableofContents/Volume41999/No2Sep1999/InterstateNursingPracticeandRegulation.aspx.>

Standards for Tissue Banking (2002). American Association of Tissue Banks, McLean, VA.

Standards and Operational Guidance for Ethics Review of Health-related Research with Human Participants (2011). World Health Organization (WHO).

Stramer, Susan L. Ph.D.; Glynn, Simone A. M.D., M.P.H.; Kleinman, Steven H. M.D.; Strong, D. Michael, Ph.D.; Caglioti, Sally, M.T. (A.S.C.P.), S.B.B.; Wright, David J., Ph.D.; Dodd, Roger Y., Ph.D.; and Busch, Michael P. M.D., Ph.D.

(2004); Detection of HIV-1 and HCV Infections among Antibody-Negative Blood Donors by Nucleic Acid–Amplification Testing; for the National Heart, Lung, and Blood Institute Nucleic Acid Test Study Group; N Engl J Med 2004; 351:760-768HYPERLINK "http://www.nejm.org/toc/nejm/351/8/" August 19, 2004DOI: 10.1056/NEJMoa040085

Schulz-Baldes, A., Biller-Andorno, N. and Capron, A.M. (2007). International perspectives on the ethics and regulation of human cell and tissue transplantation. *Bulletin of World Health Organization*, 81: 941–948.

The Declaration of Istanbul on Organ Trafficking and Transplant Tourism (2008). International summit on transplant tourism and organ trafficking convened by the transplantation society and international society of nephrology in Istanbul, Turkey, April 30–May 2, 2008.

The Nuremberg Code (1949) from trials of war criminals before the Nuremberg military tribunals under control council law no. 10, vol. 2, Nuremberg, October 1946–April 1949. US Government Printing Office, Washington, DC, USA, pp. 181–182.

The EU Tissues and Cells Directive (2005). Standards for Tissue Banking, 13th edn., 2012, American Association of Tissue Bank (AATB).

United States Pharmacopeial Convention. Sterilization and sterility assurance of compendia articles (2002). Chapter 1211 In: United States Pharmacopeia and National Formulary (USP 25-NF 20). United States Pharmacopeial Convention, Rockville, (MD). USA.

Vangsness, T. Jr., Wagner, P.P., Moore, T.M. and Roberts, M.R. (2006). Overview of Safety Issues Concerning the Preparation and Processing of Soft-Tissue Allografts. *Arthroscopy: The Journal of Arthroscopic and Related Surgery*, 22(12): 1351–1358.

Veen, M.R., Bloem, R.M. and Petit, P.L. (1994). Sensitivity and negative predictive value of swab cultures in musculoskeletal allograft procurement. *Clin. Orthop. Relat. Res.* 300: 259–263.

Villalba, R., Eisman, M., Fornés, G., Mesa, A., de Torres, P., Ariza, M.J., Gutierrez Guzmán, A. and Gómez Villagrán, M.J. (2001). Implementation of a quality plan (ISO 9002) in a regional tissue bank. Centro Regional de Transfusión Sanguínea y Banco Sectorial de Tejidos de Córdoba, Spain. *Cell and Tissue Banking*, 2: 45–49.

von Versen, R., Mönig, H.-J., Salai, M. and Bettin, D. (2000). Quality issues in tissue banking: Quality management systems — A review. *Cell and Tissue Banking*, 1: 181–192.

Warwick, R.M., Parker, R. Kearney, J.N. and Brubaker, S.A. (2010). Report of the 17th International Congress of the European Association of Tissue Banks (EATB) held jointly with the 17th Annual Congress of the British Association for Tissue Banking (BATB) including EATB/BATB/ American Association of Tissue Banks (AATB) Cardiovascular Symposium. *Cell and Tissue Banking.*

Womack, C. (2003). Ethical issues relating to supply of human tissue to the commercial biomedical sector. *Cell and Tissue Banking*, 3: 203–209.

WMDA (2006). World Marrow Donor Association, http://www.worldmarrow.org/.2006.

Zou, Shimian, Ph.D.; Dodd, Roger Y., Ph.D.; Stramer, Sussan L., Ph.D., and Strong, D. Michael, Ph.D. ((2004); Probability of Viremia with HBV, HCV, HIV, and HTLV among Tissue Donors in the United States; N Engl J Med 2004; 351:751-759 August 19, 2004DOI: 10.1056/NEJMoa032510. for the Tissue Safety Study Group N Engl J Med 2004; 351:751-759HYPERLINK "http://www.nejm.org/toc/nejm/351/8/" August 19, 2004 DOI: 10.1056/NEJMoa032510

Zwitser, E.W., Jiya, T.U., Licher, H.G. and Licher, B.J. (2010). Design and management of an orthopedic bone bank in the Netherlands. *Cell and Tissue Banking*, 13 (1): 63–69.

Index